MW00379873

Marshal Vauban
and the Defence of
Louis XIV's France

Marshal Vauban and the Defence of Louis XIV's France

James Falkner

Pen & Sword
MILITARY

First published in Great Britain in 2011 by
PEN & SWORD MILITARY
An imprint of
Pen & Sword Books Ltd
47 Church Street
Barnsley
South Yorkshire
S70 2AS

Copyright © James Falkner, 2011

ISBN 978-1-84415-927-7

Typeset by Concept, Huddersfield, West Yorkshire.
Printed and bound in England by the CPI UK.

Pen & Sword Books Ltd incorporates the imprints of Pen & Sword Aviation,
Pen & Sword Family History, Pen & Sword Maritime, Pen & Sword Military,
Pen & Sword Discovery, Wharncliffe Local History, Wharncliffe True Crime,
Wharncliffe Transport, Pen & Sword Select, Pen & Sword Military Classics,
Leo Cooper, The Praetorian Press, Remember When, Seaforth Publishing and
Frontline Publishing.

For a complete list of Pen & Sword titles please contact
PEN & SWORD BOOKS LIMITED
47 Church Street, Barnsley, South Yorkshire, S70 2AS, England
E-mail: enquiries@pen-and-sword.co.uk
Website: www.pen-and-sword.co.uk

Contents

List of Maps and Illustrations

List of Plates

Reginald Blomfield's pencil sketch of the Briançon defences (*circa* 1936).

Reginald Blomfield's pencil sketch of the Porte de Paris Gate at Lille (*circa* 1936).

Raising the Militia in a French town, 1705. Malpractice and impressment became common.

Layout of a model siege battery, *circa* 1700.

Château Queyras, guarding the high Alpine passes.

Plan of Strasbourg and the Fortress of Kehl.

Colour plates

Béthune. Captured by the Duke of Marlborough in 1710.

Mons. Detail of the 1709 siegeworks, after the Battle of Malplaquet.

Aire-sur-la-Lys with Fort St Francis.

Tournai. The radical Vauban design for the massive new citadel.

Douai. Captured by Marlborough and Eugène in 1710.

Colmar les Alpes. Fortified sentry post on the defensive ramparts.

Mauberge. The Porte de Mons (2009).

Mauberge. The defensive ditch with the Porte de Mons in the background. (2009)

Mons. Louis XIV conducts the brilliantly successful siege of 1691.

Namur. The French siege of 1692. They lost it to the Allies three years later.

Lille. Brickwork in the defensive ditch to the citadel (2008).

Lille. The massive gateway into Vauban's new citadel.

Tournai. The hard-fought siege by Marlborough and Eugène in 1709.

Introduction

'For Valour, Bounty and Probity, despite a rough and brutal exterior, without question the finest man of his century where sieges and fortification were concerned.'[1]

The name and reputation of Vauban, Marshal of France, Engineer-in-Chief to King Louis XIV, and Inspector-General of Fortifications, continues to excite attention and admiration from soldiers, historians, engineers and social reformers. A French biographer in the 1920s wrote that, 'No man has left a greater mark upon the features of his country.'[2] This is clearly so, despite the ruinous handiwork of town planners, builders of road networks, and landscape designers, over the past three centuries. A good many French towns retain their fortifications of Vauban's distinctive design, every one of typical geometry in plan, and with characteristics that, while each differs from another, offer something close to symmetry. 'A kind of neat martial logicality is demonstrated – the work of the mind applied to military strategy.'[3] This seems to fit rather well with the age in which the fortifications were conceived, designed and constructed, at a time when thought in western Europe was moving steadily towards what would become known as the Age of Enlightenment or, perhaps a little optimistically, the Age of Reason. In matters of warfare, reason may often seem to be lacking, but the work of Vauban, both where it can be seen today in brick and stone, and also in his thoughts on matters both military and civil, and recorded in his writings, appears to come close.

Opinions vary as to the number of Vauban fortifications that exist in presentable form today. Their state of repair, good or bad, is a rather subjective judgement, and what is felt to be fine condition by one observer may be just plain shabby to another. In some cases the fortifications have gone altogether, demolished as militarily unnecessary or swept away by urban development, but these are the exception and tend to have happened where the pressure of population is greatest, mostly in the north of France. It is possible to list more than 180 towns, cities, fortresses, citadels and forts that still bear, or had borne at one time, the mark of Vauban's fertile imagination and apparently boundless energy, having been designed, constructed, improved or intended for improvement to his specification. The sheer range of these fortified places, large and small, and his wider career as a military engineer in all its many and varied aspects, are a body of work representing phenomenal sustained physical and mental effort, which is not truly matched by any other soldier.

The magnificent tally of fortifications in stone and brick that Vauban left naturally excites the admiration for its sheer scale and scope, yet this can all be a little misleading. Much of what he did was developed from the eminently sensible theories and works of his renowned predecessors, notably that of Blaise François de Pagan.[4] This does not detract from Vauban's prolific achievements in fortress design, or cast a shadow over the fine reputation he enjoys. Vauban's accomplishments were well rounded, and his refined knowledge of the art of fortifications proofed as far as possible against the effects of gunpowder artillery and mining, and his understanding of what was necessary for the successful prosecution of a siege, inclined him to devote as much thought to subduing fortresses, as he did to building them. A thorough grasp of the finer points of the defensive arrangements for a fortress is invaluable for any military commander who has to lay siege to such a place.

Vauban acquired the ability to 'see over the other side of the hill', scanning the ground with his calm blue eyes, quickly assessing the essential topographic features of a place, and the best way that they could be utilized either in attack or defence. This fortunate gift was demonstrated in dramatic fashion at the French Siege of Mons in 1691, which took just fifteen days, with casualties amongst the Spanish garrison that noticeably exceeded those of the besiegers, very much against the natural order of such operations. That the garrison commander had been taken entirely by surprise at the rapid pace of the French campaign does not detract from the rapid success of the siege operations. Vauban was a patient man, and a thoughtful and astute observer; little escaped his notice, although he kept much to himself, and was stored away for future use when the time came. This proved often to be the case, as he was called upon to campaign over the same ground, and in and around the same fortresses, on repeated occasions as Louis XIV expanded the borders of France. Six years after the success at Mons, during the Siege of Ath, a fortress of Vauban's own design, his precise knowledge of the location of the sluice gates which kept at a constant level the water in the defensive ditch enabled the French mortar battery commanders to disable these devices from a considerable distance.

Vauban's attention to the unceasing demands of Louis XIV and his able Ministers for War kept him occupied for long years in the designing, re-designing, improving and rebuilding of the fortresses which were to hold France's borders secure. Most particularly his attention had to be given to the north and north-east, a region where these defences had little natural strength. France's hitherto exposed border would in the process become established and strengthened. All the same, there would be times when the French King would overreach his own enormous but ultimately finite resources, in financial, diplomatic and military terms, and the ability to achieve a sufficiently robust defence in the north would remain in some doubt.

Most towns in Europe of any size in the late seventeenth century would have some kind of formal fortification and defences, often mediaeval and obsolete, but occasionally modern and formidable, and Vauban wrote:

> The attack and defence of fortifications have always been considered one of the most essential components of warfare [...] The number of fortified positions has so increased that you can no longer enter enemy territory without encountering as many fortresses as cities [...] Today it may be said that only siegecraft offers the means of conquering and holding territory; a successful battle may leave the victor in control of the countryside for a while, but he still cannot be master of an entire area if he does not take the fortresses.[5]

In this characteristically pithy way, he summed up the importance of the siege, both as an offensive and a defensive method of warfare. Vauban was indeed a prolific designer and builder of fortresses, and must be admired as such. It seems clear, though, that he innovated to a more noticeable degree, and had more influence, in the then rather neglected art of attacking those same fortresses. Neglected, because the use of gunpowder artillery had at first rendered castles and fortified towns vulnerable, but then the development of artillery-proof fortifications had seemed to redress the balance. Defence once again came into its own, and the military engineer in defence obtained a fresh measure of advantage over the gunner in attack.

Artillery methods and tactics improved as time went on, and the ability of the defence to endure faltered once again. In the meantime, outright attack, at whatever cost in lives and blood, became an all too common practice. Vauban's most original work, accordingly, lay in that intensely measured phase of operations, the design and layout of siege trenches and works, and the understanding of how to reduce a formally fortified place by battering artillery and subterranean mining, without incurring unnecessary casualties or delay. Inevitably, some bold souls thought his methods to be too measured, if not actually slow, and they wanted to get on with things, but Vauban regretted the loss of valuable soldiers who were asked to make ill-prepared attacks with little chance of success. 'Vauban's improvements in the mode of attacking fortresses were the most considerable and the most lasting of his services to the art of war.'[6] Such logical good intentions as Vauban advocated were, just as with fortification, not unique flashes of brilliance but soldierly common sense:

> Long sieges ruin armies; empty the purse, and most commonly it falleth it out so, that it hindreth armies from better imployment; and

after a long siege, though things fall out according to a commanders desire, he will have little reason to brag of a victory.[7]

To take a major fortress was no small achievement, and a good reputation as a military commander could be built upon doing these things and little else. The measured progress of a siege had a certain comforting and ritualistic quality that was lacking in an unpredictable clash of arms in open field.

Some commanders held to the belief that a modern and properly manned fortress could resist an attacker almost indefinitely, given the right circumstances. This was rarely so, as those very 'right circumstances' would mean that the siege operation itself was a flawed undertaking, and not that the fortress had any inherent ability to endure without limit. Vauban was amongst those who saw that all defences must submit if sufficient energy, time, and resources were devoted to the task. A well-garrisoned fortress could endure, of course, but only if the besieger ran out of one of those vital elements, perhaps most often enough time, with which to successfully complete the siege. External forces played their part, but a siege was always a balance, with the effort expended by either commander weighed against the time available to achieve the desired result of each.

Sébastien le Prestre, who would be styled Seigneur de Vauban, was born in the depths of rural Burgundy, and came from unpretentious provincial stock. He had no 'interest', no influential or wealthy patron and few family connections to spur his career onwards. Instead, his early military career was that of a rebel against his young King, admittedly at a time of civil war, when Royal authority and its automatic acknowledgement as a kind of unthinking patriotic duty, was less clearly defined than it became. There was evidently a certain practical common sense about these matters in the mid-seventeenth century, that reads a little strangely today. Still, it says much for Vauban's character and particular abilities that this rather uncertain start, in the service of the volatile and rebellious Prince of Condé, was disregarded, and that he went on to become one of the most devoted and trusted servants of the King against whom he had once fought.

Louis de Rouvroi, the Duc de St Simon, a keen, if rather acid, observer of life at the Court of Louis XIV, wrote in his well-known memoirs that Vauban in the 1690s was 'A man of medium height, rather squat, and with the typical look of a soldier, but at the same time extremely boorish and coarse not to say brutal and fierce.'[8] St Simon had served as a cavalry officer as a young man, and his disparaging references to Vauban's lack of polish and plain manners seem to be a reflection of the unfashionable figure the provincial soldier cut in the glittering world of Versailles, and how this scene contrasted with his down-to-earth ways and indifference to ostentation. St Simon was a great snob, and the renowned Dunkirk-based privateer, Jean Bart, attracted similar sneering comments for wearing hobnailed shoes at Court. In any case, Vauban would probably not have disliked the reference to his having the 'typical look of a soldier', for there was certainly no disgrace in that, and while undoubtedly a provincial, he was not at all uncultured, as his writings amply demonstrate. Vauban, although installed by Louis XIV as a member of the prestigious new Order of Saint Louis, was certainly no accomplished courtier, no drone at the glittering royal Court, as the Duc de St Simon was himself once rather maliciously described. By virtue of his own talents, Vauban had the ear and confidence of the King, who was an astute judge of the men he chose for his service. Vauban's successful military career would add immeasurably to the professional standing of the military engineer, to the degree that it would be said that 'The French nobility embraced the art of engineering, and freed itself of the old prejudice to the effect that it was disgraceful to engage in warfare except as an officer of the field arms.'[9]

St Simon did open up a little in his judgements, and went on to comment that Vauban was the most honest and virtuous man of his age, 'peut-être le plus honnête homme et le plus vertueux de son siècle',[10] and that says a great deal. Vauban, with his ordinary background and few highly placed sponsors, was a self-made man in a very competitive world. He rose by his own efforts, which were recognized by great and powerful people at the time, but he appears to have trampled on few as he climbed. Having a warm-hearted nature, being kindly and thoughtful, yet methodical, energetic and undeniably demanding in his professional duties, 'He was able to reconcile success in warfare, an inherently bloody trade, with the demands of common humanity.'[11]

Vauban's career was, of course, in the coldly measured world of the military engineer. Whether in the attack or the defence, these soldiers had a demanding task that followed, to a large degree, set procedures that often led them into harm's way, 'They do not have the satisfaction of exchanging blow for blow [. . .] they have to remain cool in the midst of the most alarming dangers [. . .] the engineer must be outstandingly bold and outstandingly prudent.'[12] A measure of Vauban's success may be found in the letters he received from the King, often expressed in terms of warm regard and concern, offering thanks and appreciation for continued efforts. Louis XIV repeatedly entreated him not to expose himself too much to enemy fire, but the instructions to take more care were mostly disregarded, and eventually these had to be directed to the army commanders, who were warned, at the peril of Royal displeasure, not to let Vauban take undue risks.

Vauban's career flourished in the bright light of Louis XIV's repeated military successes, but his elevation to be a Marshal of France came rather late in life, and was perhaps delayed by his tendency to speak out on matters other than military tactics or methods of fortification. His background would certainly have told against him for a time, and to be made a Marshal of France was an unusual honour for a man of such comparatively humble beginnings, and moreover someone who was just a military engineer, a supposedly subordinate, if not an actually menial, occupation. That prejudice was breaking down as the reputation of Vauban, and word of his many successes, grew and spread. Certainly, it was widely acknowledged that the conferring of the Marshal's baton was well merited: 'To tell you in a word what I think of him, I believe that there is more than one Marshal of France who, when he meets him, blushes at finding himself a Marshal of France.'[13]

The expansion of French territory during Louis XIV's reign resulted, at a practical level, in almost incessant demands being placed on the seemingly inexhaustible energy of Vauban, and his efforts to devise and construct a viable defence for France in its enlarged form. These efforts did not go unnoticed or unrewarded, for Louis XIV did not stint when he rewarded his servants. Undoubtedly, Vauban could have died a wealthy man, had he not, in turn, been equally generous to those around him, in particular to his junior officers, those who laboured in arduous circumstances with little recognition of the real value of their services.

Generations of military engineers studied and followed Vauban's teachings and advice on how to design and construct a fortress, and how to defend or to attack those places in the most effective manner. Learned works on the science of the siege regularly appeared, and at times it appears that some of these works might have been written by the great man himself – John Muller's treatise of 1757 being a good example. There is also more than an element of plagiarism in these works, but they are valuable nonetheless, as the methods to be used in this exacting phase of war did not change greatly over the course of the eighteenth century.

Vauban also wrote extensively on political, agricultural and social conditions and development, both in France and in far-flung colonies in North America. He was at heart a reformer, interested in ways to better maintain and nurture an adequate population, able to be deployed for agriculture, commerce, and, occasionally, for war. His innovative notions on how to revise and make more equitable and effective the tax regime in France eventually brought him into disfavour with the King, for straying into affairs that were not his concern. He also had strong views on religious tolerance, and the revocation of the Edict of Nantes in 1685, which saw so many otherwise loyal French Huguenots leave, puzzled and distressed him. The growing disapproval of the King at his Engineer-in-Chief's apparent presumption was, however, tempered with a sense of his long and indefatigable service – severity was mingled with respect, and if in later years Louis XIV cooled towards Vauban, he was, at the very end, not cold.[14]

This book is principally about the soldier and his literally monumental efforts to build and maintain a credible defence system for France. At the same time, Vauban's aggressive instincts (he was wounded at least eight times during his military career, and was left with a very noticeable scar on his left cheek from a musket ball strike), and his interest in the way formal fortifications should be attacked, have to be acknowledged. 'Attack and defence are inescapable in the development of fortifications.'[15] These are not only complimentary phases of military operations, but they reflect the life work of Vauban in a very close sense. He prepared a model timetable for a formal siege of a first-class fortress, and for generations this served as a text book, setting out just what should be done in those operations. This is of as much interest as his thoughts on the duties of a garrison commander, or his work on fortress design and construction.

The defence of France was regarded by Vauban as a single and cohesive objective. The mutually supporting element of this defence looked beyond the defensive attributes of any single fortress, as they should always be linked to the activities of field armies. In the event, his efforts to prepare a viable defence was only once put to a serious and prolonged test that had a real chance of success. Yet, what a test it proved to be, with the Duke of Marlborough and Prince Eugène, at the peak of their powers and leading Allied armies flushed with success, in a determined attempt between 1707 and 1711 to break through from the recently conquered Spanish Netherlands into northern France. Like an eggshell, the border fortresses gave protection at first, but once the shell was broken, there would then be little left to defend Paris and the King in his palace at Versailles. At this particular time of peril for France, the defences that Vauban envisaged, designed and oversaw in construction, did their job well; a success that has, rather oddly, received little recognition as the prolonged passage of arms that it was.

This was the finest point for Vauban and his fortresses, but the old Marshal was not there to see it, having died some years earlier. What might be regarded as his legacy had certainly held firm. Vauban had, however, designed and built a system that was of its own time, and if anything looked backwards, for it can be seen that his engineering works, apparently the last word in scientific military design, were representative of the methods and capabilities of the seventeenth century, not those of the future. They were a skilful reworking of the ideas of others, and representative of the close of an era when defence could be made so tough that it might dictate the pace of campaigns and, sometimes, of wars themselves.

Whether working to establish a defence for France or devising methods for attacking fortresses, Vauban's career was of extraordinary length and range. It is perhaps unmatched in its breadth and detail. His efforts, his achievements, and the high reputation that he attained did much to enhance the standing of military engineers as essential participants in the conduct of war. Well into the nineteenth century, it was remarked that, while few students of the modern military art and technique would be concerned any more with the precise manner in which the 1st Duke of Marlborough had arranged his army for battle at Blenheim or Ramillies, the way in which Marshal Vauban set out the best way to attack fortresses was still regarded as the last word in rational thought, concept, and practical advice. It is, therefore, very rewarding to look once again at the military career of a great and humane soldier remembered as the 'finest man of his century', and his prodigious efforts to provide an enduring defence for France, on the one hand, and ways to conserve the lives of French soldiers when attacking fortresses, on the other.

In 1933, on the 300th anniversary of Vauban's birth, General Max Weygand wrote 'The name of Vauban is, perhaps, the one most frequently mentioned in France during all of 300 years. It is irrevocably engraved on the soil of our country by the works that he built.'[16] A strong statement, but it is hard to argue with such a distinguished French soldier when he is speaking of one of his own country's heroes, and listing the old military engineer before mentioning such notables as Turenne, Condé, Luxembourg, Saxe (who was German-born, admittedly), and even the Emperor Napoleon I. Weygand was of course referring to the prodigious range of defensive works designed, improved and supervised by Vauban, but any defence depends as much on active and aggressive action as anything else. All his designs added an element of strength to French offensive intentions, when the opportune moment came.

To walk the streets of a French town today is to be reminded of the presence and influence of the old soldier. Squares, avenues, parks, districts and hotels often carry the name of Vauban, as did warships once – postage stamps bear his likeness, and a remarkably fine statue of the great man stands in front of the Musée de l'Armée in Paris. In addition, many of the citadels and fortresses that he designed and whose construction he oversaw have survived, some in fragmentary form but others, such as the formidable citadels at Lille and Arras, Montmédy, Neuf-Brisach, Château Queyras, Mont-Louis and Mont-Dauphin high in the mountains of the south, Fort Chapus on the Biscay Coast, and the small attractively moated town of Le Quesnoy, well preserved and in imposing condition. They are fine testaments to his ingenuity and enterprise.

Yet, for all his services and untiring application to duty, at the end of his long and active life, and in chronic ill-health and low spirits, Vauban was neglected by Louis XIV. Remarkably, his death in 1707 went little noticed – no

person of eminence or note attended the funeral, a strange omission for someone who had striven so well to secure the borders of France. However, it was a
time of national crisis, with victorious enemy armies gathering on the northern
border (a border that was made more secure thanks to Vauban), so attention
and priorities must have lain elsewhere. He had risen from almost nothing, the
obscurity of a family of minor provincial worthies, to attain prominence in the
Royal service, and he had then fallen into disfavour. Despite this absurdity,
Vauban has been long remembered and held in great esteem by the nation that
he served so well, and by those interested in the art of military engineering.

In May 1808, Emperor Napoleon I had the embalmed heart of Marshal
Vauban, secure in its lead casket, removed from the small church of Saint-
Léger-de-Foucheret in the Morvan, and brought in some state to an elaborate
tomb memorial constructed in Les Invalides in Paris, where the remains of the
great Marshal Turenne already lay. The casket had fortunately been overlooked when the chapel was ransacked by a revolutionary mob in the early
1790s. This eloquent act by the French Emperor to the memory of Louis
XIV's long deceased Engineer-in-Chief indicates very well the high regard in
which the old Marshal of France was held, some 101 years after his death.

Chapter 1

Fence of Iron

'It was almost a matter of course, that an article on the attack
of fortresses, should give plans of the regular system of
attack laid down by Vauban, and never altered since.'[1]

When the young King Louis XIV came to the French throne on 7 June 1654,
his realm was, in a strict sense, unfinished and incomplete. France was only
just recovering from ruinous and divisive civil war, with frontiers that were
irregular, and in many places insecure or hardly defensible. Powerful opponents, Spain in particular, but also Austria, hovered on the fringes and looked
to take advantage of France's internal weakness. The provinces of Rousillon,
Conflans and Cerdagne in the south were just recently made French while
still technically owing allegiance to Madrid, while Catalonia was now firmly in
the hands of Spain. On France's northern border, the lands of Artois, Hainault
and Flanders were all still Spanish possessions. Towns such as Arras, Lille,
Cambrai, Mauberge and Valenciennes that are now regarded as typically
French were not so then. They were a part of the very wealthy, and therefore
highly desirable, Southern Netherlands (modern-day Belgium), that largely
Catholic portion of the Low Countries that had not taken their independence,
unlike the United Provinces of the Protestant Dutch north, in the long war
against King Philip II, Alva, Parma and their like, earlier in the seventeenth
century. The Bishopric of Liège, Luxembourg, and the Duchy of Lorraine to
the east were still independent, although owing allegiance to the Emperor in
Vienna, as were Alsace and the old Burgundian lands of the Franche-Comté.
As such, they presented a degree of insecurity, if not actual hostility, to the
interests of the French crown.

   In the south-east, the uplands of the Vosges covered the area between
Strasbourg and Belfort, and the Alps to the south and east offered more protection. The borders with Barcelonette and Savoy were potentially vulnerable,
despite the natural strength offered by the mountain chain, as the Duchy
would prove to be an inconstant ally to, and an occasional enemy of, France.
Still, French inconstancy towards the Dukes of Savoy also played its part. The
powerful forces that Madrid had in Italy, together with growing interest of
Vienna in the region, were a further threat to French interests. On a smaller

scale, the enclave of Orange in the south owed allegiance to the Princes of that House, and the Duchy of Bouillon hard against the forests of the Ardennes was still independent. The 'Spanish Road', the valuable strategic route by which the Kings of Spain had been accustomed to pass their incomparably efficient infantry northwards from Italy to the Low Countries, ran along France's eastern border, which as a result was always at risk, at least while Spain remained a military force to be reckoned with. When this proved to be no longer the case, others, the Emperor in Vienna and ambitious German Electors and princelings, would fill the gap thus left, and grow to threaten France. This threat would wax and wane with the shifting alliances and diplomatic deals that were concluded, but never go away entirely, and be incapable of being disregarded whenever Louis XIV and his Ministers conferred together in Fontainebleau or Versailles.

Taken as a whole, the frontiers of France were both ill-defined and insecure. There were man-made defences, of course, but these tended to be scattered fortresses of obsolete design, with inadequate, ill-paid and unsupported garrisons. Very often kept in poorly maintained condition, and ill-suited to modern artillery-dominated warfare, these fortresses had little capability for either providing mutual support to each other or to help a French field army mount a proper defence against determined aggression. This lack could not be addressed while France was internally in turmoil, but once this was no longer the case, a strong-willed ruler such as the new young King could, and would, move to strengthen the defence of his country.

Through the latter half of the seventeenth century, Louis XIV fought a series of wars, three major and two more minor, together with a number of lesser intimidating raids, against his near neighbours. These conflicts, from France's point of view, were strategically defensive in nature, but seemed to be openly aggressive to others. This does not imply that France alone was engaged in such aggression, as all of these neighbouring states, to a varying degree, had their own designs upon French interests and territories, and could certainly not be held up to be entirely blameless or acting in good faith for much of the time.

The marked success for French armies in the early years of the new reign was largely the work of the great Marshals of France of the day – Turenne, Condé and Luxembourg. The King certainly liked to be on campaign with his soldiers, and was not slow to offer advice and direction to the Marshals, but he did not hold himself up to be a great commander. The repeated victories carried the borders of France to their present-day extent, more or less, along the Rhine, the Vosges and the Alps to the east and south-east, to the border with the Southern Netherlands, to Luxembourg and the Rhine to the north and north-east, and to the Pyrenees in the far south on the border with Spain. In addition to large parts of Flanders, Artois and Hainault, the Duchy of

Lorraine, Alsace, the old Burgundian lands of the Franche-Comté, and the enclaves of Avignon, Barcelonette and Orange, all became part of Louis XIV's expanded domains, although Lorraine would not formally be so, while recognisably within the French sphere of influence, until well into the reign of his great-grandson, Louis XV. Defence was a comparatively simple matter for France along the long stretches of the Atlantic and Mediterranean coastlines, and on the English Channel. Still, the growing power of the Royal Navy, and briefly, that of the Dutch Navy, would always make these watery margins vulnerable to a sudden strike from the sea, and appropriate defences to cater for this would have to be maintained.

The notable military achievements in the early years of Louis XIV's reign had their own associated cost in social and financial terms, and rather inevitably required that the newly-established borders, and the territory that had been acquired in the process, should then be properly defended. This was clear military necessity and prudence, but the success of those outwardly glorious campaigns in reality achieved quite limited strategic gains. France's lengthy borders were made undeniably more strong, but in the absence of a lasting peace or a prospect of such, they would remain vulnerable to attack. It was not possible to be strong everywhere, even with France's huge resources, and the testing years between 1702 and 1713, those of the war for the throne of Spain, would prove to be ruinously expensive, with the defences of the northern border torn almost to shreds by the armies of the Duke of Marlborough and Prince Eugène of Savoy. Louis XIV's kingdom was, in the process, brought to a state of near bankruptcy, although that unhappy fate, in reality, would have to wait until the old King had been dead for several years. This was the real cost of such apparent success – in actual fact, France was made weaker by the impoverishment of its people and society, but this was hidden to most observers for, very visibly, the boundaries had been pushed outwards, and this gave the pleasing but superficial appearance of added strength.

If neighbouring states could be secured as friends and allies, through treaties, the recognition of areas of common self-interest in the face of external threats, or, not infrequently, by marriage of sons and daughters, then security could also be had in that way, through alliances and diplomacy and at relatively little cost. Such happy circumstances were rarely to be had, for miscalculation, mistrust and blatant ambition often dictated otherwise, and even staunchly Catholic Spain would in time prove to be a source of enormous trouble to France.

The mountainous passes of the Alps, the Vosges and the Pyrenees, and the tangled country of the Hunsruck, the Eiffel and the Ardennes, sheltered by the distant waters of the Rhine, appeared at first glance to impede the easy movement of large armies. As long as such relatively open avenues of approach as the

Belfort Gap to the south of the Vosges, the Saarland and the Moselle valley were held in strength by French garrisons that should certainly be so. This all seemed quite straightforward, although advanced strongpoints would have to be established to watch likely crossing places over the Rhine and elsewhere. There was an inevitable price to be paid, in the construction or improvement of these outposts, and the provision and maintenance of adequate garrisons to keep them secure. This was far from straightforward, as any exposed point would be inviting to a potential attacker. One fortress on its own, therefore, was unlikely to be sufficient; it would have to be supported by others at not too great a distance. This led to unavoidable, and ultimately unaffordable, expense. Money was dispensed on strong fortresses and distant garrisons, and effort was eventually diffused when it should have been concentrated; Vauban warned against this tendency to overstretch.

Most of the closely-knit cities of the Southern Netherlands had defences of one degree or another, and although rather antiquated they had, by and large, stood their citizens in good stead during the dreadful years of the Spanish Terror when Madrid's control was re-established in much of the north. Louis XIV did not yet have this kind of network of fortresses of strength, each one mutually supporting, particularly in those parts where France was at its most vulnerable. When the French King reached out to take those fortresses for himself, they often proved to be ineffective and their very inadequacy was a cause for concern, so that many of these conquests, gratifying though each one had been on the day, had to be strengthened if not rebuilt altogether.

It was a sobering fact that, as recently as 1636, a Spanish army had got to within an enticing 70 miles of Paris, before falling back to the northwards. In 1652, taking advantage of the distraction of the Fronde civil wars, Spain seized Dunkirk on the Channel Coast, although an Anglo-French army retook the port and fortress at the Battle of the Dunes six years later. It could be seen that 'In the north-east there is a terrible breach [...] France's age-old weakness', as Charles de Gaulle wrote in 1934.[2] The concern was slightly overstating things, as the rivers of the region were studded with fortifications at the main crossing places but, once again, in many cases these were obsolete or second-rate, and required strengthening and modernization. Furthermore, those major fortresses lying close to France's northern border were often in the hands of her potential enemies.

The military power of Spain was gradually failing, and Louis XIV, with a combination of shrewdness and ruthlessness, took advantage of this weakness by employing a neat, if rather threadbare, legal nicety. The major city of Lille was seized by French troops in 1667 as the King extended his possessions northwards into the southernmost part of the Spanish Netherlands, annexing in the process large parts of Flanders and Artois. In addition to Lille, other valuable towns like Cambrai, Tournai, Oudenarde, Ath, Douai, Mauberge, Menin and Ypres became French possessions in the process, and a fresh and more robust forward line of defence for France began to be established in the north. The King could not, however, consolidate these gains sufficiently well to hold onto them all in the face of the opposition his adventures raised against him, first of a formidable alliance led by King William III of England (who was also the Dutch Stadtholder, William of Orange), twenty-five years later, and then in the glare of the dynamic campaigns waged by the Duke of Marlborough and Prince Eugène of Savoy during the years 1707 to 1711. Louis XIV over-reached his power in his ambition for glory and for France, lost much of what had been gained in the early years of his reign, and almost came to grief. However, the end result remained a significant expansion of French territory, to what might be regarded as that country's 'natural' borders in the north and north-east as elsewhere.

Louis XIV failed, contrary to all expectations, to overawe or overpower the staunchly Protestant Dutch Republic. The stout and bleak defence put up by the outnumbered and outgunned Dutch under William of Orange in 1672 and 1673 foiled the plans of the French King to settle matters with the young republic once and for all, and he had to turn his attention back into the margins of the enfeebled Spanish Netherlands. The Dutch had enjoyed a long and, by and large, friendly relationship with France, particularly as both were in contention with Spain, for rather different reasons, but the interests of the commercially aggressive Republic had clashed with those of Louis XIV. The States-General in the Hague had to relearn quickly the grim lessons of their own War of Independence, and their tactics and methods improved markedly, in particular the skilful siege operations undertaken by their noted military engineer Meinheer van Coehorn, a contemporary, admirer, and occasional opponent of Vauban. As a consequence of this lack of success for France, no naturally strong border line, perhaps settled along the Maas, Waal and Lower Rhine rivers, was ever established in the north. To do so, however, would have been strategically impractical without proper French control of the Southern Netherlands, and this was never really achieved for anything but appreciably brief periods. Some of the early French gains – important fortress cities such as Oudenarde, Ath, Tournai, Ypres, Namur and Mons – would have to be given up, as the military and financial distress of France, and the loss of gifted field commanders through old age and the hazards of the battlefield, took their toll. Locally, this was often regretted, and the good citizens of Oudenarde, for instance, remembered their time under the French as being one of notable prosperity. Strategically, there would remain an enduring and worrying gap in France's defensive arrangements in the north, and Louis XIV was acutely aware of this, as others would be in the decades to come.

There would be French outposts to the east of the Rhine and the Alps, as at Kehl near to Strasbourg, and Pignerole and Casale in northern Italy, but these in time proved to be too expensive, too exposed, and too troublesome to hold. Louis XIV took particular care to cultivate the rulers of the Duchy of Savoy in northern Italy as a client state, friendly to, and dependent upon, the benevolence of the French King. It was, accordingly, something of a shock to Louis XIV when Victor-Amadeus II, the Duke of Savoy, allied himself with England, Austria and Holland during the War of the Spanish Succession. This was particularly so as Louis XIV's eldest grandson, the Duke of Burgundy and eventual heir to the throne of France, was by then married to Marie-Adelaide, the daughter of the Duke of Savoy. It is to the King's credit that, despite the seemingly self-seeking defection of the father, he did not hold it against his daughter-in-law, and Louis XIV was particularly distressed when she died at an early age, as did her young Royal husband, of measles.

Louis XIV also took a quite understandable interest in the internal affairs of the Southern Netherlands, and just who sat on the throne in Spain. Within recent memory there had been a potential Habsburg encirclement of France, with the Empire created by Charles V combining the manpower of Vienna and Madrid, with the wealth of the Americas and the Low Countries, so that France was beset to the north, south and east. Louis XIV's concern for the security of his enlarged territories was, accordingly, quite genuine, but to fortify the frontiers to a modern standard would prove to be a formidable, laborious, and eventually unaffordably expensive project. The French King was prepared to expend considerable sums on establishing new and modern defences in depth, but the resources of his Treasury were finite, and he would occasionally refuse consent for overly extravagant projects. Louis XIV expressed surprise, for example, that Vauban thought it really necessary to level an entire hill during the extensive rebuilding of the fortress of Ath on the Dender river. When the French then abandoned the place under Treaty terms, Vauban was ordered to tear the defences down, but managed to avoid doing so to any great extent.

Most of the major cities and towns near to a frontier would have formal defences, but by the mid-seventeenth century these were quite likely to be obsolete relics, quaint and built on and over as towns gradually expanded, and militarily now become rather ineffective as a result. Those closest to the border, and thus with an obvious defensive role, would probably have been improved and modernized over the years, but even such an important place as Lille saw its defences hedged about with suburbs, cottages, gardens and allotments under the pressure of a growing population, and friction between the military and the citizens resulted as to what was and what was not permitted in urban development and expansion. The outlying buildings would certainly have to be cleared away, regardless of inconvenience or cost to the citizenry, once an attacker approached, as indeed happened at Lille in 1708.

Often, these defences might have been enlarged and improved, after a fashion, over the years (fitful years of only occasional peace, as often as not), and they would to some imperfect degree at least have a semblance of modern military thought and design about them. Vauban's task, at the King's command, became to visit each individual fortified place in person, and assess and improve, or redesign and rebuild, as required, and as far as the deep resources of the French Treasury would permit. A coherent defence of France, sometimes referred to as the 'Pre-Carré', or duelling field, was to be put in place.[3] Soon after the capture of Lille in 1667, Louis XIV gave to the 34-year-old King's Engineer-in-Ordinary the monumental task to improve, extend and strengthen the Fence of Iron, the 'Barrier de Fer', behind which France would be secure in the north. French field armies were to be able to operate from the secure environment that well-sited modern fortresses provided 'The major long term problem French military planners faced was that of waging a good defensive campaign.'[4] It is clear that what faced Andre Maginot in the 1920s, had no less faced Louis XIV, his Ministers and Vauban some 250 years earlier.

This was quite evidently an enormous task, and one of the most notable features of Vauban's career, quite apart from the fact that he had started out as young man in rebellion against Royal authority, was his reserves of energy and unflagging diligence that he could deploy in the relentlessly demanding service of Louis XIV. His patient acceptance of these incessant calls on his time and energies is notable. The rewards that came, of course, were significant also, for Vauban was both well paid, loaded (somewhat belatedly perhaps) with honours, and very highly regarded, although the King's tolerance of his quite unorthodox views on social issues, and his fondness for offering unsolicited advice on religious toleration, and what he believed to be the undue and unequal burden of taxation, had distinct limits. Louis XIV would prove to be a generous if demanding master, but his sense of tolerance was not without bounds, as Vauban would eventually find.

The Fence of Iron that Vauban devised in the north of France would be formed in two distinct linear parts, anchored at either end on water obstacles, the Channel coast or major rivers, and might have been fitted quite well to a later prescription for national defence:

> Not as a simple slice of a battlefield on the frontier, but as a real instrument of manoeuvre [...] Even in the event of an army's withdrawal behind the front, the commander would still retain the possibility of giving battle in depth without losing the support of this fortification.[5]

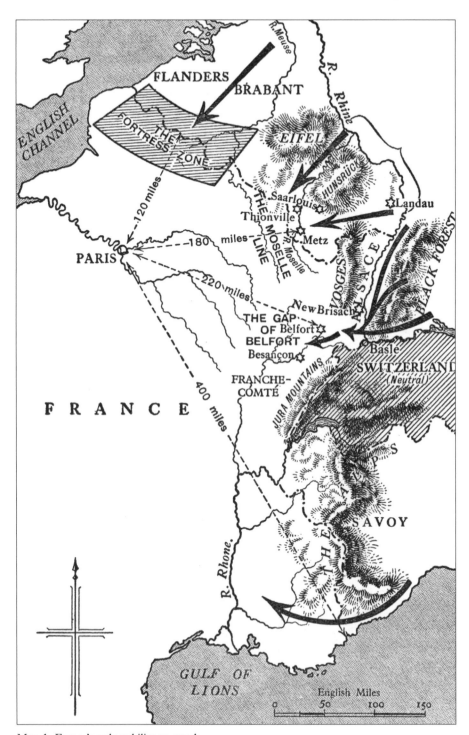

Map 1. France's vulnerability to attack.

A forward line of defence would range from Dunkirk on the coast, once that port had been bought back from England, of course, through to Givet on the Meuse. This would provide a hard shell upon which any invader would have to waste his strength and blunt the fighting capacity of his army. If, contrary to what was expected, this forward line was broken through, a second defensive line of fortresses, lying in depth, would take up the strain to absorb and exhaust the remaining energies of the attacking army. This second line went from Gravelines with its water defences on the coast, all the way to Mézières and Stenay on the Meuse.

This was clearly an ambitious plan, requiring significant effort, and proved to be very expensive to construct and maintain properly. In practice it was also flawed in strategic scope, for attempts at a really effective forward defence with French field armies operating in the southern Netherlands and in the process keeping opponents at a safe distance from the border, proved a disastrous failure. This failure exposed the fortress belt to attack, without a strong field army able to operate in unison with it. The garrisons had been stripped to the bone to bolster the strength of the field army, and they were, accordingly, ill-equipped to withstand the thrusting Allied campaign that followed the defeat at Ramillies in the early summer of 1706. However, despite repeated reverses, the dual line of fortresses eventually proved their worth, most particularly between 1708 and 1711, and saved Louis XIV and France from utter defeat at the hands of Marlborough and Eugène at a time when French morale, and military and financial resources, were at a critically low ebb. The eventual success of the Fence of Iron, qualified though it may have been, was significant, but other factors, especially that of a lack of time in which to achieve success, played their parts. However, time is a prime military asset and a lack of time, even when due to outside factors, is no real excuse for a lack of success, nor does it take away from the achievements of the defending French forces who endured much and came through without suffering final defeat.

Vauban is best remembered as a designer of fortresses, and to some, that is really all that he is remembered for. Much attention is also given to his reputed development of particular 'Systems' of defence. Although he referred to the refortification of Landau in the Palatinate as being of 'his system', as he did with the design and construction of Neuf-Brisach, in practice he had no set system for fortress design, other than to employ the classic 'Trace Italienne' as a basic template, one that was used by all other military engineers at the time anyway. 'Even a small unimportant town might resist capture for several months provided it had the Trace-Italienne.'[6] Certain features in fortress design were and remain absolute – depth (upon which Vauban noticeably placed great emphasis), protection, concealment, effective obstacles, clear fields of fire and so on. All towns have their peculiarities of topography and position, but all will be close to water, and so water obstacles, a later development of mediaeval moats, would feature prominently in all formal defensive works, and these often prove the hardest to overcome or avoid. All these components provided an irreplaceable part of a military engineer's overall defensive plan for a fortress, and Vauban's system, such as it was, consisted of intelligent application of that broad template.

The peculiarities always to be found in each separate location required that the basic outline plan should be adapted to suit individual circumstances. Vauban proved himself on many occasions to be a master of such adaption, with the ability to quickly and accurately identify the key topographical features of a place, particularly those with the scope to add most significantly to its defensive capabilities. The core task was to take the geometric design of the Trace Italienne and improve and refine the model with care and skill, to suit the precise requirements of each fortress under construction or improvement. To do so successfully, and so often, required a keen eye for ground and an open and enquiring mind, and Vauban undoubtedly possessed these qualities. The fortresses that he designed and built, or rebuilt and improved, are ample testament to his energy, ingenuity, skill and devotion to Louis XIV's service. They are also, of course, testament to the vast sums of money that the King in the heady early years of success, when his Treasury was still replete, was prepared to spend on the project.

In a very few cases, Vauban was provided with the money and opportunity to completely remodel and rebuild a fortress, as at Lille, Landau and at Neuf-Brisach on the west bank of the Rhine (Alt-Brisach on the east bank having been abandoned and demolished in accordance with Treaty terms). There were also a number of minor or subsidiary forts which received his full treatment. These were the exception, not least because of the enormous costs involved, as with his tolerance, the resources that the King and his tax-gatherers could devote to fortress building had certain limits. Vauban did develop his main themes, of course, with progressively more complex and extensive geometric designs to foil and defeat an attacker, but the central essential template of the Trace Italienne was always at the heart of the design. In that, Vauban did not differ very much from his contemporaries, and the works of such notable engineers as the Dutch van Coehorn, while different in detail, were the same in essence.

This is no surprise, for the Trace Italienne was an example of very obvious rational design, one that brooks little argument in the advantages it confers on a defender, and the challenge that is put before any potential besieging force. The designs Vauban used were not in themselves particularly novel or unique to him, but were well considered improvisations to suit the requirements of each individual fortress. 'The art of fortification does not consist in rules and systems, but only in good sense and experience.'[7] The simple technique of adaption of the original Trace Italienne by Blaise de Pagan, the notable fore-runner of Vauban in military engineering and fortress design, was in essence the same as that used in the late seventeenth century. This was then developed further, with the novel introduction of the detached bastion, commanded from the rear by artillery on the main curtain walls.

A further development, as seen at Neuf-Brisach, was an extension of this thinking to bring into use powerful bastioned towers bristling with tiers of artillery emplacements. This steady development in thought and practice did not, though, constitute a formal 1st, 2nd and 3rd Vauban set of 'systems'. The neat notion of such systems was of assistance to later commentators who sought to analyze, explain and not infrequently to criticise the increasingly complex and elaborate works of the old French Engineer. Vauban was always prepared to adapt his plans to suit local circumstances, and was certainly open to the suggestions of others: 'It is the custom among the decent men of our trade, to appeal to me [...] As I am not stubborn, I amend my plans and explain my ideas to them,' adding that 'Every fault should be treated mercifully.'[8] No two fortresses could quite be the same; the lie of the land which was occupied did not permit it, and to attempt exact duplication, as if to some robotic scheme, would have been nonsensical and to compromise on other, more important, military considerations.

On the other hand, taking on the mantle of the attacker rather than the defender, Vauban's development of a systematic and efficient method, his 'Méthode', to attack a fortress, was significant at the time, and this would be used by officers when on campaign for generations to come. He had certainly established a fine reputation as a builder of fortresses, but he took particular care to study and refine the ways in which such places were to be attacked. A 'poacher turned gamekeeper' in this respect, in Vauban's firm view it was an essential first step to reduce defences by a heavy and well-directed bombard-ment and by mining before an assault was ever to be considered, and heavy loss of life in gallant but futile attacks was to be discouraged. 'This loss,' he wrote, 'is always the result of excessive haste; we do not take half the precautions demanded by such an enterprise, and consequently instead of gaining a day we lose two – at the cost of our best troops, who perish miserably on such occasions.'[9] As with designing and building a fortress, to design an attack to overcome a fortress would follow certain set principles, but factors such as the varying topography of a locality and the strength of the defences and the resourcefulness of the garrison would demand once more that, in actual detail, every attack was distinct and different.

Chapter 2

Siege Warfare

Fortresses as a general rule fulfil one of three basic functions: to secure frontiers and deter invaders, to provide magazines and store depots from which field armies can draw supplies and sustenance, and to act as a centre of local government, a symbol of authority and centre for tax-gathering activities. As soon as a fort or fortress was built in a certain spot, the evident symbol, possibly an impudent or contentious symbol, of power and sovereignty, schemes would be laid by others to attack or gain control of the place. That much is evident from a swift glance at history. The basic intentions to hold onto the fortress on the one hand and to take it away it on the other, did not change very much over the centuries, and in essence remain the same today, wherever formal defensive structures are in place. Nor had the overall methods in use, by which a fortified city or town might be defended to best effect, or alternatively, captured with least effort and cost, changed to any great degree – brute force has a certain compelling and fascinating logic, as has starvation, deception, faint-heartedness or dark treachery.

Typically, the defender would lay out a fortified place, if the time and treasure was sufficient to do so, in as formidable a fashion as could be. Avenues of approach and access would be rendered difficult, exposing any attacker to observation and fire, and by delaying the point of any submission for as long as possible, impose a drag upon the campaign and expose the troops in the siege encampments to the rigours of the elements. The attacker, on the other hand, by careful preparations and the massing of men and munitions, would seek to neutralize and eventually overcome the defenders' arrangements however diligent they may appear, as soon as could be achieved.

The loss of time, that irreplaceable commodity, was for the attacker often the most serious consideration. Campaigning in the days before the introduction of modern metalled roads could only be undertaken in relatively fine weather; the roads and paths that swirled with dust in summer would become muddy ditches in wet weather, all but impossible to travel along. This penalty of delay might be enough to win the day for the defender, and force the attacking commander to withdraw empty-handed, to find shelter for his army as the cold weather of the autumn and winter months closed in around them.

On the other hand, the defenders were also in something of a bind, hemmed in behind their defences, usually cut off from the outside world – although on occasions this would not be so – and reliant upon their own resources, the robustness of the soldiers of the garrison, and the level of the stocks of food and munitions in the storehouses and magazines. Protected to a degree by stout fortifications and defences, the garrison had to exact a sufficiently high price in time, effort and blood from the attacking commander to either oblige him to withdraw, or to offer terms for a negotiated submission of the garrison, with guarantees of good treatment and safe conduct. The days when a defeated garrison might expect to be hanged from the walls of a captured fortress as a lesson to others were, mercifully, long over and the inclination to hold out to the last extremity that such a practice encouraged was removed as a result.

High stone walls, difficult to scale and imposing to the eye, had been the classic form for the fortress or 'castle', which had served so well from ancient times right up to the late Middle Ages. The well-known turreted castle of the chivalric era is an instantly recognized structure, imposing and reassuringly sturdy, although in present times often a little battered if not actually derelict. The real military usefulness of castles had lapsed long before Vauban was born. The development of gunpowder for military use, increasingly evident from the mid-fifteenth century onwards, brought about a considerable shift in capability and the relative powers of the attacker when ranged against those of the defender of a castle or fortified walled town. This development of effective methods in gunpowder use (earlier attempts to employ guns tactically, although promising much, delivered rather little as the pieces were too immobile to be very useable, without effort out of all proportion to the likely reward), cast into sharp focus the vulnerability of mediaeval defensive design for castles and fortified places in the then accepted sense.

With long, stone and brick walls and high towers, castles and fortified towns became quaint, almost an obsolete embarrassment, visually but superficially imposing yet expensive to maintain, uncomfortable and impractical to live in, and militarily ineffective. They seemed to offer protection and security, but in practice provided none in the face of the growing use of artillery and sub-terranean mining with gunpowder. Perhaps most famously, the fortified city states of northern Italy, so apparently powerful and secure within their stone walls, were all reduced in a remarkably short time by French Kings Charles VIII and Louis XII in the 1490s who made good use of the new weaponry, and the Papal city, Rome, in time suffered no less at the hands of mostly German mercenaries. Things were never quite the same again for the designers of fortresses and their garrison commanders, in the face of what one observer described as 'A new and bloody way of making war.'[1]

For the time being, the art of the gunner, despite the slow rate of fire of the artillery pieces and the expense of the shot and powder used, and to a lesser degree the activities of their comrades, the miners, as at the Siege of Naples in 1503, eclipsed the skills of the most accomplished fortress designers. The ratio of powder to cannonball (round-shot) necessary for effective artillery use fell significantly from 13:1 to 2:1 from the beginning to the middle of the sixteenth century, reducing both wear on the guns, which were prone to burst with distressing results, and the expenditure of expensive munitions. Fortresses were conquered, or fell into disrepair as an irrelevance, and the defender was at an apparently clear disadvantage until radical new methods could be devised to redress this new imbalance when ranged against the capabilities of the attacker.

The wheel, of course, had to eventually turn, and great thought and ingenuity was employed to make fortresses of a new and radical design, that were better able to withstand the devastating effects of artillery and mining with gunpowder. To counter these threats, fortress designers turned away from imposing stone and brick fortifications, and began the development of low and sharply raked embankments as main defences, often constructed of no grander material than hard-packed earth. Such structures offered only a low silhouette, a profile that would present gunners with as meagre a target as possible and with the ability to absorb punishment without breaking down too quickly, and deflect the fire of besieging artillery, which always had to be brought forward to the siegeworks at the cost of enormous effort. At first the earthworks were constructed to the immediate rear of the existing mediaeval walls to serve as simple supports, but then the earthworks were placed in front of the old walls, to form outer defences.

As time went on, and depending on the ambitions, pretensions and treasuries of individual sovereign princes, complete rebuilding of the obsolete defences was undertaken, the old would be demolished, and new fortifications be put in their place in the instantly recognizable geometric form of the classic 'Trace Italienne':

> As the range of guns gradually increased (owing to improvements in metallurgy and in the manufacture of gunpowder), it was found necessary to supplement the defences by means of outworks pushed out gradually further and further until they reached to a considerable distance beyond the enceinte.[2]

These earthworks would typically be between 18 and 24 feet thick at the base, hard-packed and in time faced with stone or brick but also often turfed with coarse grass to bind the material and make it stable. Earth would absorb round-shot, unlike brick and stone which would shatter, but the harder faced material was more permanent and needed less routine maintenance. Simple but effective geometric designs were developed, expanded and enlarged to whatever extent was permitted by the topography of the particular site on which they were to be constructed and, equally importantly, the depth of the purse of the prince whose Treasury was to pay for the work. The military engineers developed and refined their techniques with considerable ingenuity and skill, although there was plainly a nice tactical balance to be struck in their designs for cunning new defences, for 'If the walls be made too high, they be too subject to the blows of the artillery; if they be made too low, they may be the more easy to scale.'[3] The Trace Italienne, a classic template on which to base such designs, had no equal – properly applied, a fortress built on this principle had as good a chance of success as any.

The Trace Italienne and its subsequent derivations gave the intriguing appearance of complexity, but this was not really so as it comprised one relatively simple geometric design superimposed upon another. The indispensable defensive attributes of depth, concealment, protection, observation and good fields of fire were sought and achieved in this way. The polygonal system of fortification, employing ravelins, bastions, parapet, ditch and glacis (*see* Appendix IV for a glossary of siege terms), enabled the defender to sweep all approaches, above ground, with artillery fire and musketry. Those approaches would ideally be kept scrupulously clear, although this often proved difficult in practice, and there should be no element of dead ground that could not be covered with fire. Bastions were placed at regular intervals on the main, or curtain (courtine) wall and would enable crossfire to be kept up for mutual defence. However skilfully or quickly an attacker came forward, he would come under fire not only from the front, where it was to be expected, but also be exposed to enfilading fire coming in from each flank. The Trace Italienne, with its beguilingly intricate patterns and its derivatives became the overall template adopted and adapted by military engineers for the 300 years from the mid-fifteenth century onwards, until the advent of effective long-range rifled artillery threw almost everything back onto the drawing boards of military engineers.[4]

Advanced works, ravelins, demi-lunes and so on, forward of the main fortifications, would provide a garrison with the valuable element of defence in depth, and add the ability to keep all more middle-distance avenues of approach covered by both observation and fire. The task of the attacker was thus made more difficult, with a price to be paid to even get into close proximity of the forward edge of the main defences, the feature of which was known as the Covert or Covered Way, to begin the real work of the siege with the breaking through the main defensive wall with mining or artillery. This forward defensive element clearly distanced the besiegers' artillery from the curtain wall, the main line of defence, and well away from the citadel, the true heart of any fortress. The defenders were provided with as near perfect clear fields of fire as possible, while simultaneously having a degree of shelter from the besieging artillery. The glacis, the open slope leading up to the first line of defence, the Covered Way, would be swept with the fire of the garrison, both artillery and musketry, and heavy casualties would be expected as the price to pay to achieve a foothold at the edge of the defences. This was all a part of the soldiers' lot in life, and attacking a formal fortress, where the garrison was in good heart, was well known to be a bloody business.

Artillery was always a rather immobile arm, although improved gun carriages and the tactical development of light horse artillery from the mid-eighteenth century onwards partly rectified this lack. Firstly, only major powers and wealthy princes could afford to equip their armies with the massive guns necessary to batter a fortress, one that had been designed to withstand such weaponry, into submission. Then the enormous effort and cost of transporting a siege train of artillery to the spot from which the big guns could begin the work of breaching the defences cast an unavoidable and massive drag upon the operations of field commanders. Hundreds of wagons and thousands of draught animals would be required to move the siege train, all of which, having been gathered at some convenient spot, then had to be protected from the unwelcome attentions of enemy cavalry while on the way to the selected fortress. Not infrequently a campaign within a campaign would have to be conducted, with at least half the army besieging a fortress while the rest were engaged in bringing forward and protecting the huge and cumbersome siege guns and the associated matériel that were required. 'For God's sake, be sure you do not risk the cannon,' the 1st Duke of Marlborough wrote in 1708 to his Quartermaster-General, William Cadogan, reflecting his main concern early on in the campaign to take Lille.[5] The valuable use of waterways, in an age when the roads were usually very bad if not actually impassable, would help, but these convenient routes were often held by the enemy who also appreciated their usefulness. Many small-scale actions would be bitterly fought as one side tried to keep the rivers and canals open for use, while the other side attempted to shut them down and keep them so.

Artillery had also been in use by the garrisons of fortresses from the very start, and the design of the new defensive works would allow for the emplacement of guns to provide both frontal and flanking fire. The subsequent development of tower bastions, mounting numerous pieces of artillery under cover, a favourite device of Vauban's later designs (although first employed by the Duke of Brittany at Fougères in the 1480s), would add to the defensive strength that a well-equipped garrison could bring into play. The potential target for the gunners of the garrison was, however, quite meagre when compared to the enormous target towards which the besieger's batteries could work their destructive magic in making a breach through which the infantry could move to assault the heart of the fortress.

By the early seventeenth century, the effective use of gunpowder artillery and mining had brought about a very necessary major revolution in fortress design. In common use were low, impact-resistant earthworks of complex geometrical plan, sometimes faced with harder materials, intended to resist, absorb and deflect the power of the big guns of the siege batteries. After initial astounding successes for siege artillery, it gradually became apparent that the art of the gunner had not kept pace with the skill and ingenuity of the fortress designers, and the subjugation of a major fortress, if it could not be taken by surprise, remained an expensive, laborious and time-consuming business. Of course, that was exactly what the fortress was intended to achieve – the imposition of cost and delay upon an opponent: in particular time was gained in which other factors – the approach of relieving field armies, disease and lack of provisions amongst the besiegers, or more mercifully, negotiations for an agreed peace – might take effect.

The importance of time, so key to military operations, cannot be overstated. Fortresses provided a kind of permanent roadblock, lying squarely in the path of invading armies, imposing delay upon military operations and often dictating the pace and scope of any campaign. In this way, the judicious employment of strong fortress defences was a quite aggressive course to pursue, particularly by commanders with a less numerous army than an opponent, shackling the tactical ability of any invader to operate at will. Once again, with a short campaign season through the months of good weather, this shackling could be fatal to the best-laid plans of any attacking army commander. The other side of the coin was that the commander of an invading army, by picking off and seizing fortresses, would encroach upon the sovereign territory of an opponent, while seizing the vital adjacent river crossings. The use of the supply depots and tax-gathering opportunities in the vicinity would be taken away, while room in which to manoeuvre would be gained. In addition, contributions and supplies with which to feed hungry troops could be levied on an opponent's territory and unfortunate subjects. In this manner, a perfectly respectable campaign could be waged, without the necessary need to risk all in battle in open field, when hard-won and long cherished reputations might be found to be at considerable and unpredictable risk.

Investing a fortress was one thing, but subduing the garrison and forcing a submission was often a time-consuming affair. The price paid for such successes was of course lost time, an important consideration, but the seizure of even second-rate fortresses was undoubtedly no minor achievement. Given that there were generally recognized rules for siege warfare, aiming to civilize a fairly uncivilized business and reduce unnecessary casualties and suffering, the reputation of army commanders could rest on the successful prosecution of just such a campaign of sieges. There might well be no necessity to risk all in battle, when the capture of fortresses in a steady, almost dignified, way might very well be enough to sustain a decent military reputation for good sound soldiering:

> Let us suppose a General endowed with great bravery, but un-acquainted with the art of attacking and defending fortified places, enters into an enemy's country, and after having committed some ravages meets the army of his adversary and defeats it. (This, how-ever, is an advantage not so easily gained, since if his enemy is a wary and prudent commander, but inferior in strength, he may possibly avoid an engagement.) But what benefit will he reap from his victory, if his adversary retires into some strong place, which he knows not how to *Attac* and carry without the loss of the best part of his army? Should he advance further into the enemy's country, and leave strong places behind him, he will run the risk of being surrounded on every side, or having his convoys of ammunition and provisions cut off, whereby his army will be reduced through famine and want [...]
> It may be said that the Engineers will supply his want of knowledge.[6]

Of course, to be blocked up in a fortress, whether or not this was the result of a recent defeat in battle, was a recipe not for success but for eventual submission if the siege was conducted competently. In the same way, to leave uncaptured enemy fortresses in the rear of an army as it advanced was to court trouble. Both considerations could be seen in play in 1708 after the French defeat at Oudenarde that July. Marshal Boufflers, for all his gallant defence of Lille, had to yield after three months, but the Duke of Marlborough had been unable to push on and make the most of his recent victory, as this would have left the fortress, garrisoned and threatening, in the rear of his army and close to his extended lines of communication and supply.

So numerous were the campaigns that featured sieges above anything more dramatic, certainly not outright battles, that the story of conflict in the period of the mid to late seventeenth century might be said to be that of siege warfare and not a lot else of particular note. It would take later commanders of a more dynamic stamp such as the 1st Duke of Marlborough, Prince Eugène of Savoy, and Marshals of France, James Fitzjames, Duke of Berwick and Claude-Louis-Hector de Villars to drive forward the pace of campaigns based upon the deathly chance in a day of battle to ruin an opponent's army beyond hope of recovery, and win a war.

At first glance it might well be thought that the attacking commander always set the pace and had the more active role in siege warfare, while the garrison commander, tasked to hold a fixed point against what were often superior numbers, had the more passive part to play. This is something of an illusion, as there is nothing passive about well-conducted defence, a phase of operations that in the right circumstances can tie down and wear down an opponent very well. The defender, in fact, had an inbuilt but subtly silent advantage, in that he was fighting on ground of his own choosing, always an important military factor, ground which had been prepared with great care long in advance, as a kind of inviting killing zone into which the attacker was invited to tread. A prolonged siege would tie down the efforts and resources of an army in the limited time for campaigning before the onset of wet weather which turned the roads into impassable mud. The siege itself might not succeed at all, it might even be plainly defeated, particularly if the preparations were inadequate or improperly thought through, with consequent dire effect upon the reputations of those involved.

It had to be borne in mind that the preparation of enormously strong formal defences, for all that they were powerful symbols of sovereignty, was a very expensive and labour-intensive business. The employment of large numbers of soldiers as labourers, toiling to construct the fortresses to Vauban's designs, could not fail to have an eventual impact on the ability of the French field armies in the widest sense. Men who were trained to be very good soldiers were employed *en masse* as navvies and labourers, not only in the construction of fortresses, but in civil projects such as building canals and aqueducts. As the fortress belt took shape and grew, the cutting edge of the French army was dulled, both physically with the misemployment of her soldiers but also in a moral sense, for if all else failed, France could fall back, literally, on Vauban's fortresses. As it was, even if a fortress was taken, not infrequently this prize would be negotiated away again in the peace settlement that would inevitably follow at some not too distant point. In the end, unless a strategic gain such as a permanent extension of vital territory could be achieved, fortresses were largely bargaining counters. Louis XIV certainly extended his borders to a considerable degree, but then found this to be so when he had to relinquish into Austrian and Dutch control such key towns as Mons, Courtrai, Tournai, Ypres and Oudenarde in the Treaty of Utrecht in 1713, at the close of the War of the Spanish Succession.

Once an army commander had decided upon a siege of a certain place and had made the necessary arrangements for the huge quantity of stores, matériel, ordnance, ammunition, food, fodder and conscripted labour that would be required to be brought forward from assembly areas deep in the rear of the

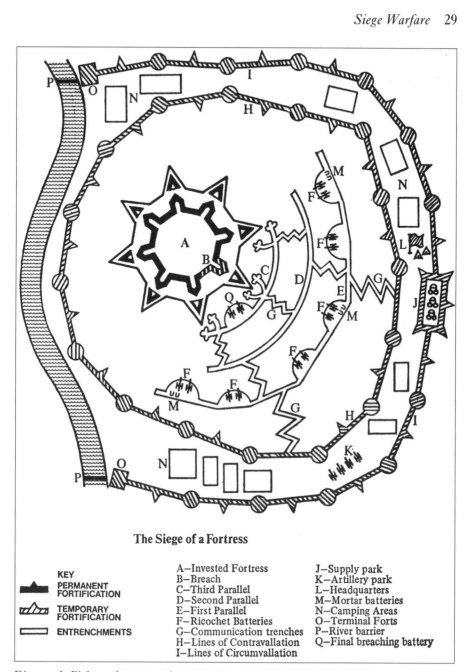

The Siege of a Fortress

KEY

PERMANENT
FORTIFICATION

TEMPORARY
FORTIFICATION

ENTRENCHMENTS

A—Invested Fortress
B—Breach
C—Third Parallel
D—Second Parallel
E—First Parallel
F—Ricochet Batteries
G—Communication trenches
H—Lines of Contravallation
I—Lines of Circumvallation

J—Supply park
K—Artillery park
L—Headquarters
M—Mortar batteries
N—Camping Areas
O—Terminal Forts
P—River barrier
Q—Final breaching battery

Diagram 1. Eighteenth-century siege operations.

army, a cavalry force would be sent to cut off all convenient lines of communication and supply to the chosen fortress.[7] This key movement was the actual investment of the garrison, severing virtually all their links with the outside world:

> The Lieutenant General who has been charged with investing a place, should provide himself with good guides and force the march, halting only as long as is necessary to graze the horses and to rest a little. He should continue to avoid revealing his objective until the approach to it makes his intention evident [...] He should detach two or three cavalry parties [...] to raid the outskirts of the fortress, these parties should attempt to make off with the animals and to take prisoners. Arriving before the fortress he should seize the chief routes into it and place his troops in battle order upon them.[8]

The cavalry would also hope to pick off any parties of troops working or foraging around the environs of the fortress, and to secure such cattle, herds, horses and fodder that were to be found in the vicinity. Unless they could be resupplied, or the besieging force driven off, the garrison and the unfortunate citizenry of the town would in the end starve, if not sooner forced into submission by bombardment and the threat of a storm of the defences 'sword in hand'. The garrison commander would be immediately made reliant upon his own limited resources, both in men and stores, while the besieger, by comparison, would be able to replenish his stocks of food and ammunition, and bring forward drafts of fresh soldiers to replace those killed and wounded in the siege works.

The ability of the besiegers to operate at will depended on whether or not the governor of the besieged garrison could call on his own field army to come forward and drive away the attacking forces. This might, on quite rare occasions, result in a dramatic confrontation by battle in open field, as was the case at Malplaquet in 1709 and Fontenoy in 1745, although more often the tactic employed would be to try to sever the lines of supply to the attacking army and oblige it to draw off as rations drew short. To counter such a move, once a fortress was invested, the besieging army would draw near and go into a fortified camp of its own, constructing Lines of Contravallation looking inwards and emplaced to guard against any sortie by the garrison, while outward-looking Lines of Circumvallation would be built to guard against any attack by a relieving force.

The construction of these extensive lines of defence for a besieging army had been a common feature since the early sixteenth century, when they were developed in Italy, and the technique was refined by both sides during the War of Dutch Independence. A French observer of the Siege of Grave in 1602 wrote 'The works are truly gigantic. Every redoubt, no matter how small, has its own wet ditch [...] the continuous line is so huge and vast that it takes nearly five hours to make the circuit.'[9] Such well-constructed lines of defence would usually withstand any attempt to breach them by a relieving army, and the fortress encircled in this way would, to all purposes, be cut off from the outside and any hope of assistance. At times, besieging armies would be themselves invested, as at Turin in 1640, when French troops held out in the Citadel, Spanish troops occupied the town, which was besieged by a French army, which, in turn, was encircled by a Spanish army in an entrenched camp trying to lift the siege. An apparently absurd arrangement, but each commander would have thought his own tactics likely to achieve the desired result, given enough time. Such lines were not at all invincible, however, as was demonstrated at the relief of Arras by Marshal Turenne in 1654, when his troops stormed the Spanish lines of Circumvallation and put their besieging army to flight, an action in which Vauban took part.

The besiegers would, in this way, construct a massive entrenched base in close proximity to the beleaguered fortress, from which the siege could be pressed forward in relative security. For any garrison commander to make a meaningful sortie was a considerable risk, although many did so, as any casualties suffered could not readily be replaced, unlike those suffered by the besieging force. That consideration had to be weighed against the likely damage to be done to the besieger's works, and the delay imposed on those operations in the process. Once again, the implacable demands of having to campaign in the months of good weather exerted a strong influence, whether for the general attacking a fortress, or for the commander of the besieged garrison using the limited means at his disposal to hamper his opponent.

At the same time, even though the resources of a garrison commander were finite, defence had to be active and not passive if a suitable price was to be demanded of the besieging army, and the cost of preparing a strong formal defence was to prove its worth. 'The defender will quickly lose the fortress if he allows the besieger to work at leisure in the country outside, for the siegeworks are like some poison which is deadly once it reaches a vital part.'[10] In rather the same way that a besieging army would construct a secure camp between the Lines of Contravallation and Circumvallation, so too would defenders make use of entrenched camps for their field armies. These would sometimes be placed in close proximity to fortresses under likelihood of threat, and by their use, a defending general, even with inferior numbers, could do much to hinder the progress of any siege from a position of relative security. Vauban approved this method, and the garrison would probably not be cut off entirely from the outside world, and could be resupplied and replenished from the entrenched camp. However, in the autumn of 1711, Marshal Villars used an entrenched camp to try to prevent Bouchain from falling to the Duke of Marlborough, who actually deployed the smaller army, and in this endeavour the French commander very clearly failed.

Vauban gave advice to his own engineers as to the matters that required particular attention when laying out the Lines of Contravallation and Circumvallation. These have a curiously modern flavour to them, when considering how to prepare any position for defence:

> Occupy all the high ground which could be prejudicial to our position; permit no hollows or defiles within musket range of our lines without assuring that they can be fired upon; avoid, and even give ground if necessary to get away from, all commanding heights which we cannot capture; profit from all natural cover, defiles, marshes, rivers, streams, and woods which can strengthen the lines or shorten the work of building them; do not be overconcerned about the symmetry of the lines, but push them out and pull them in to take every advantage of the terrain.[11]

However, the practice had developed of lavishing a significant amount of time and effort into the construction of the Lines of Circumvallation in particular, so to ensure the security of the besieging army against outside interference, while giving by comparison rather little thought and care to the layout and progress of the actual siege works. This became particularly marked amongst Dutch commanders, but the French and Spanish were also prone to this failing.

Given the difficulties of moving field armies about nimbly enough to bring an opponent to battle in the open, it is not surprising that sieges were a significant part of warfare for much of the sixteenth and seventeenth centuries. Yet, the actual day-to-day conduct of siege operations was regarded as a rather inferior business when compared with the exciting clash of huge armies in a single day of battle. Siegecraft, painstaking and diligent, was looked down upon as slightly mundane, and Louis XIV would prove to be reluctant to allow Vauban, his master engineer, to undertake siege operations in person, once he had at long last been given the exalted rank of Marshal of France. The theory was, clearly, that it would now be beneath his new dignity, with the result that the very same skills that had enabled him to rise from relatively humble beginnings would now be left unused, at a time of particular peril. Perhaps the calculation was made by Louis XIV, who rarely did things by accident, that at his age (67), Vauban's time for active campaigning was at an end. From this general attitude that siegecraft was inferior to other methods of warfare, it seemed clear that officers in the more highly regarded arms, the cavalry and the infantry, when called upon to embark on siege operations had a tendency not to take proper care, or proceed with enough caution, in case they should be suspected of insufficient vigour or a tendency to hang back in the face of the enemy. There was no difficulty with properly employed dash and initiative in an attack, as was seen at Venlo in 1702, or that at Saint Ghislain on the Tuesday night before the Battle of Malplaquet in September 1709, when Colonel Haxhausien's German brigade stormed the French defences to free the roads leading onto the battlefield. Fortified places would occasionally be taken by surprise and the garrison commander rushed into making a surrender, but these were very much the exception, unless treachery was employed.

It was apparent that the artillery arm, powerful but sluggish, had not kept up with the pace of imaginative fortress design. Sheltered by massively constructed, low and thick, earthen, stone or brick-faced defensive works in the immediately identifiable geometric design derived from the Trace Italienne, the defenders had, for the time being, obtained an advantage over the attackers, as long as their discipline, food and ammunition lasted. The fortress would hold out and impede the progress of an invader's campaign. The natural response to this impasse was the premature infantry attack, to overwhelm the defenders while demonstrating energy and impetuous valour, but with all the loss of life and probably inadequate gains that resulted. Vauban was amongst those who were disgusted by such wanton bloody expense, no matter what bravery and dash was being demonstrated. Resulting heavy and unnecessary casualties in failed attacks were common. 'Hundreds of brave soldiers lay in piles upon each other, weltering in blood, and trodden down by their companions.'[12] Such carelessly mounted infantry attacks were to be deplored, and not mistaken for true valour. Vauban was firmly against such efforts, and on occasions when his measured approach to siegecraft appeared to be too time-consuming and he was pressed to hurry things along, he refused to do so.

Quite rightly remembered as an imaginative designer and prolific builder of fortresses, Vauban was just as inventive and influential in setting out efficient, and thereby less costly, ways to attack fortified places. He devoted a great deal of thought to devising a logical way to prepare for and mount an assault on a modern fortress. Vauban's model timetable for a formal siege of a first-class fortress was set out to be:

> To invest a fortress, gather stores and construct the lines of circum-vallation and contravallation: 9 days.
> To open the trenches and reach the covered way: 9 days.
> To capture the covered way: 4 days.
> To cross the ditch to reach the demi-lune: 3 days.
> To create a breach by battery fire or mining: 4 days.
> To capture the demi-lune: 3 days.

To cross the main ditch: 4 days.
To site forward batteries and breach the main defences: 4 days.
To capture the breach and flanking positions: 2 days.
To accept the capitulation of the garrison: 2 days.
To allow for unexpected delays: 4 days.
Total time allowed: 48 days.

There was an instant problem with such a schedule; almost inevitably, this outline timetable, which was just intended to be a guide, was taken by some commanders, both as defender or besieger, as a strict model for what should be done. A garrison commander, aware that the forty-eight-day point was approaching, might feel that enough had been achieved, honour had been satisfied, and so a capitulation could be offered. On the other side of the tactical hill, the besieging commander, irrespective of the demands of a wider campaign in the field, could see the forty-eight-day programme as the time that was generally allowed for the seizing of such a fortress.

Despite all this, Louis XIV had to warn his provincial governors in 1705 against a growing tendency to give in too soon, when faced with a siege: 'They are strictly forbidden to yield their places until there is a large breach on the main rampart and they have withstood at least one assault.'[13] In practice, many commanders were ready enough to force the pace on the one hand, as Prince Eugène did rather badly at Lille in 1708, or to hang on grimly on the other, as the blinded Marquis de Laubanie did at Landau in 1704, on that occasion for a quite admirable seventy days. Vauban's successes at Mons in 1691 and Ath in 1697, on the other hand, show that the pace could at times be forced without undue casualties. He also prepared a model timetable for the defence of the rebuilt Lille Citadel, for the use of commissaries when preparing and laying in sufficient stocks of ammunition and provisions to withstand a siege. Interestingly, given his model timetable for how to conduct a siege, he only stipulated that forty days' worth of supplies should be got in. Not that matters were a foregone conclusion if the garrison was well led: 'How utterly uncertain is the course of a siege attack,' a French officer wrote, 'and how many circumstances may contrive to retard it.'

A formal siege was a huge and complex undertaking, requiring a high degree of organization and administration. It was estimated that to attack a major fortress of modern design in the late seventeenth century, a field army 40,000-strong was required as a minimum force to prosecute the siege and perform the covering operation and 10,000 labourers were required for the entrenching work, with 18,000 hand tools for use. These workmen would often be local peasants conscripted for the task, and consequently reluctant participants who would be inclined to shirk the labour or slip away when they could. Set scales required 3,300,000 sets of rations of bread, beer or wine, and meat. No less than 40,000 round-shot was required for the 24-pounder breaching guns, and 800,000 pounds of gunpowder to keep these weapons in action. Troop comforts were not neglected, and Vauban was concerned to ensure that his men had an adequate supply of tobacco: 'Essential for keeping the soldiers content,' he wrote, 'Indeed, they have become totally dependent upon it.'[14] Given the state of the roads at the time, and the inability to always have use of waterways when these were controlled by an opponent, the gathering of these men, munitions and matériel was a monumental task, one that was always vulnerable to disruption and interception by hostile cavalry raids. A reputation built upon successful siege warfare was certainly no mean thing.

Once the actual siege operations were begun, with the ground being broken and the digging of the trenches under way, a secure base would have to be established, often comprising a square earthwork redoubt, in which a ready reserve of infantry could be held to guard against any sudden sortie by the garrison of the besieged fortress:

> These works and redoubts serve for a retreat to the workmen if an enemy should make a sortie upon them; for being retreated into the said redoubts, they may resist an enemy, and stop him, till they are seconded [...] If the workmen had not a place to retreat into, they would be forced to betake to their heels.'[15]

Parallel trenches, derived from an innovation of the Ottoman armies in eastern Europe, were further developed by Vauban for use in the attack. These parallels comprised a series of entrenchments that would encircle that part of a fortress chosen as the focal point for an attack, at a more or less uniform distance, providing essential cover for breaching artillery and storming parties. The precise location where the main effort to storm the place was to be made was disguised for as long as possible. The work of counter-mining parties by the garrison, always a risk, would in this way be rendered more difficult, as would the massing of enough defenders in good time to beat off an assault with effective defensive fire. The previously common alternative course, that of a single approach trench, would signal very plainly just where the assault was intended to be made. The Dutch engineer, Meinheer van Coehorn, would protest to Vauban, on one notable occasion at Namur, that the use of these parallels was improper and almost unfair in the manner in which the defenders were misled about the attackers' intentions:

> Before the excavations of the trench actually begins, the engineers should, by daylight, take the observations that will be necessary to allow them to lay out the line during the night, and then, as soon as it

is dusk – without even waiting for dark – they should mark out with fuse lines as much of the work as they think can be finished that night [...] they should have twenty-five or thirty musketeers some fifty paces in front of them for greater security.[16]

The approach trench, known as a sap (hence the term 'sapper' for those soldiers who dug them), was described by Vauban as 'A kind of gallery completely sunk in the ground, by means of which one advances towards any works of the enemy. The uncovered sap, or half sap, is a sap which is only half-sunk.' He went on that the technique, when sapping, was of:

A man kneeling on his knees digs to get into the ground, and casts up the earth before him on both sides with a short spade, towards that part of the fortress, till he has digged 3 feet into the ground, and that he is covered [protected] with the earth, casting always the earth like a mole before him.[17]

This was hazardous work of the highest degree, and the sappers often wore armour protection for the head, neck and shoulders. Some intrepid souls preferred to do without, able to work without the constriction of armour and making faster pace, progress for which they were paid by the yard, but at greater at risk of being shot. Bounty pay was routinely offered to those who would volunteer to push the saps so perilously onwards. The lead man, digging and pushing forward the wheeled mantlet, or sometimes just a wicker-basket gabion laid on its side, was followed by his comrades close behind, piling up more gabions as protection from fire, which would increase, musketry and small calibre artillery, mortars and grenades, as they edged closer and closer to the Covered Way of the fortress. The sap would be widened and deepened by those men following the lead party, so that in time a soldier could stand erect in the trench thus created, protected to a large degree from the fire of the defenders. 'The first sapper makes a Trench of 18 inches deep and just as wide,' as John Muller wrote:

the second makes it 6 inches [more], and widens it as much; the third makes it 6 inches more, and widens it as much, and the fourth does the same; so that all four together make a trench of 3 feet wide, and as much in depth; the earth of which will serve to make a parapet strong enough to resist musket shot.[18]

When the water table was high, as it was in much of Flanders and the Low Countries, it was not possible to dig very far down without flooding the trenches (as both the German and Allied armies would find around Ypres from the autumn of 1914 onwards). So, the sap would have to be laboriously built up and stand proud, to a lesser or greater degree, of the open ground, and be protected with fascines and gabions, piled on top of one another on the side most exposed to the fire of the defenders. 'At the Siege of Bouchain [1711], the late General Armstrong carried a work through the marshes full of reeds, in one night's time, by means of hurdles and fascines.'[19]

It was not unknown for a garrison, if energetic and enterprising enough, to dig counter-approaches, creeping their way outwards from the main defences of the fortress to intercept the advancing approach trenches of the besiegers. Such counter-approaches were employed at the Siege of Phillipsburg in 1675, and by the Marquis de Laubanie in his notable defence of Landau in 1704 (Francis Todleben would also use them at Sebastopol, as late as 1854–1855, and they were not at all unknown on the Western Front between 1914–1918). The men engaged in this kind of dangerous work, whether digging approaches or their defensive counterparts, perhaps understandably, lived hard, worked hard and played hard. Drinking was a common problem, and both the work and discipline suffered as a result. 'There is one thing against which the officers ought to take every precaution; namely, the tendency of the sappers to get drunk while they are working at the head of the sap. They throw every precaution to the winds.'[20]

The system of parallel trenches, first, second and third, each one progressively closer to the defences of the fortress, was first used by Vauban at the siege of the Dutch-held fortress of Maastricht in the spring of 1673, in the presence of Louis XIV. Unlike single approach trenches, which had generally been the practice, and the head of which would naturally attract the most attention from the guns of the garrison, a parallel trench left open a number of possible points from which to launch an assault. Still, that part of the fortress to be attacked would in its turn attract the most attention from the fire of the siege batteries trying to suppress the guns of the garrison and beginning the breaching work, and so the secret, such as it was, would be a fairly open one before very long. The garrison would, accordingly, have a good indication as to what was intended and where the main blow was to fall.

Once the third parallel, that dug closest to the fortress, had been completed, an assault could be made, often under cover of darkness, on the defenders of the Covered Way. This entrenchment would be topped with stakes, or 'palisades', to add a measure of final protection from the musketry, hand-grenade throwing and artillery fire of the besiegers. If the garrison was numerous and in good spirits, the assault would probably be bitterly contested. Hand-to-hand fighting was common on these occasions, with bayonet, musket butt and grenades freely used, and local counter-attacks would be launched to drive the besiegers back down the glacis and into their parallels, where the defenders would, if the opportunity arose, pursue them to disrupt the siege arrangements, so laboriously made, and inflict still more casualties. This would all be foreseen and catered for by any competent besieging commander, and squads of second-echelon troops would be ready at hand in intervals in the approach trenches and parallels, ready to move forward into the defences and to exploit initial success, perhaps to reinforce a flagging effort, and in case of adversity to turn back a stinging counter-attack by the garrison.

A common feature of many sieges was the set-piece sortie by the garrison, part of an aggressive defence, and in effect a local counter-attack to spoil the besiegers' works, burn the accumulated stores and munitions, spike the guns and mortars in the forward batteries, and kill as many of the highly valuable sappers and miners as possible in the process. The principal aim was to delay the progress of the siege, and drive down the morale of those working in the trenches; limited success was looked for, as only an extraordinarily successful and powerful sortie would so damage the besiegers that their whole operation would have to be called off. The expected benefit of a sortie had to be weighed by the garrison commander against the casualties that he would be likely to suffer in a fortress that could not expect to receive any replacements.

Once this calculation was made and the decision taken to go ahead, sorties often took place at night, in part because of the valuable cover of darkness, which was partly offset by the greater difficulty in command and control. Also, because as much sapping work was done at night as during the day, so the chance to inflict damaging casualties amongst these valuable men was higher, while the element of surprise might also be greater. A changeover in shifts of workmen, at first light perhaps, would also be a favoured time although, if the effort was to be made in daylight midday was favoured, as the troops in the siege trenches would often be snatching a meal, with shifts of sappers changing over with all the attendant confusion and lack of alertness that this entailed:

> In the morning the French made a sally from the town [Douai] upon that post where our regiment was. It was a little before break of day. They came on silently, expecting to surprise us, but by the goodness of Providence we were ready. Our sentries gave us warning, and we put ourselves in a posture, and received them so warmly, that they immediately retired in confusion.[21]

Vauban was not that convinced that sorties were always worthwhile, in producing enough benefit in exchange for the casualties suffered by the garrison:

> Sorties are of two kinds; there are sorties in force and weak sorties; they are undertaken at different times of day and night. Weak sorties are almost invariably launched at night, sorties in force usually by day. The object of the sorties in force is to aid relief expeditions, to

destroy some part of the besiegers' trenches, to defeat part of their guard, to raid some poorly secured position, such as the one we took at Lille, to regain a poorly held position on the outer defences, such as that at Montmédy which was retaken two or three times, or finally simply as a bluster so the enemy [the garrison commander] will be able to say that he has made a sortie.[22]

He went on with careful advice on the steps to be taken to ensure that a sortie by a garrison was met in a prompt and effective manner. 'As soon as the sortie has been discovered, the workers and their guards should be ordered to withdraw, fire, fall back fifty or sixty paces, and thereafter retreat into the nearest guard position behind the other troops.' The establishing of defensive redoubts at intervals in the trenches served to give some protection to the sappers when these sorties were attempted.

However, an alert garrison commander should always be able to seize those opportunities that presented themselves, and crowded trenches on the one hand presented a tempting target, while undermanned or poorly guarded trenches were at certain risk of a surprise or 'affront'. One of Vauban's pupils wrote:

> If he [the commander of the besieging force] contents himself with putting a few workmen in the sap-heads, sudden sorties of small bodies should be made, to kill the workmen, and destroy their works; and if on the contrary the enemy keeps a larger force near at hand to support these workmen, the intended object will have been attained, of drawing the besieger in mass within reach of the heavy vertical fire [of mortars].[23]

As the siege works crept across the glacis and came closer to the outer works of the fortress, the pace of fire from the defenders would intensify, seeking to slow or halt the progress. This ability was hampered, naturally enough, by the degree of damage and the casualties that had been inflicted by the besieging batteries. These would have been hard at work to suppress the garrison and break down the obstacles and defences. To do so, by concentrating fire at the selected point of attack and neighbouring positions, was an absolutely necessary preliminary to establishing a firm position from which to dominate the Covered Way, and begin to prepare a breach in the main defences. Once again, the temptation to push the pace unduly and send in an attack before the siege batteries had done their work adequately had to be resisted.

On odd occasions, quixotic good fortune would play a significant and unexpected part, as at the siege of French-held Venlo in 1702, where the English attackers, having stormed the Covered Way and waded the flooded ditch, used handholds provided by the long grass growing on the slopes of the main defences to get over the ground with ease. The garrison commander, the Comte de Varo, had neglectfully left the grass to grow long, when it should have been regularly scythed short. 'We could never have climbed as we did,' a British officer, Richard Kane, wrote 'nor even as it was, had not the grass been long enough for us to hold by.'[24] On the other hand, at one siege conducted by the Duke of Marlborough in 1711, the besiegers dug down through the newly-captured Covered Way in an attempt to cross the defensive ditch with a measure of cover from musketry fire. They managed instead to go too deep and flooded their own works, being forced out in haste as the water in the ditch emptied out into the approach trenches.

If an outright assault on the Covered Way was not thought to be advisable or practical, then the besiegers' alternative recourse was to sap their way forward to the outer edge of the position, and attempt from there to dislodge the defenders behind the palisades with hand grenades. The defenders, for their part, would also use these simple but very effective missiles in frustrating the besiegers' attempts to occupy the Covered Way. Not infrequently, a hand grenade would be picked up and thrown back to its owner before exploding, a technique clearly not without risk, and calling for great coolness. A well-thrown grenade always has the capability to cause wide damage in the close confines of the trenches, as in 1708, when one missile thrown by the Chevalier de Guignard burned out 100 yards of gabions waiting to be filled by the besieging troops in a nearby sap. As the close-quarter contest went on and enough of the defenders had been disabled or driven out, the attackers would be able to progress to the next phase of their attack, a sudden rush of infantry to break through the palisades, where they had not been flattened by the pre-paratory bombardment, and overwhelm their opponents to take possession of the Covered Way. This was known as 'Crowning' the Covered Way, as once firmly established on the work, the sapping would be pushed out to left and right at right angles along the outer edge of the defences, to give the attackers room to mass their grenadiers for a maximum effort to cross the ditch and assault the main defences, once the breach had been achieved.

Where there remained a significant water obstacle, this had to be drained, as Vauban managed to do at the Siege of Ath in 1697, when his mortars disabled the sluices that maintained the water level. Otherwise, if this could not be done, the obstacle would have to be bridged by the laborious construction of a cause-way-like structure, made up of piles of fascines or heaped-up earth and stones. This had to be accomplished under the eyes and fire of the defenders, although if the siege batteries had done their work well enough, the fire of the garrison would have been largely suppressed, so that the construction of such a cause-way would not be an impossibly expensive task.

The Ditch, while a major part of a fortresses' obstacle plan, certainly presented something of a problem as the populace would, in time of tranquillity, use it as a rubbish dump for the refuse of the town. A ditch that was always kept filled with still water would rapidly become stagnant with attendant risks to health. So the obstacle was often left dry, until the opening of hostilities when the local sluices would be opened and the ditch filled with water. At intervals, orders would have to be given by the governor that the rubbish and filth that accumulated in a ditch should be cleared away, but the advent of war might mean that the obstacle was in a poor state to fulfil its intended purpose, especially if it was not routinely kept water-filled by the running flow of a local stream.

Once the Covered Way was secure, the grenadiers having bombed out the defending troops, the besiegers could bring forward the big guns of the breaching batteries, into position close alongside the captured works. The real bombardment of the selected spot for the breach would then begin, very often aimed at the adjacent projecting salient angle from which least crossfire would come:

> The Besieged being driven out of the Covert-Way, the next thing to be done is erecting Batteries, to make a Breach, and ruin the Defences [. . .] it is observed, that the best place for making breaches both in the ravelin and the bastion, is about 15 fathoms from the salient angle, so that the battering on both sides of the angle, the breach will become spacious and large.'[25]

Going straight for the salient angle, an apparently odd and risky thing to do, actually gave the attackers a measure of cover from defending fire, as only one

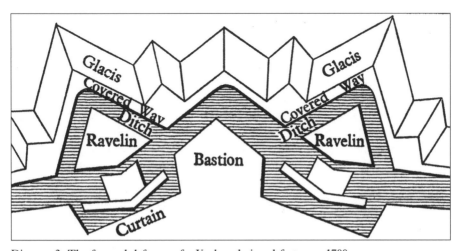

Diagram 2. The forward defences of a Vauban-designed fortress *c.*1700

piece of artillery could be mounted on the point aimed for, unlike on the adjoining curtain walls, and that could probably be disabled or suppressed by the besieger's battery fire. Otherwise, if the effort went in against the intervening wall between the salient angles, the attackers would be heading into a fire-swept killing zone.

When the breaching work got properly under way, unless a relieving army came forward to drive the besiegers off, it was just a matter of time for the garrison. The establishing of breaching batteries close to the main defences of a fortress was no simple matter for the huge guns, 24- or 32-pounders usually but sometimes massive 64-pounders, would have to be dragged along the bad roads of the time, or brought up whatever convenient waterway, river or canal was at hand and free of enemy interference. In practice the more mobile 24-pounder demi-cannon, 'the King of Siege Warfare', proved to be just as effective at the work of demolition as the larger and more cumbersome pieces, and used less powder. Once ready to be moved into battery position, to begin their work, the guns would have to be sited in pairs on foundations prepared with the greatest care so that they should not sink into the subsoil, which was not uncommon, as was found at Aire on the Lys river in the wet autumn months of 1710.

A stout wooden platform would have to be laid for each gun, and the sheer amount of material that was required was, once again, quite startling, with a single 24-pounder needing to be placed on a platform of six or seven 18-foot-long logs. Every yard of timber would, of course, have to be brought forward from the rear areas of the besieging army. Never mind food, tobacco or ammunition; at times above half an army's transport would have to be devoted to nothing else but bringing forward the huge quantities of timber that were required. The battery positions would also have to be protected from the inevitable attempts of the defenders to suppress them with counter-fire, musketry and artillery, and much of the work in establishing the batteries would need to take place under the cover of night. The mortars, cruelly effective in siege warfare, would need even more substantial foundations for their positions, due to the high trajectory at which they were fired and the resulting downward pressure with each shot. The most effective technique for creating a breach with round-shot was to break open the hard surface of the defences, and then use explosive shell with reduced charges of powder so that the shell would settle before exploding and collapse the ruined works into the ditch.

Mining was also extensively employed, where the water table and substrata allowed, and this was a particularly specialized and claustrophobically hazardous art, digging under the defences to plant explosive charges which when blown would produce the practicable breach. The earliest mining technique, that of digging beneath defences and then burning out the timber supports for the excavation and so causing a collapse from above, was still used but less frequently as the low artillery-resistant earthworks were less prone to this kind of attack.

The employment of the battering guns was first of all to suppress the defenders' artillery, then to create the 'practicable breach' in the main defences, where a soldier with both hands on his musket could mount unaided and enter the fortress.[26] This breaching work was usually undertaken at very close range, the guns having been progressively brought forward as the saps advanced. Once this breach was achieved, the defences were held to be fatally compromised, and before too long a capitulation would have to be agreed to avoid further effort and loss of life:

> Vauban's method of attack had as its object and as its result, not to leave any point upon the rampart where the defenders could live, or where they could mount a single gun. He afterwards tried at Neuf-Brisach to restore to the besieged, by means of casemates, the cover of which he had deprived them by introducing ricochet fire.[27]

These matters were finely balanced, as the garrison commander had to demonstrate vigour and zeal in holding out, but not to the point when a besieger had to storm the fortress, with all the mayhem and effusion of blood that was entailed. Less often, mercifully, the garrison commander might refuse to submit at all, perhaps through arrogance or misplaced confidence, and the place would have to be stormed, with all the attendant horrors to soldier and civilian alike, of such an extreme event. The attacking force, having been put to the trouble, effort and expense of a storm of the defences, had licence to pillage and sack the place for a time.

There was a widely understood, if unspoken, degree of common interest at this point, between the contending parties in a siege. The garrison commander, anxious to show that he had done his utmost to discharge his duty, would have resisted the sapping, mining and artillery-breaching activities as best he could. He would have made sorties, and kept the besiegers under as heavy fire as could be managed. He could usually claim to have done his best with limited resources. To give way too soon would be to invite retribution and suspicion of negligence or craven conduct, with damage to reputation if nothing more drastic. This happened to an unfortunate Danish officer in the Dutch service, who had a good reputation but was executed all the same, for giving up his post too soon in 1695.

For the commander of the besieging army, all the effort and labour of his sappers, pioneers and gunners would prove their worth when the practicable breach in the main defences was achieved, but he would want to avoid the cost, and consequent horrors, of having to storm the place. 'Enemy in position. There can only be two hours left before more attacks are made [...] It was decided by the general officers to obtain honourable terms of surrender.'[28] So, good terms would be offered to the garrison commander to capitulate, often with flowery compliments on the fine performance of his troops in adverse circumstances and so on. For the citizenry in the town, caught up in others' quarrels in which, very often, they had little direct interest, a negotiated submission and orderly return to normality, albeit with a different garrison in residence, was very desirable. Having suffered blockade and shortages, and bombardment, they would not want the garrison commander to fight it out to the last, with the possibility of sack, murder, and rapine by infuriated troops once they had fought their way into the town. As at Mons in 1691, the civil magistrates, all French speakers as it happened, were not slow to urge the Spanish garrison commander to come to terms at the right moment, and not leave things too long and invite catastrophe for all concerned.

There was also a general understanding, stemming from a revulsion at the horrors inflicted on places such as the city of Magdeburg in the Thirty Years War in Germany, or at Antwerp during the Dutch War of Independence, that the civilian populace of a fortified town should be spared, as much as was consistent with military necessity, from the horrors of war. However, the citizenry could not be protected to any great degree; hunger and danger would come to them as soon as a siege was begun, and if those that wished to do so were permitted to leave a besieged town, only those with the means to sustain themselves in the outside world could realistically take the opportunity to go. 'Passeports arrived for the ladies and women which Monsieur de Vauban (the Great Engineer's nephew) has asked for so as to permit them to go.'[29] A garrison commander would also routinely order the demolition of private houses to clear fields of fire, and the more substantial buildings would be occupied and turned into makeshift strongpoints to bolster the defences:

> Saw a lot of infantry and standards, so we assumed a siege was about to begin. We therefore began to fill the covered ways and the Places d'Armes (on the bastions) with troops, and set fire to the faubourgs and houses outside the town [...] We sent workmen to cut down the trees and hedges.[30]

In practice, a degree of destruction by bombardment was almost unavoidable, and at times this was a deliberate act of intimidation as at Douai in 1667, Mons in 1691, Brussels in 1695 and Ostend in 1706.

Local people hoping to stay with relatives in the countryside would usually find the region picked clean by the besieging army at an early stage. Outside the

walls of the fortress the population would suffer from the unwelcome attentions of armies on campaign; herds, flocks and crops routinely seized (and often
not paid for), to feed the hungry soldiers and horses requisitioned to supply
the needs of the cavalry. Able-bodied men would be commandeered to work in
the trenches for meagre wages, and their wives and daughters subject to the
amorous but often callous attentions of the soldiery.

Chapter 3

A Typical Country Squire

Sébastien le Prestre, Seigneur de Vauban, who would become one of the great military engineers of all time, was born on 1 May 1633 in the hilly Morvan district of Burgundy. The infant boy was baptized in the side-chapel of the parish church in the small village of Saint-Léger-de-Foucheret (renamed St-Léger-Vauban in December 1877), three days later, and given the name Sébastien as a compliment to his godfather, the parish priest, Père Clairin.[1] He was the second child and only son of Urbain le Prestre and his wife, Edmée (née Carmignolle), a couple of fairly modest means, who aspired to being respectable local gentry rather than anything grander, certainly with no pretensions to anything more elevated than minor provincial nobility. The family had, in fact, known genteel poverty in the not too distant past. 'We are in great trouble and want,' Sébastien's grandfather, Jacques le Prestre, wrote to relatives some fifteen years before the future Marshal of France's birth. 'If you could aid us to the best of your ability, we should be beholden to you.'[2] As is well known, poverty is an inconvenience rather than a disgrace, and the family seem to have overcome their financial difficulties in time. The closest that the boy's father and grandfather ever got to entering Royal service seems to have been with the Arrière-ban. This was a second-line local militia of rather doubtful tactical value, organized along feudal lines, and said by Vauban many years later to be 'Good for nothing except to cause difficulties by indiscipline and brawling.'[3]

The young man received rather elementary education from the priest in the village, before attending the highly-regarded Carmelite college at Semur-en-Auxois, about 20 miles to the south of Avalon. This, in effect, opened the door on the world for Vauban, who clearly had a firm appetite for education. Under the tutelage of a relative, the Abbé de Fontaine, he stayed at the college for seven years from the age of 10 onwards, and learned both to read and write well, studied mathematics, geometry, history, and acquired some considerable skill at drawing. All this might well have fitted him for the law, or perhaps the church, both respectable avenues to pursue for a promising youngster, but other factors came into play.

In 1651 Urbain le Prestre and his brother-in-law, Edmé Carmignolle, introduced the young Sébastien to the Prince of Condé, Duc d'Enghien, and renowned victor of Rocroi eight years earlier, where the vaunted Spanish infantry had been utterly defeated (a defeat from which Spain never really recovered militarily). Condé could lay claim to being amongst the most notable soldiers of the day, and both Sébastien's father and uncle seemed to have served under his command at various times in the past. The Prince was, however, now also a self-seeking intriguer and in open rebellion against the Crown. He had considerable support amongst the people of the Morvan, for local loyalties still meant much, and was looking to recruit more officers and men for his service. Condé was apparently favourably impressed with the young Sébastien le Prestre who, with no claim to fortune, had to make his own way, more or less unaided, in the world.

This was a time made particularly uncertain by the disruption of the latest of France's civil wars – 'les guerres civile' – known as the Second Fronde, the 'Fronde of the Princes'. It was also known, more dismissively by those who viewed with disdain such damaging self-indulgence by overmighty noblemen, as the 'War of the Chamber-Pots'. Many of these nobility had attempted, ultimately in vain, to curb what they regarded as the burdensome centralized power of the court and the monarchy. At this particular time, this took the form of the young King Louis XIV's mother, the Queen Regent, Anne of Austria, and her adviser and close confidante, Cardinal Mazarin. There was undoubtedly fault and grievances on both sides, but the lack of effective centralized power had a damaging effect and encouraged dissention:

> What trouble! What a frightful spectacle confronts me! The monarchy shaken to its foundations, civil war, foreign war, conflagration within and abroad; the cure on all sides worse than the ills; the princes arrested with great danger and then released with as much danger; the Prince of Condé whom we regarded as one of the great heroes of the century rendered useless to the country whose support he had been, and then, I don't know how, taking up arms against it.[4]

Popular unrest, fuelled by excessive taxation to pay for seemingly endless foreign wars, added to the difficulties at a time of deception, double-dealing, tumult and dangerous intrigue. The realm of the young King, it was said, was 'Dominated by ambitious nobles, whose only object was to get the government into their own hands, and then to share the spoils amongst themselves.'[5] Louis XIV was still legally an infant, and would not come into his majority until 5 September 1651, which was his thirteenth birthday, when he famously declared 'I intend now to assume the government personally, and hope by God's grace to rule rightly and justly.'[6]

Sébastien le Prestre, Vauban as he shall from now on be known, an aspiring soldier hoping to make his fortune with his sword, joined the Compagnie d'Arcenay, a part of the Régiment de Condé, in 1652. His immediate commander was a neighbour of the family, Charles-Antoine de Conyngham, Seigneur d'Arcenay. With the limited assistance which his family connections could provide, he gained a place as a Cadet, an honourable unpaid rank for someone who aspired to become an officer. This was due largely to the influence which his uncle, Edmé le Prestre, a Maréchal des Logis in the regiment, had been able to exert with Condé. The practice at the time was that a regiment would usually only have two Cadets on the strength, so the employment of some useful family interest on the young aspiring soldier's behalf was not without significance. Still, it is an ironic fact that Vauban, when a senior officer in the King's army, would oppose the very same system of cadetships, producing as he saw it the very worst type of soldiers with little discipline, learning or interest in their chosen profession.

There was an air of carefree youthfulness about Vauban's enlistment, a provincial young man with very parochial horizons, eager to accept the offer of possible advancement in the service of a great soldier. Young men, then and later, tended to follow the lead of local powerful magnates, and in a way this was only to be expected. No real sense of rebellion against rightful authority was demonstrated, and this seems to have been acknowledged by subsequent events. It was, nonetheless, in many ways a surprising start. At this time, Condé maintained an army on the Meuse, and was, in fact, in league with Madrid in pursuit of his own interests against the French crown. In August 1653, backed by Spanish troops, Condé advanced upon Paris, but his supply lines proved to be inadequate and he turned to attack the fortress of Rocroi in the Ardennes instead.

Vauban was noticed by Condé to be a diligent and energetic soldier who, even as a very young man, took a particular interest in the measured practices of siege warfare. This was understandable in so many ways as sieges, whether great or minor affairs, were a prominent and often pivotal part of all campaigning at the time. The young soldier first saw action at Clermont-en-Argonne, not far from Verdun, where he subsequently worked on improving the fortifications, and was at times entrusted with sole command of the whole project. This seems to have been the first in a very long list of such projects that he oversaw.

Moving on with the Régiment de Condé to take part in the Comte de Feuquières' Siege of Sainte Menehould on the Aisne river, in October 1652, Vauban distinguished himself during the course of one attack by wading the fast-flowing river under a heavy musketry fire from the defenders to secure a poorly-held outpost. The level of the water at the time would not, contrary to some accounts, have required him to have to swim across to complete the task. The town fell soon afterwards, the garrison being granted the honours of war, and after the now accepted custom were permitted to march away without giving their parole. Vauban's commanding officer was sufficiently impressed by his conduct to persuade Condé to offer him the post of an Ensign, a properly established commissioned rank, unlike that of Cadet, which was more like being an unpaid volunteer, albeit with some useful privileges. Vauban felt obliged to decline the offer, as he was unable to afford the horses, equipment and accoutrements necessary, and to pay a servant or groom. Instead, he accepted a transfer to the cavalry and served on as a gentleman trooper, being involved in a number of small-scale actions, in at least one of which he was wounded. Given leave to recuperate on this account, he was able to be present at his father's funeral in the Morvan.

The following year, 1653, 20-year-old Vauban was riding with a small scouting party when he and his comrades were surprised and charged by a larger force of the King's cavalry from the Régiment de Saint-Mauré. The Frondists fired a few shots and then scattered, riding for their lives, although most were overtaken and cut down or captured, but Vauban turned and confronted the attackers. He took advantage of a narrow sunken lane in the woods, 'un chemin creux', that prevented his opponents from getting round behind him, so that they could only approach one at a time. Brandishing his carbine in the face of the officer in charge of the Royal soldiers, a Captain de St Pierre, Vauban called out that he would submit, but only if he could do so on honourable terms, and be permitted to retain his sword, purse and horse. St Pierre was apparently rather taken with this bold declaration by the spirited young trooper and promptly accepted his parole of honour, leaving him mounted, with his side-arms, and unplundered. News of the encounter soon reached Cardinal Mazarin, who was impressed with what he heard of the young man's conduct and knowledge, and perhaps also of his recent exploits in the river at Sainte Menehould. He promptly offered Vauban a place in the King's army if he would only consent to change sides.

This was an opportunity not to be snubbed, and so Vauban agreed to enter the Royal service. He took part almost immediately in operations to retake Sainte Menehould, which was still held by Condé's Frondists, and where his recent knowledge of the state of the defences proved to be of particular value. The operations were conducted under the supervision of Louis-Nicholas, the Chevalier de Clerville, a 43-year-old Major in the Régiment de Noaillies, and a noted engineer. Had Vauban the misfortune to fall into the hands of his recent Frondist comrades manning the defences, his fate as a turncoat might well have been an unfortunate one at the end of a rope. The young Louis XIV was present at the renewed siege, and was amongst those who noticed Vauban's energy and apparent indifference to enemy fire, marking him out as probably worthy of further advancement.

Having taken service with the King, one of Vauban's first tasks was to oversee the repairing of the now rather battered fortifications of Sainte Menehould. He was also engaged for much of the rest of the year in siege operations against Saint Ghislain, Landrecies and Condé-sur-Escaut, and as the Chevalier de Clerville had become unwell and was absent on sick leave, Vauban was left pretty well in whole charge of the work. That the young man, so recently brought into the Royal service, was entrusted with these tasks at such an early stage speaks very well for his abilities. It may also, of course, indicate a general lack of good military engineers, particularly soldiers with some flair for, and real interest in, siege operations rather than demonstrating their prowess with the blade.

The young Vauban's diligence plainly met with approval, as Marshal Henri de la Ferte-Sennetière, a rough and ready soldier with a rather bullying manner, who had been in overall command at the siege of Spanish-held Landrecies in 1653, was particularly complimentary of the young man's efforts. At the Siege of Stenay the next year Vauban was wounded twice, on the second occasion by the flying debris from a mine he had just detonated, not having taken the precaution to move smartly out of the way. De Clerville was still unwell, and Vauban had been given the task to supervise the siege operations at Clermont en Argonne, where his multiple mining activities, which he doubted would be very effective if they came to be actually detonated, forced the rather faint-hearted garrison commander into surrendering sooner than he should have done.

The Fronde of the Princes stuttered to an end, for all serious purposes, in that year. On 24 August 1654, Marshal Turenne drove Condé's diminished army away from an attempt to take Arras, storming the Frondists' Lines of Circumvallation, against all the accepted practice of the day, and forcing the Prince to take shelter with his battered troops in the Cambrésis, around the town of Le Cateau. Vauban was present at the action. Louis XIV had already announced a general amnesty for Frondists in October the previous year, but he never quite forgot or forgave those nobles who had fought against him and his mother during the Regency, and had all but ruined France.

The King was less particular with the more junior rebels, and in this Vauban was undeniably fortunate. Always pragmatic, Louis XIV was inclined to forgive those Frenchmen who had fought in the service of the Spanish King or that of Condé, and in any case, Philip IV of Spain would make it a strict condition of the eventually agreed terms for peace that this should be so. Many of these men had little option but to follow the inclinations and preferences of their natural leaders, the local nobility who chose to become a part of the Fronde insurrection against what had been regarded as overly oppressive central power – power, moreover, that in the years of the King's minority, had largely been in the hands of a foreigner. Although Cardinal Mazarin was naturalized French, he was Italian-born, and was so regarded and thus reviled by many Frenchmen. In Vauban's case, his good conduct at Sainte Menehould and elsewhere was sufficiently impressive for him to be given both a cash reward and a commission in the Régiment de Bourgogne (previously the Régiment de Condé). The unit was also, rather ironically, known as the Régiment du Repentis (repentance), as it was composed almost entirely of former rebels who had mended their ways and prudently returned to their allegiance with the crown.

During 1655, Vauban was busily employed in siege operations against Spanish fortresses along France's as yet unsettled northern border. At Landrecies in July, Vauban was able to refine his mining techniques, blowing these under two attacks being carried on respectively by Marshal Turenne and Marshal de la Ferte. Condé-sur-Escaut and Saint Ghislain were both then captured that August, with Louis XIV present to oversee matters. Vauban was given the task to repair the defences, and at the noticeably early age of 22, he was made Engineer-in-Ordinary to the King, although he still had to report directly to the Chevalier de Clerville. This was a significant appointment which plainly recognized his emerging talent in this complex form of warfare, although to be Engineer-in-Ordinary was an acknowledgement of undertaking specialized service, and not a particular rank of its own accord.

Turenne and de la Ferte were again engaged in the Siege of Valenciennes, in 1656, where Vauban was once more wounded. The defences of the place were very strong, with a good-sized garrison commanded by the Comte de Menin, while Condé hovered nearby with an army some 20,000 strong, trying to interrupt the siege. The French operations were faltering, and this was dangerous when faced by someone as adept and audacious as Condé. The divided French command was unhelpful, and de la Ferte was actually taken prisoner and the army was forced to withdraw. The French troops were then besieged themselves in the fortresses of Condé-sur-Escaut and Saint Ghislain. Vauban was still convalescent with his wound, but helped with the defence of Saint Ghislain, although he had to be carried to and from the ramparts on a litter.

This casual disregard for danger when intent on the job in hand would really never leave Vauban. He had a robust and cheerful disposition, with studied indifference to what might happen, although he was always careful of the wellbeing of those around him. This attitude gave Louis XIV growing concern for his safety on many occasions, and repeated instructions were issued that he was not to expose himself too much to danger. However, this was just the daily lot of the military engineer, especially those conscientious enough to wish to inspect the progress of siege operations at first hand by tramping through the approach trenches and talking to the pioneers and workmen about how things were going. Those who chose to stay in the relative safety of the camp would be bound to come through unhurt, but the conscientious engineer was always likely to be at some hazard:

> They survived such a short time that it was seldom that you came across one who had seen five or six sieges, and still more remarkable to encounter a veteran who had served in as many sieges as this without having been incapacitated by wounds at the beginning of each operation or when it was only halfway through. Since the engineers were prevented from seeing the sieges right through to the end, they had no means of improving their knowledge.[7]

That this care for their work was not always evident amongst engineers can be seen in the difficulties that Prince Eugène of Savoy had at the Siege of Lille in 1708, when well-qualified and highly-paid engineers made a completely flawed assessment of what was required, at first, and then allowed huge stocks of stores to rot or otherwise become faulty.

Skilled engineers and experienced sappers were valuable assets, and yet were noticeably few in number, and were often misemployed:

> Men work from day to day without ever knowing what they will do in two hours time. So that everything is done in a disorderly, tentative, way; from which it follows that an approach is always ill-directed. There was a need of engineers who have a strong hold on firmly established principles; of workmen specially trained and taught; of materials sufficient in quantity and good in quality; and above all a fixed and constant resolution not to depart from rules which have been laid down when their soundness and utility have been verified by reason.[8]

On operations, the casualties in their ranks were high, as at the Siege of Montmédy on the Chiers river in 1657, the last remaining Spanish-held fortress in the north-east of France. The fortifications had been modernized and strengthened shortly before the siege commenced, which added to French difficulties. Of the 10,000 troops in Marshal de la Ferte's besieging army, only four were classed as qualified engineers, and three of these were killed while working in the trenches, within five days of the beginning of operations. Vauban alone survived, although he was lightly wounded four times, and yet he worked on in the trenches for forty days without a break. The Spanish garrison, only 700-strong and commanded by the highly capable Jean d'Allamont, held out for a very creditable fifty-seven days and during bitter fighting inflicted some

3,000 casualties upon the French. Unfortunately, gallant d'Allamont was mortally wounded by a French round-shot, shortly before the capitulation on 4 August 1657, and Vauban long afterwards remembered that the Siege of Montmédy was one of the most bleak and demanding such operations that he ever undertook.

A French officer wrote an appreciation of the skills necessary for a military engineer, skills that would change little over the years:

> Unlike the other warriors, they do not have the satisfaction of exchanging blow for blow. Not only that, but they have to remain cool in the midst of the most alarming dangers – it would be disastrous if they were panicked into mistaking one point of ground for another, because a blunder of that kind would lead to the trench being enfiladed [. . .] To sum up, the engineer must be outstandingly bold and outstandingly prudent.[9]

Vauban had been surprised at the lack of organization amongst the troops engaged in the sieges in which he took part. There was an almost constant lack of supplies and ammunition, administration in the camps was slack, poor reconnaissance was commonplace, occasionally being neglected altogether, and assaults were routinely launched regardless of the considered chances of success. 'Everything is done in a disorderly, tentative way; from which it follows that an approach is always ill-directed.' Vauban wrote: 'The batteries and places of arms are never where they ought to be.' He went on to comment critically on the attitude of some senior officers, whose thoughtless aggressive methods and lack of care needlessly cost the lives of so many of their soldiers:

> The emulation between the general officers often leads them to expose their soldiers to no purpose, trying to make them do more than they can, and caring little if they get a score or two killed so long as they can obtain four paces more than their fellows [. . .] They direct the course of the approaches as they please, and are continually interrupting the plan of attack and all the arrangements of the engineer.[10]

This lack of professional technique had become common, almost a kind of obtuse bravado, when it proved difficult for the gunners to quickly defeat modern defences. It seemed that honour required an outright attack at the first practical moment, a demonstration of valour and gallantry regardless of how imperfect the arrangements were, or the likelihood of incurring heavy casualties in exchange for meagre gains.

Marshal de la Ferte continued to approve of Vauban's energy, and granted him a commission in his own regiment, with another commission in the garrison Régiment de Nancy. The post involved no real duties to perform but enabled Vauban to draw the pay as a means to supplement his modest income. Accordingly, as he still held a commission in the Régiment du Repentis (Bourgogne), he held simultaneous posts in three infantry regiments while acting as an Engineer-in-Ordinary to the King. This was an apparently strange arrangement, but not in itself that unusual at the time. Step by step, as his reputation grew, so too did his fortune, but Vauban was generous to his soldiers and servants and would never be regarded as a particularly wealthy man. In 1658, Vauban was put in command of siege operations at Gravelines, Ypres and Oudenarde. One day he was taken prisoner by Spanish troops while on a scouting expedition near to Oudenarde, having to offer his parole not to serve again until he was formally exchanged. 'One must reconnoitre in person or have it done by sure, intelligent, men, as quietly a possible [. . .] These things are not to be neglected.'[11] In the custom of the day, the parole was promptly accepted by his captors, and the exchange was accomplished soon afterwards.

Peace between Spain and France came about with the Treaty of the Pyrenees soon afterwards. This Treaty, negotiated over the course of twenty-five meetings between Cardinal Mazarin for France and Don Luis de Haro for Spain, was, in effect, a French triumph and generally acknowledged as such across Europe. Spain had few friends of any strength, and was now irrevocably weakened both militarily and financially. The negotiations began on 13 August 1659, and took place on an island in the Bidassoa river, so that neither of the negotiators should have to leave their own territory and yet could participate in the talks. Agreement was formally reached on 12 November 1659. The overall result was astonishing, but reflected stark military reality. France regained Roussillon and Cerdagne in the south and Languedoc was made secure, establishing the border firmly on the mountain range of the Pyrenees. Pignerole and Casale were gained, giving France access into northern Italy. The northern border of France, hitherto exposed to attack by Spanish forces, began to take on more defensible shape. Parts of Flanders, Artois, Hainault and the Duchy of Luxembourg were secured. Important places for defence such as Lille, Cambrai, Arras, Bapaume, Saint Omer, Saint Venant, Landrecies, Le Quesnoy, Montmédy, Thionville, Rocroi, Marienbourg and Philippeville all became French possessions.

Louis XIV had pushed his border out to unprecedented advanced extent, with firm bases ready to support any future move into the increasingly exposed southern portions of the Spanish Netherlands. The line of the River Yser, encompassing Gravelines, Berques and Dunkirk, was not yet in French hands, but that would come in time. Dunkirk, having been wrested from Spanish control, was then ceded to England, for the time being at any rate, and in the south Louis XIV had to give up any lingering claim to Catalonia. The King

bastien le Prestre de Vauban, Marshal of
rance. Louis XIV's indefatigable Inspector-
eneral of Fortifications.

King Louis XIV of France, The Sun King,
circa 1660.

ouis II de Bourbon, Prince of Condé. Brilliant
ut capricious. Vauban served in his rebel
rmy during the Second Fronde.

Cardinal Jules Mazarin. Italian-born diplomat
and politician. He brought Vauban into the
Royal service.

Henri de la Tour d'Auvergne, Marshal Turenne.

William of Orange, King William III of England.

François-Michel le Tellier, Marquis de Louvois, Louis XIV's formidable Minister for War. A staunch supporter of Vauban and his plans.

Jean-Baptiste Colbert. Louis XIV's Controller-General of Finance, and Minister for the Navy.

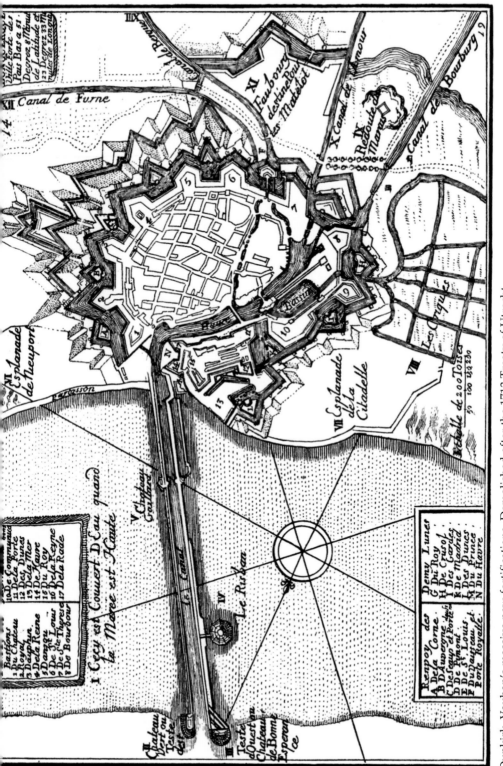

Dunkirk. Vauban's massive new fortifications. Demolished after the 1713 Treaty of Utrecht.

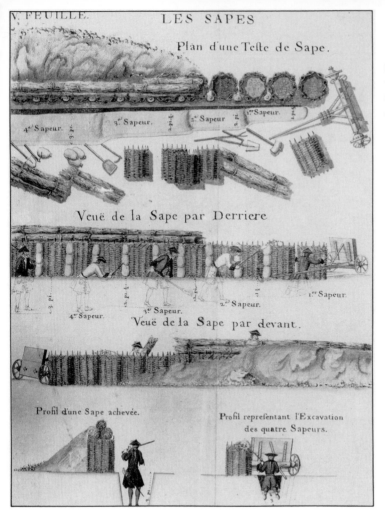

Siege operations. Sapping techniques, an illustration from Vauban's *Traité de l'Attacque des Places*.

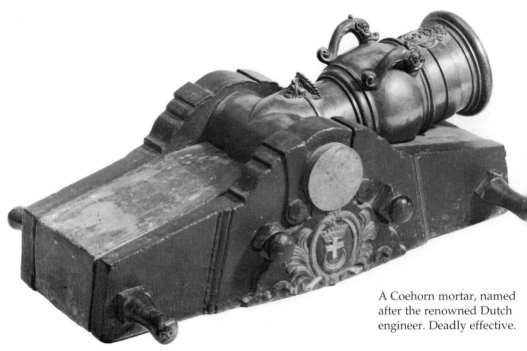

A Coehorn mortar, named after the renowned Dutch engineer. Deadly effective.

n Churchill, 1st Duke of Marlborough.

Prince Eugène of Savoy.

ançois de Neufville, Marshal Villeroi.
feated at Ramillies in 1706, he lost the
anish Netherlands.

Claude-Louis-Hector, Marshal Villars. With
Vauban's Fence of Iron he defied
Marlborough, 1709–1711.

Reginald Blomfield's pencil sketch of the massive Porte de Tournai, at Lille (*circa* 1936).

Reginald Blomfield's pencil sketch of the water defences at Gravelines (*circa* 1936).

Reginald Blomfield's pencil sketch of the Briançon defences (*circa* 1936).

Reginald Blomfield's pencil sketch of the Porte de Paris Gate at Lille (*circa* 1936).

Raising the Militia in a French town, 1705. Malpractice and impressment became common.

Layout of a model siege battery, *circa* 1700.

Château Queyras, guarding the high Alpine passes.

Plan of Strasbourg and the Fortress of Kehl.

received Condé's submission to his authority on 27 January 1660, when the turbulent and egocentric nobleman, acknowledging that now even he had a master, declared that 'He would like to buy back with the best part of his blood, all the trouble he had caused.'[12]

Louis XIV had a marked fascination with sieges, seeming to like the measured and almost stately process in the reduction of the defences of a fortress, far removed from the unpredictable cut and thrust of an all-out battle. He liked to watch the progress of the operations, and to be with his soldiers, for whom he plainly had a real interest and distant affection. Also, he wished to be on hand to take the surrender of the garrison, when that gratifying moment came.

The King had gained not only Spanish territory, victory and a peace, but also a Spanish bride – the notably attractive silver-blonde-haired Infanta Marie-Therese, Philip IV's daughter, once rather unkindly described as 'A saint but not very bright.'[13] Bright or not, the Infanta brought with her the undoubtedly alluring promise of a dowry of 500,000 crowns. This vast sum was well beyond the capability of the Spanish Treasury to pay, as was widely known, and would provide Louis XIV with a convenient excuse for further territorial expansion before very long. This may well have been foreseen, and the fact that Marie-Therese had originally been promised in marriage, more or less, to Archduke Leopold of Austria was conveniently overlooked.

Life was not all hard campaign, worry and toil, for Vauban also managed the time and opportunity to find a bride. On 25 March 1660, he married Jeanne d'Aunay (Osnay) whose family could claim to be long-established and worthy, but now evidently rather impoverished nobility as the bride's father, Claude d'Aunay, was the Baron d'Epiry. Vauban agreed to settle some of his father-in-law's more pressing debts as part of the marriage settlement, an arrangement of which his own shrewd mother seemed to heartily disapprove, as she was absent from the ceremony. A rising man in the King's army, Vauban was certainly something of a catch for a young woman of obscure family connections.

The marriage contract described Vauban as 'Ingenière ordinaire du Roy, Capitaine Lieutenant du regiment d'infantrie de Compagnie de M. le Maréchal de la Ferte Servitre, et Capitaine d'une Compagnie en la Garnisonne de Nancy.'[14] As the wife of a prominent soldier, Jeanne would discover, as many others have done before and since, that married life would be one of spending long months living quietly at home apart from her husband, initially at the rustic but imposing and fortified Château d'Epiry, as he crossed from one corner of France to another on the King's business. On one occasion the Minister for War, Louvois, would petulantly warn Vauban not to waste the time to stop at his own large country château at Bazoches (purchased in 1675), even though he would have to ride past the village on his way. The advice

Map 2. France in 1648, before Louis XIV's campaigns of expansion.

seems not to have been heeded. Still, despite the long separations, the marriage was apparently happy, Jeanne was made an executrix of Vauban's will, and the couple had two daughters; Charlotte (born 1661) and Jeanne-Françoise (1678), while a son died when he was only two months old. This affection did not prevent Vauban from engaging in a number of liaisons with young women while he was away, in the custom of the day, and he acknowledged several natural children in a more confidential will that was drawn up in March 1703:

> There is a girl in the neighbourhood by name Mademoiselle Baussant, living in the Rue St Vincent, who claims to be enceinte by me [...] as she is a girl of some birth, this must be effected secretly.

There is besides a poor Irish lady, by name Madame Districh, who also claims to have had a child by me, to which she swears vehemently; although I have as much reason to doubt her as I have the others, I would not risk the salvation of my soul for it; for that reason I beg Friand [Vauban's Secretary] to give her also 2,000 livres.[15]

Friand was instructed strictly to keep these matters confidential, to be divulged to a very few. The ladies may well have been embroidering the truth, but the old soldier clearly found it difficult to deny the possibility of paternity outright. 'I find the claims difficult to believe,' Vauban asserted, 'but all the same I make provision for them.'[16]

As an engineer of some considerable note and reputation, Vauban found that his services were in demand by two of the King's principal Ministers, Jean-Baptiste Colbert, Minister for Marine, who wanted the harbours and seaward defences improved, and François-Michel le Tellier, Marquis de Louvois (having succeeded his father in office as Minister for War in 1666), who was more concerned with the security of the land frontiers of France. There was a distinct element of rivalry between the two men. After an unfortunate episode when Vauban was wrongly accused of misappropriating public funds at the refortification of Alt-Brisach, and in which Louvois intervened to have the charges dropped, Vauban worked largely under his direction, although often also called upon to prepare plans for seaward defences.[17] He would eventually be put in charge of the refortification of the port of Dunkirk, which was recovered from Charles II of England in 1662, on payment of the magnificent sum, in instalments, of 5,000,000 livres. This would be a massive and complex undertaking that was not really complete until 1706 (and was subsequently and rather belatedly demolished under the Terms of the Treaty of Utrecht agreed in 1713, at the close of the War of the Spanish Succession).[18]

Cardinal Mazarin died the year after Vauban's marriage, in March 1661, and his brilliant but baleful influence over the young King was gone. Louis XIV became his own man, assumed the role into which he was born and to which he would prove to be remarkably well suited, even though this was often at the expense of his near neighbours. France occupied a powerful strategic position, with an economy fast recovering its vibrancy after decades of turmoil, and a population of 18,000,000 at the time. By contrast, the peoples of Spain and Austria numbered only 6,000,000 each. England was militarily of little account, as yet, and Germany was fragmented into principalities and the elected representatives and archbishoprics of the old Holy Roman Empire. Sweden and Denmark were far away to the north and no longer the force they once were, while the young Dutch Republic was mostly interested in enlarging its trading empire.

A statesman in Holland noted rather ruefully of Louis XIV and his ambitions, that here was 'A King, vigorous of body and spirit, who knows his mind, and who acts on his own authority; who possesses a kingdom populated by an extremely bellicose people.' He added that it would require 'miraculous moderation, if he stripped himself of the ambition which is natural to all princes [...] to extend his frontiers'.[19] There were ways other than aggression to extend territory, and Louis XIV proved to be an adept at diplomatic nimbleness, but always from a position of relative strength. In 1662 Charles IV, Duke of Lorraine, made over the Duchy to France on his death, in return for his own son being made a Prince of the Blood, and to succeed to the French throne in the admittedly rather unlikely event that the Bourbon line should die out. The following year, as a token for this submission, Marsal was occupied by French troops and the fortifications of Nancy were largely demolished.

No matter what Ministers were in office, with their petty jealousies and departmental bickering, the ambitions of the young King remained wide and lively. Vauban, skilled as a military engineer, would be at his service, initially overseeing the levelling of the fortifications of Nancy, agreed under the treaty terms with the Duke of Lorraine. He was then given the task to design the greatly enlarged fortifications of Brisach on the eastern bank of the Rhine. This was a major undertaking, working on an extended outpost for France, and certainly the most significant task he had yet been entrusted with, and a good indication of the degree of trust that was placed in his abilities.

Chapter 4

The War of Devolution

By early May 1667, Louis XIV had decided on provoking another war with Spain. The rather thin pretext for renewed conflict was that the massive dowry of his Spanish-born wife, Marie-Therese, had not been paid by her father, King Philip IV who had died in the autumn of 1665. Under an obsolete, but undoubtedly rather convenient, Law of Devolution, the 'Jus Devolutionis', Louis XIV claimed that a major part of the Spanish Netherlands should come to Marie-Therese, as the daughter of the first marriage of Philip IV (her older brother, Balthazar, had already died), rather than going to Charles (Carlos) II, the weak and almost invalid son of the Spanish King's second marriage, or for that matter to Charles' own younger sister. This was quite incorrect, as the law, which was actually more in the nature of a custom rather than anything else, was intended to apply to private property, not to sovereign rights over territory.

The King, apparently sensitive to suggestions that this claim had little validity, took the time to dictate a justification of his wife's rights, and for the associated declaration of war on Spain, 'A Treatise on the Rights of the Queen.' The whole argument had just enough constitutional baggage attached, when seen in an uncritical light, to be of use in legalistic argument, and there were some obscure procedural precedents to hold onto, to enable a cloak of rather doubtful respectability to be cast around Louis XIV's aggressive moves against his neighbours in the north. In fact, the King needed little encouragement or excuse; he was energetic and ambitious, and had apparently enormous resources. 'He was young,' a Dutch observer wrote, 'rich, well-served, blindly obeyed, and eager to distinguish himself by foreign conquest.'[1]

There was a robust counter-argument that could be used, and this held that Marie-Therese had set aside her claim at the time of the marriage to Louis XIV, to which the equally forthright rebuttal was that as her dowry had not been paid in full, her renunciation was in consequence, null and void. No longer militarily significant, the increasingly moribund Spanish Empire was, in effect, an easy target for the ambitious young French King. To see things from Louis XIV's King's viewpoint, there was also the possibility, if not actual likelihood, of a renewal of Habsburg encirclement of France, seen to greatest effect in the wide reach of the late Emperor Charles V, and now, if of more limited extent, still a lingering concern at Fontainebleau. So, to extend the French territories to the north would serve several purposes, both as a defensive move, and in search of martial glory and renown, so that there seemed to be good sound reasons to do so on all counts. The answer to concerns expressed over the French King's aggressive attitude is also given, 'France was constantly threatened from the north, and Louis XIV was determined to put an end to that menace.'[2]

The rich domains of the Spanish (Southern) Netherlands were a particularly tempting prize. The region was populous, prosperous and strategically important, but sat relatively exposed along France's northern border, a border that, from the French point of view, was vulnerable to external attack, and consequently should be strengthened with good and well-trained French garrisons. To encroach further into Spanish territory was, in consequence, a strategically attractive way, at apparently little risk or cost, to make even more secure the borders of Louis XIV's realm in that region.

The occupation of the Spanish Netherlands, in part if not whole, was desirable, not least because of the richness of the region with its tax-gathering possibilities, and no doubt this appeared to be perfectly obtainable, at scant comparative cost, in the face of the flagging power of Spain. In addition, if the King wanted also to enforce the continued compliance with French wishes of the United Provinces of Holland, only twenty years independent from Spain, defiantly Protestant and with a burgeoning seaborne trading empire, then this was the route that his armies would one day have to take. Otherwise those troops had to make their way across the territory of the Arch-Bishopric of Liège, with flanks that would be potentially exposed to the Dutch garrison in Maastricht, or to interference from a number of increasingly assertive German Electors and princelings across the Rhine to the eastwards.

Some Dutch politicians already favoured a straightforward division of the Southern Netherlands, ignoring Madrid's wishes or claims of sovereignty entirely, with the southern fortresses of Luxembourg, Cambrai, Douai, Aire, Saint Omer, Bergues and Furnes going to France, and the northerly remainder being quietly annexed to Holland. Many of these places were, of course, already in French hands. On this occasion, the Dutch were busily engaged in a naval war with England. With their attention necessarily focussed on other things, they chose to ally themselves with France, in the pragmatic hope, not without some realistic prospect of success, of gaining at the expense of Spain. Portugal was also persuaded to engage the Spanish militarily, and so to keep the attention of Madrid busy and away from unfolding events in the Low Countries.

The French King went on campaign on 24 May 1667, shortly after concluding a confidential treaty with King Charles II of England. This would ensure the compliance of that monarch not to become involved in the hostilities, as long as French naval support for the Dutch was withheld. As would be expected, Louis XIV set out on the campaign road in considerable style, and he was accompanied by a large and magnificent entourage. The elegant company, not all of whom shared the King's enthusiasm for life in the country, included the Queen and two of his current mistresses (although the ladies, who must have lent a decided colour to the martial occasion, were left in comfort at Compiegne for a while). Louis XIV was attended, rather more relevantly, by a well-drilled army some 35,000 strong, commanded by such skilful commanders as the Prince of Condé, now at last readmitted to Royal favour, and Marshal Turenne. 'All that you have seen of the magnificence of Solomon,' a French officer wrote admiringly of the King's progress, 'and the grandeur of the King of Persia, does not equal the pomp displayed.'[3]

There was no such nicety as a formal declaration of war on Spain, but initial opposition was pushed aside, and much of Flanders, Artois and Hainault was soon in French hands without a great deal of difficulty. These lands, hitherto a Spanish possession would, in large part, now become French as payment in kind for Queen Marie-Therese's infamous absent dowry. The impotence of Madrid in the face of such confident assertiveness was starkly evident. Important towns such as Arras, Courtrai, Tournai, Ath, Oudenarde and Douai (where Vauban was shot and wounded on the left cheek), soon fell to Louis XIV's generals. The heavy, and really unnecessary, bombardment of Douai, however, meant that much of the place was in flames when Louis XIV was presented with the keys by the submissive magistrates of the town. The Queen was shown, in contemporary depictions of the scene, as looking calmly on from the rather spartan comfort of her coach. Operations against well-defended Dendermonde were unsuccessful, however, after the countryside around the place was flooded by the Spanish Governor, who ordered a prompt and judicious opening of the sluices that controlled the local waterways. For once, the French commanders were caught out, but Vauban was still recovering from his wounds received at Douai and was, as a result, not engaged in those particular operations. The lessons of the failure at Dendermonde would, however, have been noted and well learned.

The King was of course present at the taking of the greatest prize of all, the capture of the city of Lille. The place was strongly fortified, and manned by a well-trained garrison 3,800 strong, in addition to a locally recruited militia of perhaps rather mixed quality. The quixotic niceties of campaign were evident, as the commander of the Lille garrison sent a polite note to Louis XIV complimenting him on his arrival in the siege lines, and asking to be told just where the King would locate his quarters, so that he should not be fired upon from the guns of the city's defences. The smart reply came that the French

King might always be found wherever his soldiers were, and that was that. The exchange of messages continued as the Governor regularly sent parcels of ice from his own ice-house to freshen the King's food while enduring the relative discomforts of the encampment. Louis XIV asked that the portions, which were in fact rather small, might be increased, to which the dry answer came that the Governor was reluctant to comply with the request. His own supply was quite limited, and as he expected the siege to take a long time, he did not wish to inconvenience the King by having to altogether cut off the supply of ice sent to grace his simple table. The exchange seemed to have ended with the Governor winning the point, at least where these niceties were concerned. Militarily, he was less fortunate.

The Siege of Lille began in earnest on 28 August 1667, and when complete the Lines of Contravallation and Circumvallation were an impressive 18 miles in length, being finished only in mid-September. Ground was broken for the siegeworks, and trench-digging of the approaches then started, and Vauban described the procedure adopted in some detail:

> The first night's workmen should be drawn from the regiments responsible for the guard or from those off duty, preferably the latter. Get together as many as possible, dividing them into little groups of fifteen or twenty men under an officer or a sergeant who will supervise them. Each should take a shovel, a pick, and a couple of simple fascines [...] they should follow behind the guard until they arrive upon the ground where the trench is to be opened, at which point it is a good idea to reassure them and to tell them exactly what they are going to do [...] When the engineer arrives at the head of the intended trench he should place the first workmen with his fascines on the line, then the second, the third, the fourth and so on, until the whole brigade [the working party] is in position. He should then warn them to be silent, to lie down on their fascines, not to start work until they are so ordered, and under no condition to allow anyone to come and mix with them [...] After he has posted the brigade the engineer will give the order to begin work at the same time and all must cast the dirt up on the side towards the fortress.[4]

The Chevalier de Clerville, still in post as the King's Commissary-General (Director) of Fortifications, was nominally overseeing the operations against Lille, but Vauban played the more active part. He was again frustrated at the lack of imagination and thought that was given by his colleagues to keeping losses as low as possible. He later drew from memory two detailed plans of the approach trenches which were aimed at the salient defensive angle covering the St Maurice Gate; the first showed the simple single approach that was actually put into use, with the French intentions clearly signalled to the defenders who, as a result, could concentrate their fire to good effect, and the second option which was of Vauban's own devising. This gave a broader, and much less obvious, manner of attack, with intentions not clearly shown to the defenders, and more like his later use of parallels.[5]

On 25 September 1667, the Gardes Françaises on the right, supported by the Régiment d'Orléans, and the Régiment de Picardie on the left, stormed a part of the Covered Way. At least one spirited sortie was made by the Lille garrison, although Vauban rather dismissively felt that this was sent in just so that the Spanish Governor could show to the world that he had done his best to resist and nothing more. A demi-lune, protecting a bastion, fell to the French the following day, and the Governor acknowledged that the defences were breached beyond hope of recovery. He prudently asked for terms for an honourable capitulation. These were granted, and the 2,500 survivors of the garrison were permitted to march out and go to Ypres, while the citizen militia were ordered to return to their homes. Louis XIV entered Lille immediately, having been handed the keys by the magistrates in an elaborate ceremony, while Marshal Turenne was directed to move on to swiftly take Alost.

By his good conduct in the operations against Lille in particular, Vauban gained a commission as a Lieutenant in the Royal Guards, in addition to a pension of 2,400 livres per annum (which seemed to have been only irregularly paid), and permission to sell, at a profit, his existing commission in the Régiment de Picardie. Only those who had a claim to nobility could hold a commission in the Royal Guards, and a little neat footwork was required to establish this for the undeniably provincial Vauban: 'The nobility of the petitioners [Vauban], was sufficiently well-known and established, and that their father, grandfather and great-grandfather had always lived as befits noblemen.'[6] As it was, he had no private income of any significance, and could see very well that he could not meet the expense of the commission in the Royal Guards, the uniform costs and the range of servants necessary to maintain the rank in such exalted company being quite prohibitive. Vauban soon sought permission to sell that commission too. Although the intention to sell out of the Royal Guards so readily might be thought to have been rather a snub, the King knew his man and his situation, understanding the reason for this 'extraordinary request'; he gave consent, and Vauban arranged to sell the commission to another officer, one Lieutenant Bailly, for no less than 20,000 livres, although this sum, as with the pension from the King, never seems to have been paid in full. As it was, Vauban would have to complain on several occasions that his pay was seriously in arrears, but the frequent large cash awards from the King for his successes in war must have eased matters to a certain degree.

Eager to secure his newly-won possessions, Louis XIV had plans drawn up to massively strengthen and modernize the defences of Lille. Some of the other captured towns and districts, such as those of Douai, Ath, Oudenarde and Tournai would have to be negotiated away over the coming years as the price of a peace that became increasingly necessary, but he never let Lille go. The Chevalier de Clerville, respected but out of favour and seemingly rather ineffectual, prepared a plan for the new enlarged fortress, but this was not thought to be satisfactory. The fact that the Minister for War had taken a dislike to the older man no doubt played a large part in all this, rather than in any inherent defect in what de Clerville suggested. There was, however, a certain air of not wishing to offend an old retainer, but also of not letting him interfere very much either. 'You may let M. le Chevalier de Clerville speak as he pleases about the things he wishes to,' Louvois wrote to Vauban, 'let him talk, but never carry out any of the things which he says.'[7] The King directed Vauban to draw up an alternative scheme, and this was approved, much to de Clerville's disgust, and the younger man was accordingly entrusted with the prestigious task of designing and supervising the construction of the huge project. He wrote rather waspishly that:

> The Chevalier de Clerville, before his departure, planted a dozen stakes at random in my presence, merely that he might say that he had drawn the trace of the citadel, but, as a matter of fact, not one of them is of any use.'[8]

De Clerville, who had enjoyed a distinguished career and held a very good reputation but now clearly eclipsed by a more gifted man, went into obscure but comfortable semi-retirement as Governor of Île d'Oléron. There he was pretty well ignored until he died, disappointed and irrelevant, ten years later.

Vauban was also appointed to be the new Governor of the Lille citadel, while the Marquis d'Humières was made the Governor of the city itself, and Vauban reported to him in that role. Given the enormously prestigious task to actually oversee the rebuilding of the fortifications of the fortress and the city to his own prepared plan, Vauban was allowed the services of two engineers, forage for his own horses, and 500 livres additional pay each month – not a particularly lavish arrangement, it seemed, considering the scale of the project. The prestige that the task conferred, however, given the importance with which the King viewed the capture of Lille, was immense, and settled quite literally in stone the reputation of Vauban as a military Engineer of the first rank and a man to be reckoned with.

A master-mason in Lille, Simon Vollant, was awarded the contract for the work to be undertaken, and was given the title 'Engineer and Architect of the

Armies'. The construction commenced in 1668, remarkably soon after the capture of the place, employing the services of no fewer than 6,000 workmen, both tradesmen and unskilled labourers, amongst whom were many soldiers who, not surprisingly, did not relish to any great degree the drudgery of the task. Their particular skills lay in other directions, and, as a complete aside, the French army noticeably began a slow decline in its effectiveness, in consequence of such increasingly frequent misemployment of trained soldiers as labourers. Technical difficulties were soon encountered, which really might have been foreseen – perhaps de Clerville would have done so, but it cannot be known for sure. The unstable sandy subsoil for the foundations made work slow, as did some faulty materials, delays were inevitable and there was discontent in the labour force over poor pay and conditions. Sometimes this was so bad that armed guards had to be posted over their lodgings to prevent the workers from absconding in the night. 'To prevent the desertion of bricklayers, which infuriates me,' Vauban wrote:

> I have taken, subject to your consent, two of M. le Maréchal's guards, most reliable men [. . .] In the evening we shall discover who are missing, and in the morning they will set out and seek them in the heart of the villages, and will drag them by the ears back to their work.'[9]

Vauban was active in seeing to these mundane but important problems, but he was also concerned at the inadequacy of the compensation being offered to those citizens, in whatever place, whose houses were being demolished to make way for the new enlarged fortifications. He wrote in February 1669:

> The valuation of demolished buildings which has been made here is in no sense reasonable, and this is only too evident, for the owners prefer to demolish the houses themselves and sell the materials here and there at a low price, since even that price they find to be double the valuation figure.[10]

If people were knocking their own houses down and making off, however understandable this might be, there was an air of uncertainty and lack of control which was not conducive to the smooth progress of the construction of the vast new works that were intended. Discontent amongst the displaced citizenry was such that it was thought prudent to disarm the town militia, at least for the time being. They were, however, reformed when matters calmed down, and some of these militiamen, or their sons and nephews at any rate, rendered excellent service to Marshal Boufflers when Lille was beset by France's opponents in the critical days of the autumn of 1708.

The rebuilding and remaking of Lille was a tremendous undertaking, and transformed the city and the fortress. In the end, Vauban was only able to provide the Minister for War with a full set of plans of the newly-completed defences of the city and citadel in 1674. This was quite timely, as war with Spain was looming close once more. The demands upon his time and energy were considerable; tasked with undertaking more and more projects, the King's Engineer certainly became overworked. That there were gratifying rewards there is no doubt, but the strain did occasionally tell:

> The discomfort of my cold was greatly aggravated by long journeys on horseback. I have almost killed my horse with long marches, and as a matter of fact, I have been obliged to dismount more than fifty times, owing to the pain in my head and the giddiness caused by my cough.[11]

The work of enlarging and improving the defences of Lille was a demanding task. The relatively simple defences that had been there in 1667 when the city was captured, were enlarged and strengthened out of all recognition, with formidable outworks and the construction of a new and powerful citadel. This structure, on its own a good 90 acres in area and with no less than 60,000,000 bricks in construction, lay on the north-eastern side of the newly-enlarged fortress. The citadel comprised and comprises to this day, a massive pentagonal shape, with six forward bastions and extensive water defences drawn from the nearby Deule (Dyle) and Marque streams. Amongst the innovative inner defences were subterranean courses which fed a water-filled ditch. Sluice gates placed at intervals were immune to artillery and mortar fire or interference, and ensured a constant level of water. This was a formidable obstacle, one which was proved of worth in 1708, in 1796, in 1914 (briefly), and even as late as May 1940 at a time of the most sombre need for France.

Vauban's care and attention to the designs he prepared extended to the layout of the various interior parts of the fortress. Such seemingly mundane matters as the living quarters, kitchens, storehouses, workshops and stables received his close attention, which was given not just to the main defences. His model design for barracks and cookhouses ensured better than customary conditions for the soldiers of the garrison. The magazines, packed as they would have been with ammunitions and explosives of all kinds, were always vulnerable to enemy fire and are a good example of his care, for 'If the magazines blow up, we all go up with them' as one famous general would say.[12] So well thought out was their design that not one of Vauban's magazines ever did go up under enemy fire. Vauban's concern for the soldiers stretched beyond such solid benefits, even to the small degree that he calculated just how much tobacco was likely to be consumed by each man in his pipe over a given period, to ensure that an adequate supply of this luxury, deemed to be so necessary for the maintenance of good morale, was maintained.

Simon Vollant had so distinguished himself by his diligence and energy during the project to improve the fortifications of Lille, while working under the supervision of Vauban, that he was then given the task of improving the fortress of Menin. This was despite the fact that Louvois seemed to think that he was mad.[13] The Minister for War had also heard gossip that Vollant and another engineer had accepted bribes from contractors, and he reported this to Vauban, who responded with typical forthrightness and a certain hint of outraged dignity:

> I will take the liberty of telling you that affairs have gone too far to stop here [...] Appoint some honest man who will probe everything to the bottom and then report to you on it [...] As for me, I am no less accused than they, and as being perhaps more guilty [...] Listen to all that can be said to you and to investigate it in order to learn the truth, and if I am found to be guilty, then, since I have the honour to be more closely in touch with you than the others and as you honour me with your more intimate confidence, I shall deserve severer punishment [...] at least the rope. Knowing my own scrupulous probity and sincere fidelity, I fear neither the King, nor yourself.[14]

So far as can be seen, that absolved Vollant from all suspicion, and Vauban heard nothing more from Louvois on the whole subject.

The success that was achieved by Louis XIV's commanders, particularly in the Southern Netherlands, quite understandably caused some wide concern amongst France's neighbours. In consequence, within a year of the capture of Lille, England, the States-General of Holland and Sweden formed the League of Triple Alliance, an undoubtedly powerful and influential combination with which to better restrain the King's seemingly dangerous ambitions for further expansion of his domains. The invasion of the Franche-Comté in the east which commenced under the command of the Prince of Condé on 4 February 1668, a lightning French operation taking little more than two weeks, added to these concerns. Rochefort, Besançon and Salus submitted to the French, and Dole was occupied on 13 February. Construction of a large new citadel was begun on Mount Etienne, at Besançon. Still, under the terms of the Treaty of Aix-la-Chapelle which was concluded on 29 May 1668, Louis XIV was obliged to give up the occupation of the Franche-Comté, but at the same stroke managed to retain most of his gains in the Low Countries – Charleroi, Oudenarde, Tournai, Binche, Ath, Douai, Courtrai, Armentières, Bergues, Furnes and Lille. Marshal Turenne, however, was outraged that so much was negotiated away, writing to the Minister for War that this was 'A knock-down blow for France.'[15]

In fact, as would soon be seen, the Franche-Comté could simply be re-occupied at any convenient time by French troops, so that little of real substance had been given up. Louis XIV had gained possession of key fortresses along his northern border in the meantime, most significant undoubtedly being that of Lille. Although in a strict sense possession of these fortresses did not immediately confer sovereign rights over the surrounding districts, in a practical sense that was just what took place, possession always being nine points of the law, and almost the whole of Artois and southern Flanders had become in the process a French possession. France had made more secure her northern borders against aggression, although simultaneously Louis XIV's neighbours were more concerned at further aggression, and were now very much on the alert, if not actually hostile. This was a nervous state of affairs that did not auger very well for a period of prolonged peace in the near future.

The States-General of Holland, however, were now regarded as having double-crossed the French who, with some arguably good reason, had posed as their old allies against Spain, by concluding the alliance with England and Sweden. Had this arrangement not taken place, Louis XIV was brought to believe, he might very well have secured the whole of the Spanish Netherlands for France. This reduced state, left over almost as an afterthought but a very valuable afterthought all the same after the successful War of Dutch Independence, was regarded by many as a strategic irrelevance other than for the immensely desirable trade and tax revenues that the rich and populous provinces yielded. However, the region also provided Holland with a valuable barrier, a defence in depth, against possible French aggression, and the maintenance of this strategic benefit and the security of such places as Liège, Julich, Cleves and Spanish Gelderland would remain a cause of concern and contention for many years. France was also, it was thought, under threat from this same direction should an invader use the Low Countries as the route by which they would attack. The experiences of 1815, 1914 and 1940 amply demonstrate that this was no idle or overly manufactured reason for the concern, which was clearly genuine. So, Louis XIV, outwardly for the most valid of reasons connected with the defence of northern France, sought to further extend and consolidate his already firm grip on the region as Spanish power and influence waned.

During their long and bitterly contested war of independence from Spain in the late sixteenth and early seventeenth centuries, the Protestant Dutch had received considerable assistance from largely Catholic France. This was astute French self-interest rather than anything finer, as Spain's misfortune was seen,

Map 3. The Netherlands in the late seventeenth century.

with good reason, as France's gain, and a certain encroachment on Spanish territory and influence had been under way. Now, that valuable assistance from France was something of a diminishing memory, and the robustly independent attitude of the Dutch, particularly where their trade tariffs were concerned, was an irritant to Louis XIV. In the meantime, the structural weakness of Spain as an Imperial power, exhausted, overextended, overreliant upon supplies of bullion from the Americas and plainly now unable to adequately protect its vast possessions, was evident. The United Provinces of Holland were seen to be commercially strong, and particularly so at sea, yet they were militarily weak and quite isolated, being at loggerheads with Protestant England, although Sweden did offer some support. The French King was persuaded by his advisers, principally the arguments put forward by the brilliant Marshal Turenne it seems, to try to bring the Dutch Republic to heel once and for all. A huge subsidy would be offered to both England and Sweden to stay out of the coming conflict, and their rulers quickly proved unable to resist the proffered gold, regardless of the solemn terms they had so recently entered into with Holland under the terms of the now seemingly irrelevant Triple Alliance.

The French Minister for War, Louvois, was well aware of the thought and care that Vauban gave to how siege operations should be conducted, at a practical, standing in the trench, level. He gave instructions to Vauban, in those rather few spare hours he might have, between the almost constant round of inspections he was required to undertake and which led him in 1669 to Antibes, Toulon, Perpignan and Villefranche de Conflent in the south, to prepare an aide-mémoire for the guidance of junior officers to use when engaged in siege operations. This confidential document, *Memoire pour Servir a l'instruction dans la conduit des sieges*, was published in 1669, and the contents were thought to be so valuable that its circulation was limited to trusted recipients only, although this restriction was understandably hard to enforce. This later became the basis for the notable *Traité de l'Attacque des Places*, which, together with a rather less memorable memorandum on the defence of fortresses, *De la defense des Places*, was republished in Leiden in the 1740s.

Vauban was also engaged during 1670 in drawing up plans for the defence of Turin, on behalf of France's ally, Charles Emmanuel II, the Duke of Savoy. That autumn, he was sent back to Flanders to inspect the fortresses in the area, and quickly aroused the suspicions of the Spanish Governor of Nieuport who assumed, probably quite rightly, that Vauban's enquiries and attention were not entirely driven by simple idle curiosity. Hot words were exchanged on one of these excursions, and he was lucky not to be shot at.

Chapter 5

War with the Dutch

Towards the end of April 1670, Louis XIV set out on a grand tour of his newly-acquired possessions in the north, gained at the Treaty of Aix-la-Chapelle – those parts of Artois, Hainault and south-west Flanders that had fallen to his victorious generals in the campaigns of the preceding three years. It was politically expedient for the citizenry of the region to see their magnificent new King in all his finery, and gave Louis XIV the happy chance to view progress with the refortification of Lille. The King was accompanied by a huge cavalcade of noblemen and noblewomen, retainers and servants, and an escort of 20,000 troops – the plain intention was once more to impress the people with the power and prestige of the French monarchy. The Royal coach on this occasion contained not only Queen Marie-Therese, beautiful but fading, but also two of Louis XIV's current mistresses – Madame de Montespan and Madame de la Vallière, as none of the ladies relished the thought that they might not be needed, and so be left behind.

The long column of coaches and wagons carried plate, pictures, exquisite tapestries and carpets, furniture, linen and ample stocks of fine food and wine. Wherever the King stopped, the magnificence of the court was to be, to some rather limited degree, recreated. The weather was poor, and the rain soon turned the unpaved roads to tracks of apparently bottomless mud. Campaigning armies were used to such trials, but progress was slow as the cumbersome vehicles of the Royal entourage sank to their axle trees and stuck at the crossings of the Sambre river near to Landrecies. The elegant occupants of the coaches, both male and female and mostly unaccustomed to the rigours of campaigning, were in horror at the thought of being stranded in what appeared to be a desolate wilderness. Louis XIV was more robust, and seemed not to mind in the least having to sleep on the floor of a simple cottage, with the leading ladies of his entourage sharing a mattress in an adjoining room, while his own coach was dragged onto drier ground by relays of heaving, and no doubt cursing, soldiers. At first, Queen Marie-Therese refused to leave her rather cold carriage for the more dubious comforts of a local cottage. On at last being persuaded to do so, she was almost pulled over into the mud by one of her ladies-in-waiting who had sunk to her knees in the mire, and was gamely attempting from that semi-recumbent position to hold the Queen's train up and prevent it becoming wet and dirty. Going on such a tour clearly had its attendant trials.

The Treaty of Dover, negotiated between Louis XIV and Charles II, had detached England from attending to any obligations to come to Holland's aid if it were attacked, and a rather similar agreement was reached with Sweden. Assurances were given that, no matter what the outcome of hostilities, the continuance of the Dutch Republic, albeit in some reduced form, would be certain. Tensions between Louis XIV and the States-General grew progressively more acute, and were made worse when, in 1671, the Dutch placed a rather provocative embargo on the importation of French brandy and wine. This was in part a retaliation for the imposition of a double rate of duty on goods being brought into France from Holland, but what had begun as a trade war became distinctly more serious when Louis XIV decided upon military action to curb the pretensions of the Dutch Republic. More significantly, he was looking to extend the French sphere of influence northwards to encompass what remained of the Spanish Netherlands, and to secure the ports of the Channel coast. To subdue the Dutch at this time, and bring them under French influence if not actual domination, would allow a free hand in the exposed Spanish Netherlands, without interference or protest from The Hague.

For many years, the Dutch had regarded the military power of Spain as the most pressing threat, and their memories of the long war to throw off the rule of Madrid lingered on. In some ways, the support of France, as a means to divert Madrid's attention and hobble Spanish military capability, had been the bulwark of Dutch security rather in the manner of 'The Enemy of my Enemy is my Friend.' That was all well and good, but as the years went on, and the Dutch grew in wealth, influence and confidence, Spanish power, concurrently and for very different reasons, lessened. The possibility of a threat to Holland from France grew to be more apparent, and the States-General began to look upon the Spanish Netherlands less as a lurking threat to their security, but more a useful bulwark to protect that very same security.

French military preparations were plain, and early in December 1671 the States-General wrote to Louis XIV, asking in what way they had given such offence. It was all too late now to try to negotiate a settlement, for on 6 January 1672, the King wrote back to The Hague in clear and uncompromising terms, having, of course, already decided on war:

> We increased the number of our troops in order to employ on the fortifications the infantry in garrison there, and to protect our subjects from the aggression which threatened then owing to the extraordinary levies of infantry and cavalry that you raised, and the fleet you stationed off our coasts [. . .] By doing this we have obeyed the

laws of prudence, and provided the protection that we owe our
people.[1]

Despite such lofty and seemingly unimpeachable sentiments, this was little
more than picking a quarrel with a smaller and weaker neighbour as a matter of
strategic opportunism. With the Dutch subdued, Louis XIV would clearly be
in a better position to proceed to achieve his aims in the Spanish Netherlands.
Cold-blooded calculation, as so often in international affairs, was clearly in
play, but the demands of the King had succeeded also in alerting the other
states of Europe to the wider potential threat from France, and this would
prove to be a very counter-productive policy in the long term.

For the time being, Louis XIV was in a strong, seemingly unassailable
position. The Duchy of Lorraine had been occupied by French troops in 1671,
so that flank was secure. The Emperor in Vienna, sensitive to the Ottoman
threat from the East, was unlikely to get involved in fresh war, so long as
Imperial lands in Germany were not put at risk. When everything was considered, despite as yet ill-defined long-term consequences, Louis XIV
appeared to have almost a completely free hand to act as he wished in the
north. The States-General, partly through inertia and complacency, could
muster few friends and allies, other than the ambitious Elector of Brandenburg
who indicated a willingness to become involved if his own interests could
prosper in the process. Instead, a defensive alliance was concluded with Spain
on 17 December 1671, an act of desperate convenience between old adversaries,
but Sweden had already accepted French gold to stay out of any renewed
hostilities and England was unlikely to be anything but hostile, and looking to
reap advantages in opportunities for overseas trade once the Dutch were
weakened.

The immensely valuable Dutch Smyrna Fleet, laden with the exotic luxuries
from Byzantium and the East, was attacked by a squadron of English ships
under command of Sir Robert Holmes off the Isle of Wight in March 1672.
The Dutch, understandably alarmed and affronted at this attack, began to
increase their forces on land and at sea. England then declared war on the
United Provinces on 27 March, closely followed by Louis XIV, who had already
secured the compliance of the Electors of Cologne and Munster to allow French
troops unhindered passage as they marched northwards against Holland. On
6 April 1672, Marshal Turenne began to advance with 23,000 troops against
the Dutch, marching forward from Charleroi, through the territory of the
Archbishopric of Liège. Louis XIV joined the army three weeks later, and war
with the Dutch was duly formally declared. The French forces, reinforced by
30,000 men under the Prince of Condé (who had wintered his troops at the
expense of the unfortunate people of Lorraine), moved down the lines of the

Sambre and Meuse rivers to Neusse on the Rhine. A third army, under the command of Marshal Luxembourg, manoeuvred in support. These confident opening moves were aimed at the Dutch-held towns of Rheinburg, Orsoy, Emmerich and Wesel, on the Lower Rhine to the north of the Bishopric of Cologne. Condé would have preferred to attack the key fortress of Maastricht and secure that city first of all as a secure base, but Louis XIV was determined to achieve an early success. 'It has appeared to me,' the King wrote,

> so important for the reputation of my armies only to begin my cam-
> paign by some brilliant feat, that I have not considered an attack on
> Maastricht sufficient for the purpose [...] I have considered it more
> in accordance with my purpose and better calculated to enhance my
> prestige to attack simultaneously four places on the Rhine [...] I do
> not know the strengths of the garrisons of these places, but we will
> do our best.[2]

The Dutch seemed to be of the same opinion as Condé, and being chiefly concerned for the security of Maastricht they had concentrated a strong force to hold the fortress. This was understandable tactically, but in fact a strategic error, and the Dutch outpost at Orsoy, just downstream from the confluence of the River Ruhr with the Rhine, was besieged between 25 May and 5 June. Having secured the place without too much effort, the French then attacked Rheinburg, with Vauban supervising the operations against the defences of the town. The exposed and ill-fortified Dutch frontier at the Tollhuis and Lobith was then reached, and the French army halted to regroup on 12 June. The result of all this was that the main Dutch line of defence along the border with the Spanish Netherlands and the Archbishopric of Liège had been neatly outflanked.

There was dissention in the Dutch high command; they had been out-manoeuvred, and this was clear for all to see. The formidable obstacle of the Rhine still lay ahead of the marching armies, but in a very well-handled operation, the French got over the river without serious hindrance or delay. Cavalry swam the fast-flowing river, and a bridge of boats was hauled into position by pioneers. The outnumbered Dutch on the far bank fought well, but were driven off by troops under command of the Duc de Guiche:

> We were still swimming the river, when the enemy saw us, waded
> into the water and attacked us [...] the battle hung in the balance
> when just in time the King ordered our cannon to fire, and that
> forced back the enemy. I saw young Brasselay, a Cornet in the
> cuirassiers, thrown from his horse and start to swim with one arm,
> holding his regimental colour aloft with the other.[3]

With the Dutch detachment in hasty retreat and the crossing-point over the Rhine secure, Louis XIV crossed the river during the evening of 12 June using the pontoon bridge, and without getting his feet wet. The whole operation, at such little cost, was generally regarded as a significant achievement.

At this stage of the campaign, the conduct of the French troops towards the people in the districts through which they marched was, on the whole, very good. The local Dutch appeared not to resent too much the approach of the French troops, who were clearly under orders to be on their best behaviour. Provisions, livestock and forage were taken by foraging parties, as usual and was expected, but almost always in exchange for hard cash, and the local farmers were clearly not averse to this trade even if the purchasers were French commissaries. 'Everything was bought that the Dutch were willing to sell.'[4] Unfortunately, such admirable order and discipline would not last very long.

Organized resistance by the Dutch field army, which was a mere 15,000 strong, appeared to crumble in the face of the French advance. The town of Deventer fell, Utrecht was occupied on 23 June 1672, and Nijmegen surrendered on 9 July. Smaller posts hastened to give themselves up, or were abandoned as indefensible. Much of the southern provinces of Gelderland, Utrecht and Overjissel was soon in the hands of the French and their ally, the Elector-Bishop of Cologne. It seemed to everyone that Amsterdam, just 20 miles away from the advancing French troops, Leiden, and even The Hague must also fall, and when that happened, the shortlived republic of the United Provinces of Holland would have become simply another client-state of the French crown. Large parts of its territory and fortresses, if not all, would be occupied by Louis XIV's troops, and the republic become virtually just an extension of his ever-enlarging domains. Whatever was left would be an enfeebled mini-state without defences, unable to form alliances or trade without interference, and forever at the beck and call of the French. As a useful addition for Louis XIV, what little remained of the security of the Spanish Netherlands would be undermined and left at the mercy of the French King's intentions and ambitions.

Downcast by repeated reverses, the Dutch offered terms for a cessation of hostilities, but these overtures were disregarded, a serious strategic mistake by Louis XIV who, had he only agreed to what was offered which included the giving up of numerous fortified places, would have achieved without further effort all that he sought. 'By means of all these places the King could in wartime readily master Bruges, Ghent and Antwerp,' Vauban wrote, concerned at what was being blithely ignored, and he went on to urge that peace be made now, 'while Europe is still standing in amazement.'[5]

The moment passed, and the States-General were goaded into action by public outrage at the woeful conduct of the campaign so far. After the brutal lynching by a mob of the De Witt brothers, whose policy had so manifestly failed Holland, the 21-year-old William of Orange, as Stadtholder, was appointed to the sole command of the Dutch field army and control of the campaign. This might have been a poisoned chalice of high order, had the young William not been the doughty character and implacable opponent of the French that he proved to be. It was far from clear at the time, but the hitherto victorious campaign for Louis XIV turned a bleak corner at this point. To the astonishment of those who watched in certain expectation of continued French triumphs, the Dutch, in their bleak determination, now began to break open their sluices and breach the sea-dykes, to flood the land and drown their flocks, herds and crops, sooner than that they should submit.

In an atmosphere of desperation bordering on acceptance of total war, the States-General had fallen back on their final defence, 'the Water-Line', where only an older enemy, the salt sea, could shield them. In fact, a similar strategy had been adopted to foil Spanish commanders during their eighty-year war against Madrid and this had proved quite successful, but all this seemed to have been forgotten, and the French commanders were now taken entirely by surprise. What had been meted out to the troops of Alva and Parma was now served to the French. 'The determination to flood the country was certainly rather violent,' Louis XIV wrote with grudging admiration, and a perceptive understanding of what was really at stake, 'but what would one not do to save oneself from foreign domination.'[6]

Huge tracts of Dutch farmland were soon under several feet of salt water, and only the main roads, elevated on embankments, remained fairly dry, but these were in most places barred by fortified posts held by William of Orange's troops. There was no fallback position for these soldiers; if they failed to hold where they stood, the French would get through to Amsterdam and beyond, and would win the war. To add to this peril, it soon turned out that some of the breaching work on the sea-dykes was ineffective, and was delayed or even sabotaged by farmers and peasants desperate to save their livestock. The difficulty was not a new one, as during the war with Spain, 'Guards had to be placed near the sluices to prevent them being closed by dissenting farmers who would lose their land.'[7] Draconian summary penalties, even death, were pre-scribed for anyone interfering with the breaching work, but enough damage was done all the same, with some 200 square miles of inundated territory laid to watery waste to seriously hamper the French advance. The fighting for passage along the few dry roads, which offered them at least an element of mobility, was desperate: 'It is difficult,' a weary French officer wrote, 'to understand how such a country can exist. It is impossible to tell whether land or water dominates.'[8]

Marshal Turenne had not thought it necessary to send his cavalry advanced guard to take possession of the town of Muyden, where the main sluice gates of the Dutch water system now shielding Amsterdam were in place. A French detachment under the Marquis de Rochefort was belatedly sent to seize the town, but they were driven off after sharp fighting and with heavy losses. On 26 June, with the resulting impasse and slowing of the pace of the campaign, the Dutch sought peace once more, but Louis XIV's envoys arrogantly presented the envoys with impossibly penal terms. These demanded that the border of the United Provinces was to be set at the Waal River, and fortified places on that line should be occupied by permanent French garrisons. Furthermore, a huge financial subsidy was to be paid to France in recompense for having had to go so reluctantly (as it was put) to war, and preferential terms were in future to be offered to French traders.

The Dutch envoys in their turn played for time, pretending to be waiting for instructions from The Hague, and then, after ten days' prevarication, they rejected the terms presented by the French. Louis XIV promptly ordered a move against 's-Hertogenbosch but heavy rain set in, and the countryside was already awash with the flooding, the soldiers were becoming short of provisions and could still only try to move along the elevated roads, on the narrowest of fronts. The garrison of 's-Hertogenbosch, stoutly commanded by an Irishman, Colonel Kilpatrick, resisted well, and no real attempt to storm the town's rather outdated defences could be made. The French troops had little choice but to retire, in a clear degree of disarray, at the unexpected rebuff by the Dutch garrison.

The French King went back to St-Germain at the end of July 1672, leaving Marshal Luxembourg in overall command of the operations. 'The King,' the Minister for War wrote, 'having realized that all the approaches to Holland are at present inundated, and that until the frost sets in it is not possible to penetrate them, has ordered the advanced guards to be withdrawn.'[9] Louis XIV had troops sent from Munster and Cologne into Friesland and Groningen in the north, but the whole campaign was clearly languishing, as was shown by the attempt to capture 's-Hertogenbosch having to be abandoned so readily. Vauban had been busily engaged throughout this time in inspecting the Dutch towns captured in the early stages of the campaign, and advising which should be retained and improved for defence. No fewer than forty of these places were intended to be held by France, and garrisons had to be found for them, significantly diluting the strength and effectiveness of the field army. Now, he was instructed to leave the campaign, which evidently was not likely to progress very far for the foreseeable future, and return to attend to the refortification of Lille. Vauban was, however, as diligent as usual, and able to send to Louvois numerous outline plans, which he had already devised for the strengthening of the captured Dutch posts. These plans would have to remain on the shelf.

The French troops in southern Holland now found themselves moving through the wet autumn months towards winter, in a drenched and barren land where movement was difficult and there was no forage. Some regiments had to be sent back to the Rhine, where Imperial and Brandenburg forces were slowly gathering; this concentration gathered pace as the French campaign continued to languish. Meanwhile, 'The rain falls without stopping,' wrote Luxembourg; 'at the moment it falls as if they were pouring it out in buckets, and I assure you that a man needs to be made of iron to bear it [...] All the roads are impassable and no one would dream of moving.'[10] The French field army was all but stranded. A fresh attempt to advance on Amsterdam across fields that had been made hard by a sudden frost had to be abandoned in the face of a thaw that turned vast areas of land into watery wasteland once more, with the tactical movement of troops and passage of supply wagons all but impossible.

The Dutch were not fighting on their own now, as Spanish troops were in place on the Water-Line by late 1672. Concern had grown in Madrid at the renewed French incursion into the Low Countries, an encroachment that, while directed by the tactical demands of active campaigning might yet prove difficult to roll back once peace came again. Dutch prospects, as a result, had significantly improved. The French commanders continued to try to operate in appalling conditions. 'I have caused all the dykes to be sounded,' the Prince of Condé wrote, 'by officers sent for the purpose. The only dyke uncovered is the big one from Woerden to Leiden, and on that the enemy have rebuilt the fort [...] the fort is inundated all around; there is nowhere any approach save by the big dyke.'[11] A bitterly cold winter was coming and the mood of the campaign changed for the worse, with shivering French troops venting their frustration in outrages against the local people. In return they were picked off and murdered by the peasantry whenever they strayed too far from their sodden camps. Small-scale clashes, fierce and draining, were fought between French troops and the Dutch and their allies with increasing frequency as the weeks went on.

Spain formally entered the war, but Louis XIV had by then given up the seemingly pointless task of subjugating the obstinately-held Dutch heartland. Minister for War, Louvois, wrote in disappointment tinged with some quite unreasonable bitterness, that 'If the Dutch were men, they would have made peace long ago, but since they are such beasts, we had better prepare ourselves for [more] war.'[12] It is always best to be careful what you wish for, and Louis XIV and his Ministers and commanders had wished for this war which yielded so little for them. Treasure and effort, and the lives of many good soldiers, had been expended, and still no gain achieved that added very much for the lasting security of France. What had been gained, however, was the lasting suspicion and enmity of William of Orange; undoubtedly a bad thing. Now, the French King turned the attention of his Marshals back to Limburg, and to the Meuse valley, where a ruthless campaign of devastation was carried out to hinder the future deployment of Dutch or Spanish troops, and the great fortress of Maastricht. The home territory of the United Provinces of Holland might not be had, but the seizure of that city and fortress would be an undoubted prize for France, of limited worth perhaps, but a prize nonetheless.

Emperor Leopold I of Austria had persuaded the Archbishop Elector of Trier to permit Imperial troops to occupy Coblenz, and the neighbouring fortress of Ehrenbreitstein, at the confluence of the Rhine and the Moselle. In this way, the French strategic posture facing Holland and the Spanish Netherlands was in danger of being outflanked. This, of course, was just what was intended, and soon afterwards Imperial troops occupied Phillipsburg, and Louis XIV's troubles grew when the Elector of Brandenburg, concerned at French interest in the Rhine crossings and encroachment into the territory of Cleves, formally allied himself to the United Provinces. Gradually, France's neighbours were gathering their strength to counter the ambitions of the King.

In June 1673 Vauban requested a spell of much-needed leave to visit his family home, but was summoned instead to join the operations against Maastricht. The French, turning their backs on efforts to subdue the Dutch, deployed a formidable force some 45,000 strong, with a battering train of fifty-eight large siege guns. Clearly, no home leave was to be expected at the time, and 'I perceive that I have made my request too late,' Vauban wrote rather ruefully.[13] The siege operations were quickly under way, and thousands of peasants were conscripted to labour on the Lines of Contravallation and Circumvallation. The undertaking was formidable, for Maastricht was a large and well-designed fortress with five hornworks and numerous demi-lunes, all protected by inundations and a flooded ditch. In addition, the 6,000-strong Dutch garrison was the right size for the task at hand and was well-equipped and provisioned; commanded by Major General Jacques Farieux, an experienced officer of fine reputation who could be relied upon to do his best. Few of Vauban's methods for a formal siege would have been all that novel, or a great surprise, to a professional soldier like Farieux.

As was becoming usual, Vauban was entrusted with the day-to-day command in the trenches. These works were opened on the night of 17–18 June, although as a matter of routine etiquette the orders were issued in the name of Louis XIV. 'The operations were directed by a siege head [Vauban] who received the direct orders of the King, and accounted to nobody but him.'[14] At Vauban's particular request, the general officers were not permitted to interfere in the siege operations, and only had command of the troops actually guarding the entrenchments and those of the covering army. Past experience had shown that their involvement in the actual siege was often not of great assistance. Vauban had no doubt as to the scale of the task before him. 'I know of nothing more difficult to surmount,' he wrote,

> than the outer edge of the ditches – the counterscarp. Whether you take it at the first attempt or not, the effort is certain to entail heavy losses, especially if you fail, which happens all too often [...] It is always the case that in the siege of a fortress that puts up a resistance you lose three times as many people in taking the counterscarp as you do from then until the final reduction of the place. The loss is always a result of excessive haste [...] at the cost of our best troops who perish miserably on such occasions.[15]

The main effort against the defences of Maastricht came from the south. The Dutch resisted stoutly, and the fighting was costly, with Charles de Batz de Castelmore, Comte d'Artagnan (the hero of Alexandre Dumas' novels), amongst those who were killed in the trenches on 24 June. The French attack that day, that of the Feast of St John the Baptist, went in across the flooded ditch, and a demi-lune was seized after some sharp fighting. James, Duke of Monmouth (illegitimate son of Charles II of England), and John Churchill, the future Duke of Marlborough, also took part in the affair, as part of the contingent of English troops loaned by Charles II at a handsome rate into the French service. Both Englishmen attracted the notice of Louis XIV, on account of their gallantry on this bloody occasion.

The assault, which was made on the orders of Louis XIV, was upon a prominent demi-lune in front of the Port de Bruxelles, and was made under cover of darkness. Resistance was light at first, as the defenders had apparently been caught unawares, but the Dutch recovered quickly and after blowing a well-placed defensive mine, a smart counter-attack drove the French back, with the exception of a group of thirty soldiers who held on grimly to the very edge of the works. The survivors of the party at last had to withdraw after Monmouth failed, despite a valiant effort under heavy fire, to capture a fortified path that led down to the ditch. As daylight came, a full-scale counter-attack was made by the garrison which drove the French soldiers away, in what had been a very bloody affair for both sides. 'I don't know what it is,' Vauban wrote later in some exasperation, 'showing off, pride or just idleness, the readiness we show to expose ourselves outside the trenches.'[16] Monmouth and Churchill fought alongside a young French officer, Claude-Louis-Hector de Villars, a cavalryman who was seeking to gain some experience in siege warfare. As a Marshal of France, he would put Marlborough and his colleagues to the most severe test thirty years or so later, in the dark woods to the south-west of Mons, close to the small hamlet of Malplaquet.

Vauban had expressed his exasperation at those young officers who, while gallant enough and anxious to demonstrate their bravery and valour, were inexpert in the techniques of siege warfare. They were impetuous and impatient of delay, for whatever well-founded reason, but seemed to consider themselves to be adept in these complex and measured matters, always eager to offer what was usually ill-judged advice to those who really were more expert in the art:

> It is not surprising that among the many who believe themselves to be engineers, or who claim to be, there are so few who are able and deserving of that title. The profession is great and very noble, but it demands a genius especially made for it and continuous application throughout many years, something that nature and the vigour of our sieges accord but rarely.[17]

On this occasion at Maastricht, the skilful use of narrow trenches and parallels, simultaneously taking several different angles of 'approach', foiled the Dutch attempts to mount an effective defence for long. 'The way in which the lines were drawn,' the King wrote, with evident satisfaction,

> prevented the enemy from attempting anything. The enemy, astonished at seeing us approach him with so many troops and in such a fashion, adopted the plan of attempting nothing since we advanced with so many precautions, for the fortress was approached almost in battle formation, with great parallels long and spacious, so that owing to the parapets the enemy could be attacked with a very strong front. The Governor and the officers who were with him had never seen anything of the kind, although Farieux had found himself besieged in four or five fortresses, but only where the attack had been by saps so narrow that it was impossible to hold them against the feeblest sortie [by the garrison].[18]

This effective technique was reported to have been adopted by European engineers from that in use by the Ottoman armies, mostly notably at the Siege of Canae on the island of Crete. It was neither entirely novel or new, and had certainly not been invented by Vauban, having also been employed in 1637 at the Siege of La Capelle and at Gravelines in 1644. Simply, the employment of parallels to disguise the main point of attack was just a very neat piece of soldierly common sense. Jean-François de Chastenet, the Marquis de Puységur, an influential French soldier and military theorist, wrote 'I am all for the Turkish practice, according to which they attack by successive parallel lines which occupy the same width as the front of the fortress which is under attack.'[19] The additional feature that seemed to have most effect was that the saps were routinely set at a series of alternating angles, zig-zags in effect, and this prevented defenders from firing down the length of the trench and inflicting casualties. Again, this technique was little more than soldierly common sense.

The parallels would not always completely circumnavigate the entire circuit of the fortress, but more often just confront that portion to be attacked, and of course, sufficient of the adjacent defences to disguise the real intention. Care also had to be taken, and stressed as particularly important by Vauban, to hold strong reserves of infantry nearby, ready to repulse any sudden sortie or counter-attack by the garrison. Caution and economy of force was to be practised, and there was to be no massing of troops prematurely in exposed or advanced positions, thereby offering tempting targets to the defenders' artillery:

> The method consists in moving step by step closing ground and gradually enveloping all the works of the place by lines always well knit together and supporting one another, if it can be helped; never massing troops at one point; never risking a considerable portion of the army in hazardous assaults, as used to be done before this time.[20]

Vauban was always looking for ways to make the attack more effective. He pressed the real necessity for the engineers, scarce in numbers and valuable assets that they were, to all the same be in close attendance at the sapping and entrenching work. This was plainly good practice, and kept the pioneers and labourers at their work and avoided idling or drunkenness. The inevitable effect was that of incurring casualties amongst these same specialists who were hard to replace and whose loss Vauban always bemoaned.

All garrisons had their sharpshooters on duty, vigilant men with carefully chosen muskets with slow-matches well alight, or later on, good flints at the ready, looking to pick off any inviting and unsuspecting target. Vauban's own tendency to get as close as possible to the action, as seen when he was shot and wounded in the face at Douai, frequently drove French commanders, under strict orders as they were not to allow him to come to harm, to something close to a state of despair. Vauban had been warned before by Louvois, against exposing himself too much to enemy fire: 'You will realize the displeasure of His Majesty should anything untoward happen to the Sieur de Vauban.'[21] However, the siege operations against Maastricht proceeded well and were ahead of the normal timetable. Jacques Farieux, the Governor of the place, expressed his despair at the difficulty he had in mounting a prolonged defence: 'It had fallen to him to stand six considerable sieges, but that he had seen none like this, and that from the first day he had lost hope of being able to do anything.'[22]

On 1 July 1673, once the defences of the Porte de Tongeren had been taken, Farieux submitted, after a resistance of only thirteen days, appreciably sooner than had been expected. Despite this, the fighting had been severe, and he and his troops were permitted to march out with all the honours of war, without giving their parole, with drums beating, colours flying and the slow-matches of the musketeers glowing brightly. Vauban was exhausted by the effort, but was given the immediate task of repairing the battered defences of the fortress and city. There was clearly to be little rest: 'The King,' Louvois wrote rather impatiently only a fortnight later, 'is beginning to be slightly annoyed at not receiving your plans for the fortification of Maastricht.'[23] Despite this kind of rather fatuous complaint, Vauban's reputation was more secure after such a resounding success, and Louis XIV awarded him the gratifying sum of 4,000 livres for his part in the successful siege. The new defensive works were so effective that a Dutch attempt to recapture the fortress, just two years later, had to be abandoned after forty-one days, an unusual instance of a formal siege failing.

Military duties and the stream of demands on his time and services that came from the King and Louvois kept Vauban away from his family and matrimonial home at Morvan for long periods. He found occasion, however, to write to the Minister for War on the effectiveness of perriers, the stone-throwing mortars that projected deadly showers of fist-sized missiles to a great distance with disconcerting accuracy. It was noted that the stones fired in this way would penetrate even hard-packed earth to a depth of 6 inches and more. To troops exposed without overhead cover, the effect was devastating. 'The stones fly through the air as in a cloud, then flog the ground with a force I can only compare with that of pikes landing point downwards.'[24] On the other hand, if those same stones had bounced and ricocheted their way around the defences rather than burying themselves deep in the ground, it seems likely that more casualties, injuries requiring more time-consuming attention rather than actual fatalities, might have been caused. Either way, they were a highly useful tool of war.

Vauban also sketched out his developing ideas for the rational and cohesive defence of France, with mutually supporting fixed fortified positions backed up by mobile field armies by means of the Pre-Carré, or Fence of Iron. Writing to Louvois:

> The King ought to give a little thought to squaring off the bound-
> aries of his lands. This confusion of friendly and hostile fortresses is
> all most unsatisfactory [...] whether it is accomplished by treaty or

by a successful campaign, you must continue to preach the need to
tidy up the boundaries.[25]

Any project for a rational defence on these lines, of course, required enormous
expenditure in money and labour, and pragmatically giving up territory that
was only of marginal value while retaining that which was of most importance.
The resources of France were great but not infinite. Vauban would stress to the
King and his Ministers that overextension, just acquiring territory that could
not then be adequately defended except at ruinous cost, would have the
consequence of a gradual but inevitable weakening of the whole defensive
structure for France. Still, victorious campaigns had a certain and quite natural
allure to them, which all too readily would lead on to further and yet further
victories. These things were very tempting, when such success and apparent
glory was to be had. It seems that what in the event was actually undertaken,
over a period of many years and at varying levels of urgency or priority, was
not a cohesive or formal plan but a rather piecemeal fortification of those places
captured by Louis XIV's gifted field commanders. The appearance of a
thought-out plan was certainly there, but it had more to it as an afterthought,
with, just perhaps, the same effect when put into practice.

Such lofty considerations, almost abstract in the short term, were for the
future. In the meantime, Vauban was sent to inspect the work at Nancy and
(Alt) Brisach, and then went on to command the siege operations against the
Spanish-held fortress of Besançon in the Franche-Comté. This place, high on a
rocky spur above the River Doubs, could, in turn, be commanded from nearby
high ground, tactically a dangerous disadvantage. The garrison capitulated on
22 May 1674, after only nineteen days, and Vauban was once more given the
task to repair and strengthen the defences, the citadel of which was only fully
completed in 1688. The defences on Mount Chambron, from where artillery
could command the town, were also strengthened but Vauban was actually not
in favour of making these defences too strong, as that would make more difficult any attempt to retake them if they had been lost to an opponent. There
was, plainly, an element of double if not actually muddled thinking here – the
heights were either worth defending, and doing so properly, or they were not.
If they were well defended, an opponent should not be able to seize them in
sufficient time to affect the operations against the fortress.

The Austrian Emperor had now entered the war, and the Elector of
Brandenburg, whose troops had initially been pushed back by the French,
became active once again. The Great Elector, as he was known, was very
determined and had clear ambitions, and his reach and influence would steadily
grow in effect as the years went by. Louis XIV still had the rather marginal
support of Charles II of England, but little real activity in the war was expected

from that quarter. French troops were now gradually being withdrawn from Dutch territory for deployment elsewhere. Important places such as Utrecht had already been given up, and Zutphen, Arnhem and Nijmegen would be abandoned, along with the towns of Cleves, Overjissel and Deventer. Maastricht, important and powerful, alone of all the trophies remained to Louis XIV to show as a result of all the effort made. This was a sobering moment, a real setback for the King, which was cloaked with rather threadbare declarations of a success.

On 11 August 1674, the Prince of Condé won his last victory, soundly defeating a Spanish army at Seneffe, but this was at a heavy cost and lasting damage was not inflicted upon his opponents as they fell back, depleted but still in the field. The Spanish and their allies then counter-attacked with notable spirit, and the weakened French forces were taken at a disadvantage, although Louvois rather ill-advisedly scoffed in a letter that 'I have seen with the greatest surprise that at Tournai [where the French commanders had their quarters] they have got it into their heads that the enemy was about to attack.'[26]

Despite such blithe scepticism, the French-held fortress of Oudenarde on the Scheldt river was indeed under threat. Vauban, now promoted to Brigadier of Infantry and busily engaged in conducting a survey of the fortresses in the region, was sent to take command of the garrison at this critical time. This was the sole occasion that he had an active command of troops when conducting a defensive operation in earnest. Vauban appears to have relished the task, and the garrison conducted themselves very well under his leadership. Despite his declared dislike of sorties, a number of these were made to successfully spoil the attackers' entrenchments. Vauban even managed, by careful manipulation of the sluice gates, to flood their battery positions and approaches, a trick that others could employ and would actually be used rather well against him at the Siege of Mons in 1691. All the same, an English officer remembered that the successful operation was not nearly so clear cut:

> The siege was carried on with such application and success, that the besiegers were in a few days ready for a storm; but the Prince of Condé prevented them, by coming up to its relief. Upon which the Prince of Orange, pursuant to the resolution of a council of war the night before, drew off his forces.[27]

Frustrated, the Dutch and their Spanish allies had to draw off as an opportunity to engage Condé and Marshal d'Humières with any sign of advantage did not present itself. Condé commended Vauban for the manner in which Oudenarde had been defended, and he was assured that the King was aware of and very much approved his conduct.

To the west, Bergues and Dunkirk were also at some risk, and Vauban hurried there, only to be waylaid on the journey. Louis XIV again expressed his concern that Vauban should not take undue risks in the discharge of his duties. This anxiety became more acute when it was learned that he and his escort had been ambushed on the road near to La Bassée. Vauban was not injured but several of his escort were hurt in the skirmish, including his nephew who was wounded, and a groom whose arm was broken. 'The King forbids you,' Louvois wrote rather tartly, 'under pain of his displeasure, to expose yourself to such risks.'[28] However, the Minister's letter bordered on the absurd as the pace of instructions sending Vauban hurrying from one place to another, in response to the demands of the war, never slackened. He had to move without the protection that commanding generals often obtained, by their requesting passes from an opposing commander to be allowed to take a particular road or route free from the danger of being accosted by hostile cavalry patrols.

The French managed to secure much of the line of the River Meuse in the summer of 1675, moving through Mons and then Namur, then onwards with the seizure of Dinant which submitted on 29 May and then to Huy on 6 June. This was a bold and confident move, putting the French commanders back into a good strategic position. When they approached Limburg, the 1,000-strong garrison commanded by the Count of Nassau-Siegen put up a stout-hearted resistance, but after the Covered Way was lost and three mines were exploded to start a breach, the place submitted on 20 June. As a counter-move, the French garrison in Gavre, protected only by obsolete defences, came under Dutch attack on 23 July 1675, but the Comte de Chantilly and his troops put up a good defence and held out for a very creditable three months.

Meanwhile, Imperial troops had entered Alsace, once again threatening the whole French strategic posture, and Louis XIV had lost the services of two of his best field commanders – the Grand Condé, erratic but brilliant, retired due to ill-heath, while Marshal Turenne was killed by a round-shot strike to the breast at the Battle of Salsbach, near to Strasbourg, on 27 July. Vauban, newly returned from a rare spell of home leave in the Morvan, was touring the defences of eastern France and prepared plans for the strengthening of the defences of Metz, Toul and Verdun in particular. His plans were incomplete when he was instructed to hasten to Courtrai, and then to Le Quesnoy, but on his arrival there it seemed that there was little of great urgency for him to attend to. In time the defences of Metz were improved, although this was apparently not completed to Vauban's precise design, which brought the wrath of Colbert (something to be feared) down onto the head of the resident engineer, Niquet, who had dared to try to deviate from the agreed plans:

'Understand that it is not your place so much as to lay a finger on the work designed by the Sieur de Vauban.'[29]

Plans were now being laid to attack Cambrai and Valenciennes. Vauban recommended that Condé-sur-Escaut and Bouchain be taken first, with the two towns then being used as forward bases from which to strike onwards. 'It is the best blow to strike in the present state of affairs [...] we must think of consolidating our forces. You cannot very well do this except by taking the fortress of Condé, which assures you of possession of Bouchain.'[30] The advice was accepted, but the season was late and the weather had turned bad. Movement was difficult, and matters were delayed over the cold winter months as a result. In April 1676, Condé-sur-Escaut was captured by French forces after five days of tough fighting for the Covered Way and demi-lunes. The attacks were supported by artillery mounted on rafts of Vauban's own novel design, which crossed the adjacent water obstacle defences. Next, Bouchain, subjected to a tremendous bombardment of round-shot and mortar bombs over four days, fell on 11 May after little more than a week's resistance, and Aire followed suit on 31 July. Improvements were immediately put in hand by Vauban, whose promotion to Major General was now announced. The strengthened defences at Bouchain, in particular, were highly effective and would play their part in the campaign of 1711, proving very difficult to overcome at that time.

Vauban was sent on a further round of inspections, and this found him once more in Verdun at the end of the year, clearly feeling the ill-effects of the bitter wintry weather:

> The vilest and coldest weather imaginable. Everything was ice-bound, and I came near to breaking my neck a score of times [on the road] [...] If this weather goes on, the King will get very little out of any work undertaken this winter, and I, for my part, will be glad enough to come through it without getting my nose and ears frost-bitten.[31]

Meanwhile, a Dutch attempt to recapture Maastricht failed against a stout resistance put up by the French garrison under command of Lieutenant General Jean Sauveur de Calvo, a Spanish officer in the service of Louis XIV. De Calvo's accomplished defence of the fortress in the face of a formal siege, one which was well conducted and properly provisioned, was an unusual and instructive example of a success for the besieged against the besiegers.

De Calvo even felt able to exchange some racy banter with his opponent, over the difficulties he faced in the campaign. He declared that, as it was reported that the Dutch commander had announced his intention before too long of saluting de Calvo's famously attractive mistress with a fervent kiss on the cheek, 'He would give him,' de Calvo wrote in a gently bawdy vein, 'licence to kiss her all over if he kissed her at anywhere at all within three months.'[32] Despite such an alluring inducement to success, when several spirited attempts were made to storm the outer defences, all proved to be unsuccessful and where gains were made they were costly, and very well-handled French counter-attacks drove the Allied troops out again:

> At break of day, the attack was begun with great resolution [...] the bastion was again taken, and in it the commanding officer, who in service to himself, more than to us, told us that the centre of the bastion would soon be blown up, being to his knowledge undermined for that purpose [...] After about half an hour's possession of the bastion, the mine under it, of which the French officer gave us warning, was sprung.[33]

Whether or not de Calvo's lady-love, who may or may not have been particular in these matters, would have welcomed the gallant attentions of the Dutch officer was never put to the test, as the siege of the Maastricht fortress was abandoned soon afterwards.

Valenciennes was invested by the French on 5 March 1677, with Vauban taking command of the siege operations. The move was cloaked with so much seemingly needless secrecy at first that he wrote rather irritably to Louvois that 'It is rather a curious thing to see that everyone knows what you intend to do, and that it is only to me that any secret is made of it; apparently I am to play an insignificant part in it, and my opinion is to count for nothing.'[34] There was more than a note of uncalled-for impatience here, and perhaps injured pride, as other officers had already received their instructions while those intended for Vauban were still in preparation. As it was, the operation was not a greatly taxing undertaking and the garrison, expecting no relief, gave way on 17 March, after a surprise attack in broad daylight sent in by Marshal Luxembourg at Vauban's suggestion. The forward defences in a ravelin were overwhelmed with the sudden force of the assault, and the soldiers of the garrison broke and ran for shelter. The attacking French soldiers, as a result, were able to establish themselves in some nearby houses and, defying ill-coordinated attempts to evict them, called forward reinforcements. The defences were clearly breached, and the magistrates of the town pleaded with the Governor that he should submit straight away, and so the garrison surrendered themselves as prisoners of war.

Vauban and other senior officers received large cash rewards from the King, as was customary, and he was also gratified at last to also receive some of his considerable arrears of pay. The town of Cambrai was now isolated, with a string of recently secured French-held fortresses to the north, and the garrison could expect no immediate assistance. Louis XIV came to take charge of the siege operations, at least in appearance at any rate as Vauban actually gave the instructions, and toured the entrenchments each day. The defences of the town were old and unsophisticated, just a mediaeval wall flanked by towers, and with no protecting outworks or defensive ditch. Work started on breaking ground and digging the trenches on 22 March, and the almost indefensible town was given up on 5 April, with the Spanish garrison withdrawing into the more formidable Citadel.

The attack on the Citadel of Cambrai was conducted from the town side, but the operation had not progressed very far when an impetuous French officer, Captain Du Retz, persuaded the King to permit him to lead an outright assault in broad daylight on the nearest and most prominent demi-lune. He appeared to be frustrated with what was regarded as the slow rate of progress. Vauban protested that the artillery had not been able to achieve very much yet, and that it was too soon for such an attempt, 'Sire, you will lose lives that are worth more to you,'[35] but his comments were all to no avail, and Du Retz and his party of stormers set off. They captured the demi-lune quickly enough, but these forward works were often designed to become a trap for anyone forcing their way in as the rearward side would be deliberately left open and was exposed to the fire from the untroubled main defences. The Spanish soldiers of the garrison poured in a terrific musketry and a shower of hand grenades from their positions and the French soldiers, despite a stubbornly gallant but fruitless effort, had to withdraw after two days of the most bitter fighting, and with the loss of 440 men. They had nothing at all to show for their effort, and the useless expenditure of blood and powder.

Louis XIV acknowledged that he ought to have heeded the warnings of his Engineer, and that the attack should not have been made. As if to drive home the lesson, Vauban then put in a far more measured and noticeably less flamboyant attack, with proper artillery support, and retook the demi-lune two days later with the loss of only three killed and wounded. The big guns then began their remorseless work, as did his teams of miners, and once two breaches were made in the adjoining bastion, the Governor capitulated on 17 April 1677. The garrison had put up a good defence during the twenty-nine days of the siege. They were granted the honours of war, marching out with colours flying and drums beating bravely, two days later. Louis XIV asked that the Spanish Governor be introduced to him, so that he could congratulate him on his own brave conduct and the valour of his troops.

Despite all these gallant niceties, the submission of important places such as Valenciennes and Cambrai had come somewhat sooner than might have been expected. The garrison commanders were generally held to have been able to do more if they had applied themselves better, but the operations of the French, the attack supervised by Du Retz being perhaps an exception, had been very well handled indeed. Meanwhile, Vauban was appointed to be a Maréchal de Camp, a significant promotion, and was sent to oversee the operations against the minor fortress of Saint Ghislain. In what was becoming an almost routine instruction, the field commander there, Marshal d'Humières, was warned by Louvois that 'His Majesty approves your taking M. de Vauban with you, but he urges strongly upon you the necessity for his safety, and he is not to be allowed to undertake work in the trenches.'[36] The refrain was now a common one, and remained a little absurd. The heavy demands on Vauban's services, which rather inevitably put him in harm's way if he was to discharge his duties properly, remained just the same.

Much of the region was firmly in French hands now, and the way lay invitingly open for further advances. Saint Omer had been invested since February 1677, but still held out with a Spanish garrison. An attempt by Dutch troops under William of Orange to relieve the place was turned back in a bloody encounter with a French force, under command of the King's brother, the Duc d'Orléans, at Cassel on 11 April 1677. The Dutch army's left flank was broken by the Marshal d'Humières' attack, while the centre and right of the army was held firmly in place by Marshal Luxembourg. Although battered, the Dutch then moved eastwards and attempted to take Charleroi, but failed to do so in the face of skilful manoeuvring by the Marshal. Eight days later the French secured possession of the counter-scarp at Saint Omer, and the 1,500-strong garrison capitulated on 22 April, being permitted to march away to Ghent. Vauban was not present, however, as he was still fully engaged in the trenches before Cambrai, before going on to take part at the Siege of Saint Ghislain.

The elderly Chevalier de Clerville, sidelined and all but forgotten, had died, and 45-year-old Vauban was appointed to the vacated post of Inspector-General of Fortifications in his place. Vauban now had the formal responsibility for the design, construction and upkeep of all the fortified places of France. He did feel some unease that he would become enmeshed in paperwork and bureaucracy to the detriment of his activities in the field, but Louis XIV brushed these reservations aside; he wished Vauban to accept the post, and there was accordingly no more to be said.

The bountiful cash rewards which Vauban received from the King, particularly at such triumphs as the capture of Maastricht, had enabled him to purchase a suitably grand country home, the château of Bazoches close to his place of birth. Up to then, Vauban and his family had lived in La Tour d'Epiry, apparently a rather comfortless place, but they now aspired to something better and more elegant.[37] The estate at Bazoches had been owned at one time by Vauban's great-grandfather, the Comte de la Ferrière, and latterly by the now impoverished Comte de Mellun, so he presumably knew the property well. A certain measure of his success was, no doubt, that he could demonstrate this by restoring the property to the family.

By the beginning of 1678, Louis XIV had grown tired of the prolonged war with the intransigent Dutch, and he sought peace on whatever advantageous terms could be arranged. He was understandably anxious to hold on to the gains made over the previous few years at the expense of Madrid – primarily the towns of Ath, Cambrai, Bouchain, Saint Ghislain, Condé-sur-Escaut, Saint Omer and Valenciennes. In the meantime, the campaigning had to go on to maintain the pressure upon his opponents to agree suitable terms. The French armies at first feinted towards the north-east against Luxembourg, Namur and Mons, but then turned to threaten Ypres. In response the Dutch moved troops from their garrisons in northern Flanders to reinforce the garrison, only to find that the French had taken ill-defended Ghent with little difficulty, in only nine days. The citadel there submitted to Louis XIV on 12 March. The Spanish Governor, Don Francisco de Pardo, offered the capitulation with every appearance of complaisance together with an elegant compliment: 'I give up Ghent to Your Majesty, it is all I could desire.'[38] This rather rapid sub-mission caused a certain amount of surprise, and some pointed comment was expressed that nothing like enough had been done by the Governor and his garrison to resist the attack. The French army moved southwards, and Ypres was in turn invested just six days later. Once more, Vauban had control of the siege operations, while Louis XIV lodged comfortably nearby with his retinue.

Morale amongst the French troops was high after recent successes, but the 3,500-strong Dutch garrison in Ypres, where the fortifications had been improved in response to the growing threat, resisted well. The citadel was of a pentagonal shape, and the curtain wall protected by a series of demi-lunes. The low-lying nature of the ground to the south side made digging difficult, with the French entrenchments beginning to fill with water as soon as ground was broken. Conditions were bad, and progress was slow. Accordingly, Vauban decided to concentrate his attention to the east of the town where the terrain was a little more elevated and therefore drier. This side not only held the citadel, the strongest part of the fortress, but the main thrust of the besiegers' efforts was made perfectly clear to the garrison at an early point by the con-centration of activity – always a dangerous thing to allow, and quite contrary to Vauban's normal teaching and practice.

The trenches were opened under Vauban's supervision on 22 March. The King, as usual, wished to see what was going on, and once more demonstrated a healthy disregard for personal danger – a virtue that was certainly admired by his soldiers – under what proved to be heavy fire from the fortress. Great care had to be taken that he came to no harm on his excursions to see his troops at their work, and one French musketeer chided the King for being too far

forward one day, with the brusque comment, 'Is this the place for you?'
Vauban, who had quite enough to handle without these risky Royal excursions
into the trenches, wrote that:

> Whatever care you may take to construct your trenches, there is
> never any place in them where you are completely safe from all
> hazards. You are incessantly exposed to the ricochet of the balls
> which most often – only raking the top of the parapet without being
> stopped – fall into the trench killing and maiming [...] Since there is
> so little safety in the trenches might we not well consider whether the
> sovereign, who may be present at the Siege of some fortress, should
> share the risks of his troops? Certainly, he cannot expose his sacred
> person, even when necessary for the good of his state, without
> causing a whole people to tremble [...] It is not for me to find fault
> with the actions of my sovereign, but as my conscience obliges me to
> speak freely on anything that may serve for the conservation of his
> person, and especially on subjects relating to the craft I profess, it
> would be even less proper for me to remain silent [...] I categorically
> assert that His Majesty ought never to appear in the trenches.[39]

More than anything else, it seems that Louis XIV and his party just got in the
way, whatever their intention was, and whatever benefit the morale of the
soldiers may have gained by their visits. Quite understandably, no one would
wish to point out to the King that he was simply adding to the worries of his
commanders, and probably slowing the pace of the operations, when his
intention was the complete opposite. As had been seen, Louis XIV frequently
admonished his field commanders that Vauban should not be permitted to
expose himself to undue risk by going forward in the trenches, but his own
conduct seemed to undermine such strictures. So neither man appeared to give
very much attention to the concerns of the other on the subject, as both had
firm views on what was and what was not appropriate, and were not inclined to
pay too much heed to the advice of others on such matters.

Nikolaas Hoedt was the able commander of the Dutch artillery in Ypres.
Vauban's trenches to the east of the fortress came under heavy bombardment
from the gunners from the very start, and one well-placed shot killed sixteen
members of the Gardes Françaises, while another struck the side of the building
in which the King had his quarters. Vauban then opened a new line of attack,
this time coming in from the north along the line of a canal, where the slightly
elevated banks enabled the sappers to make better progress well out of the wet
and low-lying fields all around. The Covered Way was reached on 25 March,
and the Governor, aware that no relief was likely, duly capitulated. He and his
troops, including Hoedt, were permitted to march away without giving their

parole; the capitulation had come quite early, it was acknowledged. However, impressed with the skill demonstrated by the Dutch artillery commander, Louis XIV offered Hoedt a commission in the French army, but the gunner refused to switch his allegiance. When Vauban was tasked to improve the defences of Ypres, he decided that the old citadel was so poorly positioned and incapable of an effective defence that it should just be demolished, and he had it resited completely.

The French King declared his terms for a general resumption of peace with the negotiation of the Treaty of Nijmegen, and this was signed with the Dutch on 10 August 1678.[40] Four days later an expensive battle was fought at St-Denis, not far from Mons, with some 8,000 casualties, as neither of the army commanders, William III or Marshal Luxembourg, had learned of the agreement for peace. On 17 September, terms were also agreed between France and Spain. The Cambresis and the Franche-Comté regions would remain in French hands, and the defences of Besançon transformed under Vauban's direction: 'Make of Besançon ever after one of the finest strongholds in Europe, on which the King may depend.'[41] Maastricht and Ghent were returned to the Dutch, along with several other important towns in Flanders, such as Charleroi, Courtrai, Ath and Oudenarde which were returned to Spanish control, but France kept hold of Valenciennes, Bouchain, Condé-sur-Escaut, Aire, Saint Omer, Ypres, Cassel, Cambrai, Mauberge and Bavay.

The previously weak, even dangerously porous, borders of northern France had been significantly strengthened in the course of the war. Major gains had been made more secure, including the line of the Oise river, always a potentially vulnerable avenue into France, with possession of the fortresses of Philippeville and Marienbourg. The continued occupation of Laon, Soissons and Rocroi gave added strength and depth. Vauban, responsible now for the formal defence of France, was tasked to look at ways to improve the defences of this region. Louis XIV finally agreed terms for peace with Emperor Leopold on 6 February 1679, and French possession of Nancy and Freiburg was confirmed, and what had undoubtedly been an almost uniformly victorious war for France, despite the real disappointments of the campaign in the Dutch southern provinces, was at a tired end. Importantly for Vauban's project for defence, territory in depth and towns of the first importance for this purpose had been permanently secured as French possessions, not just as places occupied by garrisons for the time being.

The new Inspector-General of Fortifications drew up a detailed memorandum, setting out an outline for a cohesive scheme of defence for northern France, the region strategically of the most importance, and now enlarged sufficiently to allow for a viable defence in depth. Vauban was eager to see that a proper system of fortification for the region be established, and he had certain concerns at what, of necessity, had been negotiated away, to achieve an end to the war. He wrote, significantly, for the future security of France:

> The frontier towards the Low Countries lies open and disordered as a consequence of the recent peace. There is no doubt that it will be necessary to establish a new frontier and fortify it so well that it closes the approaches into our country to an enemy while giving us access to him.[42]

The interest Vauban took in offensive operations, as well as the defence, is quite clear.

What he proposed was the establishment of a double line of modern first-class fortresses to be constructed and improved all the way from the Channel coast to the Meuse river. Of the newly-established borders in the north and north-east, Vauban wrote:

> The fortified points that compose it will secure the river-crossings for us and provide communication between the local government districts; that the fortified places should be large enough to contain not only the munitions required for their own defence but also the supplies needed if we invade enemy territory. If we assume all these to be necessary conditions, it appears that the frontier would be very well protected if its defences were reduced to two lines of fortifi-cations, on the model of an army's order of battle, as follows.[43]

This double line, which would become known to many as the Pre-Carré (although the term clearly had a wider meaning and the defence system constructed is more aptly described by the other term, a 'Fence of Iron'), ran for some 120 miles in length. It would comprise fourteen fortresses of modern design in each of the advanced and depth lines, and be strengthened at frequent points by water obstacles such as rivers, canals and areas capable of inundation at times of need, while an improved road network would allow the rapid movement of troops from one point to another as a likely threat developed.

> The first line would be made up of thirteen fortified towns, and two fortresses: Dunkirk, Bergues, Furnes, the fort of le Knocq, Ypres, Menin, Lille, Tournai, the fort of Mortagne, Condé, Valenciennes, le Quesnoy, Mauberge, or some other place on the River Sambre, Philippeville, and Dinant. The second line, of thirteen places, would comprise: Gravelines, Saint Omer, Aire, Béthune, Arras, Douai, Bouchain, Cambrai, Landrecies, Avesnes, Marienbourg, Rocroi and Charlesville [...] and all of them large and strong. In addition, the first line should be strengthened with canals and waterways from the

great canal of Ypres to the Lys, and between the Lys and the
Scheldt, along whose banks entrenchments could be dug in time of
war, which, together with all the other fortifications listed above
would secure all the region behind them, while at the same time the
canals would provide valuable assistance for the movement of goods
and commerce.[44]

The scope and scale of what Vauban proposed was enormous, not only in the
amount of construction and reconstruction that was intended, but also in the
cost that was entailed. There were opportunities to improve the prospects for
future campaigns, of course:

> Once the frontier is stabilized in this way, and the frontier places
> finished and well supplied, they will be extremely strong and the
> very best of their kind. Moreover, we have every reason to hope that
> we shall be more often on the offensive than our enemies, so that
> there will be no need for further fortifications. I am of the opinion
> that we should build no further fortifications outside these two lines;
> on the contrary, I think that in the course of time it would be best to
> destroy all fortifications that do not form part of these lines, or are
> situated deep inside the kingdom, for they serve only to encourage
> rebellion.[45]

Louis XIV, whose Treasury had not yet reached a state of exhaustion, although
that would certainly come in time, lent a willing ear to the project which was
approved, in modified form.

The onset of renewed peace, albeit quite a temporary state of affairs while
each side drew up fresh schemes for advancing their own interests, enabled
Vauban to begin to put into practice his schemes for a well laid-out defensive
barrier in the north-east region. Louvois, for his part, did his best to ensure
that the money saved by not having to actively campaign was devoted instead
to the strengthening of the frontier. Louis XIV could now view with relative
complacency the newly realigned border he shared with the Spanish Netherlands. Not only was Spain either on friendly terms with France, or at worst a
spent force militarily, but the many marshy rivers in the region, such as the
Meuse, Escaut and the Sambre, bolstered by the now strengthening belt of
fortresses firmly in French hands, gave a distinct measure of security in a
region which had previously not had such. This remained the case, of course,
as long as no powerful hostile power was in possession of, or operating freely
in, the Southern Netherlands, and this vital strategic consideration would
induce Louis XIV into making a most regrettable error in 1702, when his
youngest son had taken possession of the throne in Madrid. The matter was

even more acute for France in the terrible aftermath of the dramatic defeat of Marshal Villeroi's army at Ramillies, in May 1706, when French troops were almost entirely driven out from the region.

Elsewhere, the difficult tracts of country to the east, such as the Ardennes, the Hunsruck and the Moselle valley, bolstered by the massive water barrier of the Rhine and the depth provided by the plains of the Palatinate, the Franche-Comté region and the Duchy of Lorraine, gave a fair measure of security. So, too, did the difficult uplands of the Vosges, and then south past the Belfort Gap to the formidable barrier of the Alps, with the Duchy of Savoy courted as a friendly power to watch over the passes which led from northern Italy. In the far south, the barrier of the Pyrenees provided a natural secure stone wall as a safeguard when looking towards Spain, requiring only a few fortresses at strategic points. Given all this, with Vauban hard at work on the defences in the north, the security of France could be seen as having been much transformed and improved over what it had previously been.

Chapter 6

An End to Glory

In the same year that he was appointed to be Inspector-General of Fortifications, Vauban completed and submitted his designs for the rebuilding of the defences of Mauberge, Longwy and Menin. He was then sent on a tour of inspection in the south, visiting Lyon, Antibes, Toulon, Cette and Perpignan. The engineer Niquet, so insubordinate in the past at Metz but undeniably skilled, was summoned to come south also, to supervise the improvements at Toulon. He continued to cause mischief, and once again incurred the wrath of Colbert, being locked up on one occasion as a warning. Niquet was not alone, as the further from Versailles the more tendency there seemed to be for individuals to suit themselves in their actions and ignore their instructions. On several occasions, Vauban found that he was required to exercise his skills in these more outlying areas as moderator among the officials and functionaries he met, who were far from central authority and had taken to petty jealousies and bickering amongst themselves. He wrote to Louvois of his findings:

> I have prepared several naval and fortification schemes adequate to the importance of these places and of the enemies that they have to fear. I have settled a number of things that required my attention, made peace among the staff, and drawn up a plan for the arsenal, with which we are all pleased, inspectors, engineers, naval officers and master carpenters. I trust the King will be so too, and after that it will only rest with His Majesty that this work should be carried out.[1]

Vauban had been forbidden by Louis XIV to travel by sea, on account of the risk posed by the piratical cruises of the Barbary corsairs in the Mediterranean Sea, and he complained to Louvois of the poor state of the roads of the region over which he had to travel: 'It cannot be said that one travels post, one crawls, and frequently takes to one's legs [...] I am heartily weary of it.' His progress was commendable, however, and, once in the Pyrenees, Vauban selected Mont-Louis, almost an eyrie amongst the high rocky crags, for a fortress with a square citadel and four bastions, in addition to a massive and unusual crownwork that encompassed the old town. This remarkably fine site remains, at 1,600 metres above sea level, the most elevated such place in France.[2]

Vauban had written to Louis XIV, urging that the city and fortress of Luxembourg stood out as a dangerous omission in the defensive arrangements that he was busily planning. Despite his concern at not overstretching French military strength by trying to hold indefensible places, the city was deemed to be sufficiently key to be worth the taking. French troops blockaded Luxembourg, although they did not attack the garrison, in the summer of 1681. The move proved to be premature, and after a few months the French withdrew.

Under the 1648 Treaty of Westphalia, towns in regions such as Alsace had been left with most of their ancient rights and privileges intact, and they enjoyed a large degree of local autonomy. With the shifting fortunes of war, some of these same places had sided with France's opponents, and were left on the losing side and now potentially vulnerable. Louis XIV created a Chamber of Reunions in 1679 to 'invite' the civic authorities of Alsace, Lorraine and the Franche-Comté to consider his claim to sovereignty over them. Not surprisingly, there was a general understanding of where their best interests lay, and they found in the King's favour without too much hesitation. Minor states were persuaded, by a mixture of blandishments and threats, to acknowledge allegiance if not actual fealty to Louis XIV. French policy was to be increasingly driven by the desire to secure the crossings over the Rhine, particularly that at Strasbourg and the adjacent fortress at Kehl. During the summer of 1680, virtually all of Alsace came under French control, and Saarlouis, a newly-fortified town on the Saar river on the south side of the Hunsruck, was designed by Vauban. Far to the south, the Principality of Orange (from which William III's family took their name), on the River Rhône, was seized.

Vauban was engaged in inspecting the extensive work at Dunkirk and other Channel ports, such as Boulogne and Cherbourg, when he was given the task to repair and strengthen the rather dilapidated defences of Strasbourg, which was recently occupied by French troops. He arrived in the city on 4 October 1681, and under the plans rapidly submitted to Louvois, the old town was to be enclosed by brand new fortifications with multiple bastions. His scheme, contained in 'un gros volume d'écriture', did not meet with Royal approval at first, indicating that the resources of Louis XIV's Treasury were not infinite, and that this fact was striking home. Louvois wrote to him in a rather irritable tone, complaining that the plans sent were 'Too elaborate and magnificent [...] You must find ways of simplifying them [...] reduce the cost. His majesty has too many fortresses to build to continue making handsome gateways.'[3] Colbert also had occasion to comment rather caustically that Vauban was accustomed to great expenditure in fortifying towns, implying that the expense was not always justified and that he had too great an appetite for grand projects in localities where they were not really required. This was not so, for Vauban was concerned to concentrate effort to best effect, and yet, the expenditure on his projects still remained considerable.

Late in December, Louvois wrote to Vauban sending him southwards once more at best speed, without stopping on the way, the customary phrase being 'the King commands you'. This time he was to go and attend to matters at Casale in northern Italy. The fortress had only recently been acquired by France from the Duke of Mantua for the quite magnificent sum of 2,400,000 livres, but, as it transpired, Vauban found no great emergency to attend to when he got there. He then went to French-held Pignerole, then to Provence, and then back to the Franche-Comté, inspecting the work in each locality, assessing what progress was being made, and encouraging, praising or admonishing, as required, the engineers and workers wherever he went.

It was fairly clear that the agreement contained in the Treaty of Nijmegen of 1678 had not done enough to resolve the tensions between France and Spain. Matters that would have to be settled at some point were merely put to one side while the opponents either caught their breath (as with Spain), or consolidated their gains (in the case of France). Incidents and minor clashes on the newly-established borders in the north increased in frequency, and on 31 August 1683, the Governor of the Spanish Netherlands was presented with an ultimatum by Baron d'Asfeld that he should submit to terms that were dictated by Louis XIV or face a military offensive. Some 20,000 French troops crossed the border the very next day without waiting for an answer, indicating very clearly that preparations for renewed war had been under way for some time. In October, however, war was formally resumed and Louis XIV sent his army into the Spanish Netherlands once more, laying siege at first to Dixmude and Courtrai. Imperial Austria chose not to become involved this time, but Madrid could count on Dutch assistance, and the States-General provided 8,000 veteran troops to support the Spanish in the campaign.

Vauban was actively involved in the renewed siege operations. The Marquis d'Humières had command of the field army, and under the customary strict instructions from Versailles, did his very best to ensure that the Engineer exposed himself to enemy musketry as little as possible. The Marquis wrote in almost plaintive terms from the camp to the Minister for War, in November:

> I have not been able to prevent M. de Vauban from going into the town [during the attack on Courtrai]; he promised me faithfully that he would not stir out of his lodgings, but would receive there reports from his engineers of what was going on [...] We very nearly fell out over it, you know he cannot be controlled at one's pleasure.[4]

The Spanish defence of Courtrai lasted a meagre four days, and Dixmude fared little better, both places being taken by the close of the campaign in November 1683.

Louis XIV had intended to move next against Luxembourg, but he chose to call off the operation when the threat of Ottoman aggression against Vienna came again. It was clearly not thought to be acceptable, for the time being, to be applying pressure while Christianity was under attack. Renewed Spanish belligerence, mixed with French opportunism, would change things once more. The highly capable Marshal François de Crequi, Marquis de Marine, imposed a blockade on Luxembourg in late December 1683, and on 3 January 1684, he received orders from Versailles to make a determined attack on the city. As before, the careful stockpiling of stores and munitions well in advance enabled the French to move more swiftly than their opponents. The formal siege of the city was begun when the fortress was invested by the Marquis de Lambert on 22 April. Vauban, although newly appointed to be Governor of Douai, was once more placed in command of the work in the trenches at Luxembourg, and the anticipated capitulation of the garrison would add significantly to the depth of the formal line of defences for the north-eastern borders of France.

The Luxembourg garrison was commanded by the Prince de Chimay, an experienced officer who had some 3,600 troops, but some of these were ill-trained and poorly equipped militia, and only one regiment was said to be of good quality and properly trained. Marshal de Crequi commanded the besieging army, 27,000 men, with sixty-three large siege guns and mortars, while 20,000 peasants were conscripted from the locality to labour in the trenches. In addition, Vauban had a formed company of engineers and miners, some sixty strong. Because of the difficult nature of the ground, the siege works were constructed mostly to the north-west of the city. Yet again, Louvois sternly warned the army commander not to permit the Inspector-General of Fortifications to unduly expose himself to danger:

> His Majesty recommends to the Marshal to give Sieur de Vauban all the time necessary to conduct the works required to reduce the place in such a fashion that it may be done with as few losses as possible. His Majesty also recommends to the said Sr Marshal, to give such orders as needed to prevent Sr de Vauban exposing himself without need.[5]

The King's comment regarding the need to limit casualties is instructive, indicating that Vauban's recommendations on this aspect of siege warfare had been taken to heart, and careful but steady progress was becoming more the accepted practice than hitherto. As usual, this cautionary word to de Crequi regarding the Engineer's own safety proved to be all but impossible to perform, as he insisted on inspecting the progress of the trenches at first hand, daily tramping through the mud to see what progress was being made, and encouraging the engineers, sappers and workmen as they inched their perilous way forward.

A heavy bombardment of the Luxembourg defences was begun. By 11 May, Vauban could report that the work on the approach trenches was progressing well, although the hard substrata around the city made the work difficult for the miners, who worked under the supervision of the Chevalier de Goulon. Several spirited sorties were made by the garrison, and although these were driven back with heavy losses, they inevitably slowed the progress of the siege. Attempts to extend the trenches under cover of darkness proved disappointing, and an initial misalignment of the works required additional work to remedy. Furthermore, the strength of the bastion towers constructed by the gifted Spanish engineer, Louvigni, proved to be something of a shock to the French besiegers. This lesson was not lost on Vauban, who took careful note and incorporated the bastions into his designs with increasing frequency from then on.

On 14 May, a rather ill-judged attack on one of the tenaillions was beaten off with heavy French casualties, while an attempt to trick the garrison into an early blowing of their defensive mines below the glacis was equally unsuccessful. The young son of Marshal d'Humières, Colonel of a regiment of Foot, was on hand to take part in the siege and to better learn his trade as a soldier when involved in siege warfare. He insisted on looking over the parapet of an approach trench to see how close they had come to the defences, and a vigilant sentry in the garrison saw him and promptly shot the young nobleman dead.

Vauban was equally careful to enhance the ability of French sharpshooters when suppressing the fire of the defenders manning the Covered Way, by using elevated wooden platforms. This technique was duly reported to Louvois, who promptly scolded him in a letter: 'Take better care of yourself [...] Your present occupation compels you to expose yourself quite enough, without amusing yourself by taking pot-shots.'[6] As usual, the Engineer paid little attention to this advice, and on one notable occasion when he was conducting a rather close reconnaissance of the glacis, he called out to a Spanish sentry who was watching him that he was a friend, and the soldier, taken in by the Frenchman's calm nonchalance, lowered his musket and waved him on. The King soon heard of the escapade, and was not at all amused; Louvois also sent a reprimand, but this appears to have been ignored once more:

> The Sieur de Vauban, Marshal de Camp, was one of the first on the counter-guard, and gave there with his ordinary sufficiency orders,

very beneficial for the security and continuation of the lodgements, which were made there. All the foot, which were at this action, acquitted themselves very well.[7]

At last, a breach in the main defences was made, after heavy bombardment and some skilful mining. Casualties amongst Vauban's treasured miners and pioneers had been heavy, many falling victim to well-aimed hand grenades. He also recalled afterwards that one mortar often had more effect at this kind of work, when suppressing the fire of the defenders, than four long-barrelled cannon; the fearsome effect of the showers of stones fired from the perriers was well-known, certainly.

Careful preparations were made for a general assault on Luxembourg, and scaling ladders were ostentatiously brought forward into the third parallel, ready for use. The Spanish Governor, de Chimay, asked for terms on 31 May 1684, and celebrations for the success began in the French camp, but these were a little premature. After lengthy negotiations over the terms, the garrison formally capitulated on 3 June, and Luxembourg was given up to French troops. Compliments were exchanged, and the garrison was permitted to march out with all the honours of war, their colours, arms and baggage intact:

> All the garrison, their families, domesticks, and servants, shall go forth of the town in full liberty, with their moveables and effects, and without having their baggage visited [inspected] [...] they shall not in any sort be molested by our troops for the space of four days; during which they may take the way of Louvain, or of Malines, without being in any way opposed.[8]

Vauban's efforts in the siege were rewarded with a gift, a 'gratification', from the King of 8,000 pistoles, but the pace of operations had been relentless: 'I am so tired and sleepy,' he wrote, 'that I no longer know what I am saying.'[9] Such was his exhaustion that he took to his camp bed for four days, but all the same, was immediately given the task to repair and improve the battered defences of the fortress. The Marquis de Lambert was appointed to the governorship of the place.

Vauban took the time to write to Versailles with warm recommendations for the services of his own engineers and miners during these siege operations; diligent men who tended to be casually overlooked when honours and rewards were distributed. 'They deserved so much the more,' he wrote, 'and had worked in so deliberate and courageous a manner, they would have allowed themselves to be killed to the last man before one of them would have complained.'[10] Vauban had for some time had a particular project in mind, that of establishing a dedicated permanent corps of properly trained engineers, and he wrote to Louvois, who had already complimented him on the success in the Siege of Luxembourg:

> Be so good as to obtain authority to raise the company of sappers I have requested so often; otherwise, I cannot conduct sieges in the orderly way in which I would if I were supported by trained men, always under my own control.[11]

His efforts were eventually rewarded with the formal establishment of a Corps of Engineers, and their reputation and professional expertise became so high and well established, that they were long held to be pre-eminent in military circles.

The Siege of Luxembourg had seen the first widespread use of 'Cavaliers' – a 'sort of little firing platform' – elevated wooden structures that were placed at intervals to enable the attackers to dominate and suppress with musketry the defenders manning the Covered Way. 'We began a platform on the right to look backwards into the Covered Way, and there were seven or eight soldiers killed.'[12] A long-favoured technique was to have the best shots actually using their muskets, while their less adept comrades kept them supplied with loaded weapons from behind, as Vauban wrote:

> We attempted to make a lodgement in the angle of the covered way of the redoubts on the left. To do this the sap was pushed forward [...] to the head (edge) of the covered way at which they raised several gabions one on the other and filled them with sacks of earth – a sort of little firing platform capable of holding two or three fusiliers, who were raised 7 or 8 feet higher than the top of the parapet of the counter-scarp, being able to cover the entire covered way with fire. This forced the enemy to abandon their position. Although these two nests could only hold four men, their fire was continual because grenadiers in the trenches kept loading and passing their fusils.[13]

Platforms of this kind could, of course, also be used by troops in a garrison to enable them to fire into the closest approach trenches from an elevated position: 'The arquebusiers, who were regularly relieved by fresh troops, kept up a constant fire, so that the defender dared not show his head above the parapet.'[14] For the besiegers, however, to be able to dominate the Covered Way in this fashion and eventually force the evacuation of that vital position, would remove the need for an expensive assault, or to have to extend the saps forward from the third parallel to 'crown' the works, as it was known, with additional subsidiary parallels branching out to right and left along the edge of the Covered Way.

Once this dominating position was firmly established, and the infantry holding the Covered Way having been driven off, killed or captured, the large guns of the besiegers' batteries could be dragged forward to begin to create, at close range, the practicable breach that would spell the approaching downfall of the fortress. This would be a critical moment for the garrison, and often called for a spirited counter-attack by the garrison to recapture the Covered Way, and re-establish the security of the fortress, before the guns of the siege train got properly into place. 'The besiegers having got possession of the covert-way and perfected their lodgements in it, will fall to work at their batteries for making a breach [...] this work must be opposed.'[15]

Spain was in no position to pursue a vigorous campaign in the Low Countries or in the Franche-Comté, and was likely to only lose even more by fighting on. Emperor Leopold I in Vienna was asked to intercede, and negotiate a peace with the French on Madrid's behalf. It was agreed that Strasbourg and Kehl would remain in French hands, and that all the gains in Alsace, Lorraine and the Franche-Comté under the policy of the 'Reunions' would stand. Luxembourg, Chimay, Bouvines and Beaumont were recognized as given up to French garrisons for the time being. This was all formalized when the Treaty of Ratisbon was concluded on 15 August 1684, and peace, uneasy certainly, but at least a peace, returned to western Europe once more. Spain was exhausted by war, and Madrid had for too long had to count on the support of allies who proved to be broken reeds or fair-weather friends. Louis XIV emerged stronger still, and had been able to hold on to most of his recent gains.

As it turned out, the key fortress and city of Luxembourg, greatly strengthened to Vauban's design though it had been, would have to be given up within thirteen years at the close of the Nine Years War, much to general regret. Still, the rewards for his work came in plenty; he had been appointed Governor of Douai in 1683, a position that he was allowed to sell for a handsome sum three years later when he resumed the Governorship of Lille citadel. However, there are distinct traces that, for all the devotion to the King's service and undoubted zeal in pursuing the many objectives he was set, Vauban was chafing that promotion came to him rather more slowly than he might expect. He was a man who had rarely been afraid to speak his mind, and he wrote to Louvois in a rather peevish, almost sarcastic, tone in 1684:

> I get letters from all sides to congratulate me for the King has had the goodness to make me a Lieutenant General; it is even to be seen in print in the Gazettes of Holland, and the historical journal Woerden; but nevertheless those who ought to know best tell me nothing of it.

So, if you please, Monseigneur, let me either be repaid the postage of
the eighty or a hundred letters that I have had to pay for, or obtain
from His Majesty that I should be made Lieutenant General indeed,
so as not to give the lie to so many worthy people.[16]

The longed-for promotion came, but not until four years later, in 1688.
Rumours of the promotion had circulated all the same, and Vauban's wife,
Jeanne, when standing as a godmother to a child on 15 August 1684 was
described rather grandly, but quite erroneously, as 'The wife of the High and
Mighty Lord Sébastien le Prestre, Knight, Lord of Vauban, Lieutenant
General of the Armies of the King.'[17]

Military matters were not the only concern for Vauban, as he was with some
reluctance drawn into the ultimately abortive work to provide a supply of fresh
water to the newly-built palace at Versailles. In particular, Louis XIV wanted
to increase the flow of water to the ornamental fountains in the grounds.
Vauban's advice was sought and he suggested that an inverted siphon, or a
water-tower, from a canal at ground level would be more effective than to try to
construct the vast and lengthy aqueduct that was proposed to run from the
River Eure at Pontgouin, along a course of 80 kilometres across the Maintenon
Valley and marshes (the château at Maintenon was already supplied in this
exact way, by a siphon). Louvois now had charge of public works and, with
an alert eye on his Royal master's wishes, attempted to rebuff Vauban's suggestions by contradicting his detailed calculations over the advantages of a
siphon, but he failed in this and instead got hopelessly entangled with his own
fallacious arguments. He then dismissed the Engineer's objections to the
project with the simple declaration that the King wanted an aqueduct, and that
was all that there was to be said: 'Only an aqueduct on arches is to be thought
of [. . .] to this alone you must devote your attention and give your advice.'[18]
Despite this exhortation, the hugely expensive aqueduct was, perhaps unsurprisingly, never built despite a great deal of wasteful effort misemploying
20,000 soldiers as labourers. Although the cutting of the first turf was accompanied by lavish celebrations, conditions were bad, with the marshes of the
Eure chronically malarial – sickness was high, and a good corps of veteran
troops was ruined in the project. Massively impressive, but forlorn and ruined,
the ivy-clad vaulted remains of those portions that were constructed may still
be seen with a few, surprisingly lush, trees growing on the upper structure.

This strange folly duly set aside, Vauban was soon more productively
employed, being sent to supervise the rebuilding of the fortifications at Belle-
Île, just to the south of Quiberon, off the Biscay coast. Matters did not proceed
smoothly at all, as the contractors proved themselves to be either incompetent
or corrupt, quite possibly both, with one going bankrupt while another

embezzled the workers' pay and then absconded. Yet another was described rather scathingly as 'Much given to wine, and besides this a little quarrelsome, and something of a scoundrel.'[19] Despite these difficulties, Vauban designed and had constructed a neat and symmetrically attractive seaward-facing fortress, built over a period of some six years between 1683 and 1689.

The momentous Revocation of the Edict of Nantes was enacted by Louis XIV in October 1685. This was a move of apparently ill thought-out religious intolerance, which had been preceded by bouts of oppression of the non-Catholics, and drove into exile many thousands of Huguenot French; men and women who had hitherto been perfectly loyal to the Crown (as their conduct in the Fronde civil wars had shown), yet would not or could not bring themselves to convert to Catholicism. 'The French persecution of the Protestants raging with the utmost barbarity [...] Innumerable personages of the greatest birth and riches leaving all their earthly substance, and barely escaping with their lives.'[20] In this almost casually damaging way, many veteran officers and soldiers, thrust out of French armies and civic employments, went and took service with Louis XIV's potential opponents; England, Holland, Sweden, Hanover and Prussia, to the detriment of the King's ambitions. Two of Vauban's own most promising young engineers, Captains Goulon and de la Motte, were amongst those forced to flee and take service abroad.

The War of the League of Augsburg (also known as the Nine Years War) began in 1688, and Louis XIV would soon miss the skill and valour of those exiled Huguenot soldiers:

> M. de la Motte, Captain of Miners, after having rendered excellent service at the Siege of Mainz, took it into his head as he left, that his conscience would no longer permit him to serve without com-promising with the demands of his former religion.[21]

However, the Edict of Nantes had originally been enacted by King Henry IV of France, in the face of pronounced clerical opposition, and the revocation undoubtedly had deep popular support amongst many of Louis XIV's Catholic subjects. Still, the effects of the loss of otherwise loyal French men and women, and the accompanying increase in the pool of military skills available to France's opponents, would become widely recognized and acknowledged.

The obvious other side of the case was that, due to a marked degree of similar religious intolerance, considerable numbers of good English, Scots and Irish Catholic soldiers found themselves excluded from serving in their own countries, and made their way into the French service, where they enjoyed a fine reputation for many years. Prominent amongst these exiles was James Fitzjames, Duke of Berwick, the illegitimate son of King James II of England, born when he was still Duke of York. As an Englishman, Berwick was unique in becoming a Marshal of France, and was one of Louis XIV's best field commanders. The simple fact that he adhered strictly to the Catholic faith espoused by his parents undoubtedly aided his career.

Vauban's concern at the enforced expulsions of Huguenots from France, or their forced conversion to Catholicism (often under conditions of great brutality which reduced the true worth of such conversions to virtually nothing), was deeply felt. 'Kings are, it is true, masters of the lives and property of their subjects,' he put in a note to Minister for War, Louvois, in 1686:

> but never of their opinions, since the sentiments of the heart are beyond their power, and God alone can direct them [...] His Majesty should state that having seen the sorrow of the ill-success of the conversions, and the obstinacy with which most of the newly converted cling to the so-called abandoned religion, [...] re-establish the Edict of Nantes, purely and simply, on the same footing as it formally was.[22]

Louvois was astute enough, and had enough regard for the Inspector-General of Fortifications, not to pass the contents of the note to the King, who was bound not to appreciate what would appear to be blatant and uncalled-for interference. Still, the Minister for War wrote a sharp and sarcastic reply to Vauban, who was at the time enjoying a rare period of leave at his country home: 'I have never known you to make such a blunder as you seem to have made in this memoir, I concluded that the air of Bazoches has clogged your wits, and that it would be a very good thing not to let you stay there much.' It was not difficult to find more work to occupy Vauban's attention, and orders duly flowed from Versailles setting him off on his travels once more.

Over the two years that elapsed since Vauban's argument with Louvois concerning the details of the shelved Maintenon aqueduct project, he had continued his work inspecting the fortresses along France's borders and preparing them for improvement. Amongst these projects was Mont-Royal, in the Moselle valley. Vauban's innovative design for the fortress was to use unusually long curtain walls, on which tower bastions would be placed at intervals. These had been encountered at Luxembourg, each heavily equipped with artillery firing from casements through embrasures in addition to having a gun-platform on the roof. Mont-Royal was to become a formidable fortress, securely set on an island, and requiring a garrison of 4,000 troops. Vauban's concern for its actual viability and security, unless fortresses at Coblenz, Trarbach and Trier were also held, on this occasion proved to be right, and it eventually had to be demolished. He also travelled again to inspect defences in

Lorraine, Franche-Comté and Alsace. Vauban was once again concerned that such places, well in advance of the main fortress belt, would be untenable, as would Landau in the Palatinate and Kehl near to Strasbourg, requiring the expenditure of considerable effort to defend, probably without lasting success, for any extended period. Garrisons would have to be found, tying down soldiers who might be more productively employed elsewhere, and they would be at undue risk while only adding marginally to the overall defensive structure that was in the process of being created.

Vauban also had to give his attention to other major civil projects, such as the construction of the Canal de Languedoc, where work had been proceeding, rather fitfully, for over twenty years. Vauban considered the project to be too limited in scope, and wanted the waterway to be made deeper and wider, and extended to connect to the rivers Garonne and Rhône. One of his subordinates, the incorrigible Niquet, differed once again and volubly expressed his contrary opinions to the point of insubordination. Exasperated, Vauban bluntly told him to just get on with the work anyway.

Vauban wrote to his nephew, Dupuy-Vauban, with words of advice fit for a budding young engineer of some promise beginning to make his way in the world: 'Learn your fortress thoroughly and deliberate every day of your life on the means of defence which you could employ in the case of attack.'[23] He also devoted a good deal of his attention to the project to improve the defences of Landau on the River Quiech, even though this was one of those places that seemed to him to be too exposed and therefore of debatable value. 'I have taken the opportunity,' he wrote when submitting his proposals for the King's approval, 'of this project to propose a system, which though it has some appearance of novelty is really only an improvement of the old.'[24] Vauban was referring once again to the construction of tower bastions. As it turned out, the fortress, for all Vauban's reservations as to its real value, amply proved itself in 1704. In that year, under the valiant command of the blinded Marquis de Laubanie, the outnumbered French garrison there held out for a very creditable seventy days, and slowed to something approaching a crawl the progress of the Duke of Marlborough, after his triumph over Marshal Tallard at Blenheim in southern Germany that summer.

In 1687, Vauban was given the task to modernize and strengthen the defences of Belfort to the south of the Vosges mountains. A new bastioned trace was constructed, over twice the size of that which it replaced. A curtain wall protected the lower town, again strengthened with the now familiar tower bastions, additional detached bastions which were known as counter-guards, and with demi-lunes providing protection for the Covered Way. The actual work of reconstruction went on for some thirteen years, until 1700, and still more improvements had subsequently to be added, to guard against fire from nearby high ground, with a strong hornwork eventually being built on the north-east side of the fortress.

Uppermost in Vauban's mind remained the vulnerability of the border with the Spanish Netherlands, and the outdated defences of Bergues and Ypres (at the time still in the hands of a French garrison) were known to be in poor condition. Repair work was begun, but in the course of this, in the autumn of 1689, Vauban fell ill while attending to the project at Ypres. Although Louvois urged him to come to Paris to consult the best doctors, Vauban preferred instead to travel to his home at Bazoches in January 1690, where a strict diet of fresh milk taken for twenty consecutive days rather surprisingly appeared to restore him to health. Vauban employed his time while convalescent in writing another earnest treatise on the merits of inviting the Huguenot refugees to return to France and being brought back into the Royal service, but if the King ever saw the well-intentioned tract, he took no notice. Vauban's services remained much in demand though, and for most of the year, despite still feeling rather unsteady on his legs, he was engaged on a tour of the fortresses in Flanders and supervising the continuing construction work at Sedan, Luxembourg, Thionville and Mont-Royal.

Although he was concerned at what might be regarded as the slow pace of his promotion, Vauban was undoubtedly appreciative of the marked degree of favour shown to him by Louis XIV, and of the generous way in which his successes were rewarded with gifts of money. With one of these purses he had been able to purchase the château at Bazoches, where he established a gallery or studio in which trainee engineers could learn and refine the arts of military design and fortification.[25] Vauban also frequently offered support to officers who had been less fortunate than himself, and those who, having lacked the ability or the chance to catch the attention and favour of the King or that of his Ministers, languished in neglected garrisons on poor pay and with few opportunities to shine. Gifted with a naturally generous nature, Vauban wrote: 'Is it not right that I should thus make restitution of what I receive,' he wrote, 'in excess from the bounty of the King.'[26] He also prepared a proposal for the King's consideration, to stoutly fortify the city of Paris with an outer ring of defences and large magazines and storehouses within the city, so that a lengthy siege could be withstood. As so often, the plan was good on the face of things, but money was not made available, and the promising project came to nothing at the time.[27] Louis XIV was clearly less than enthralled by the proposal, as he was always sensitive to the latent power of the numerous populace of that city to make trouble for the Crown, as had been shown quite clearly during the Fronde. To allow that same citizenry to enjoy the protection of major formal defences, effectively making them immune from Royal influence, might not be altogether a good thing.

While engaged, more or less continuously, with the construction of France's formal defences, Vauban continued to devote his attention to the most effective means of laying siege to such fortresses. These operations had commonly taken place at considerable cost both to the sappers labouring in the trenches, and to the troops undertaking the actual assault. Such a heedless lack of technique and discipline, while gradually diminishing, was still present. Conspicuous by their dress and eager to take an active part and so gain notice and promotion by performing rash acts of valour, it was the officers, often the best and most valiant, that took disproportionately heavy losses as ill-prepared attacks went in upon inadequately degraded defences. There was always a quite natural desire to make progress (particularly as the campaigning season was usually short, depending upon fine dry weather), and it would certainly not do for a young officer to be thought to be hanging back in the King's service. Vauban had the mental robustness, both to see that such an attitude was immature and counter-productive, and to say so openly.

The lesson, however, was learned (where it was learned at all) rather imperfectly, and officers anxious to adhere to the implacable, impatient, demands of commanding generals would continue to be sacrificed along with their men in headlong assaults and hotly contested breaches. John Muller, a student of Vauban and his methods, wrote in 1757 of the method to be employed when mounting an attack 'sword in hand':

> When a town is not strongly garrisoned, *or the General thinks the foregoing method too tedious* [Author's italics] the *Attac* may be made as follows – The Third Parallel in this case should be at least as far forward as the mid-way of the glacis, having its parapet in step-fashion, that the troops designed for the *Attac* may pass easily over it, without any confusion. A great quantity of fascines, gabions, and other materials, must be got ready and placed at the back of this Parallel. A strong party of grenadiers is ordered, and placed in the Parallel, five or six deep, and the workmen behind them on the reverse of the Parallel, having their tools and materials by them. Likewise, all the adjacent parts of the Trenches must be well furnished with troops to support the grenadiers, if there is occasion [to do so], and fire whenever the enemy appears. The grenadiers must be provided with hatchets to cut the palisades in case the guns have not broke them. Before the *Attac* is made, the guns and mortars are to fire briskly for some time at the defences [...] All the troops begin to move, and passing quickly over the parapet of the Parallel, march quickly to the

Covert-Way, which they enter through the Sally-ports or passages cut by the guns, or else the grenadiers cut the palisades with their hatchets, and being entered charge the enemy so vigorously as to oblige them to retire [...] the Batteries fire continually upon all the defences of the Covert-Way, either to silence or abate the fire of the enemy, as much as possible and to oblige them to think more of their own safety, than opposing the Besiegers.[28]

Muller went on to say that, since Vauban devoted so much thought to a rational way of attacking fortresses, and his views carried such weight in military circles, such attacks were both unnecessary and rare:

His chief study being always to preserve the troops as much as possible [...] if the garrison is strong, and commanded by a governor who knows his business, it would be imprudent to make such an attack.

Unfortunately, history would amply demonstrate that for all the Marshal's teaching on the subject, impatient generals, or those with time treading hard on their heels, would go on attacking in this way, often with success but not infrequently meeting bloody failure.

The fertile imagination of Vauban was not confined to devising cunning ways to attack or to defend fortresses. He had become increasingly unconvinced of the effectiveness of infantry armed with pikes, when opposed by those armed with a preponderance of matchlock, and later, more efficient flintlock muskets. Many others expressed the same interest and concern, of course, with the conservative camp by and large wishing to stay with the tried and tested weapon, the pike, and to save the expense of a mass re-equipping of armies with expensive muskets. Even so, the ratio of pikemen to musketeers had been falling for many years, and this trend accelerated as the greater efficiency and effectiveness of the flintlock over the much more cumbersome matchlock had become evident. Once musketeers could be depended upon to build up a sufficiently devastating volume of fire, aided by the platoon firing technique which was increasingly widely adopted in all armies (but only slowly by the French), the argument was at an end. 'I am not an advocate of the pike,' Vauban wrote, 'for more than twelve years I have railed against them.'[29] The day of the pike was clearly coming to an end. Even so, French ministers, concerned at ever-growing costs, were reluctant to go one step further and change from the matchlocks to flintlock muskets. Their soldiers showed their clear preference by hurrying to pick up the fallen flintlocks of the enemies on the battlefield, at places such as Steinkirk in 1692, while throwing away their own matchlocks.

A persistent concern was the vulnerability of infantry in the open to any sudden charge of massed cavalry. This was a strong argument for the retention of the pike, but the pikemen could in other circumstances be slaughtered by well-drilled musketeers standing off and out of reach of pike thrusts. Still, once the musket, whether matchlock or flintlock, was discharged, the infantry were once again vulnerable to cavalry attack, and so the pike appeared to show its value again. The plug bayonet was developed, but this was really just a dagger whose wooden handle was stuck into the end of the musket barrel to make a rather inferior and short quasi-pike for defence against horsemen. The plug bayonet, once fitted, also prevented the musket from being fired, and so was unsatisfactory, even when used with care. The solution was the development of the socket bayonet, enabling the infantry to both defend themselves from mounted attack and to maintain their rate of fire at almost their usual volume (the socket bayonet when fixed would slow, but not prevent, the reloading process). Louvois wrote to Vauban in 1687, on the merits or otherwise of bayonets:

> I have seen officers [. . .] who have assured me that in the infantry of the Emperor [Austria], there is not a single pike [. . .] I beg you to explain to me how you contrive a bayonet at the end of a musket which does not prevent one from firing and loading.[30]

Louis XIV inspected the new weapon in 1690, but declared himself to be unconvinced of its real worth. The introduction of socket bayonets into French service was slow as a result and did not begin until three years later, when platoon firing also began to be introduced. Vauban gave a good deal of thought to improvements that might be made, not only to the weapons carried, but also to uniform, equipment, the rates of pay, the medical services, and the way in which soldiers were recruited, or more often than not, simply impressed into the ranks from the militia in defiance of the terms of their service.

The strains of almost constant warfare told upon the quality of the French infantry, particularly as many men were often being misemployed as labourers and pioneers when not actually actively engaged on operations. This deterioration became progressively more acute as the long wars of Louis XIV went on, and would be particularly noticeable in the months following the huge defeat for French arms at Ramillies in 1706, and to a lesser degree after Oudenarde two years later.

Chapter 7

Nine Years War

With the formation of the League of Augsburg in 1686, Austria, Brandenburg and other German states created a defensive alliance against France, although Louis XIV, unsurprisingly, saw things quite differently, and considered the League to simply be an aggressive step against him. After the victory over the Ottoman armies at Mohacs in the following year, and then at Belgrade in 1688, the Austrian Emperor, Leopold I, was newly confident and assured that he no longer had to face a serious threat from the East. He gradually but decidedly moved against French-held territories along the Rhine. Prince Joseph-Clement, nephew of the Elector of Bavaria, was elected as Archbishop-Elector of Cologne on 26 August 1688. He had the support of the Emperor, but the election was in the face of Louis XIV's expressed objections. These objections were disregarded, and the Elector of Brandenburg's troops entered Cologne to support the installation of Joseph-Clement. Almost inevitably, trouble was the result, and the Emperor must have been well aware that this would be so, but attempts at mediation over the dispute proved fruitless. As a counter-move, French troops were sent to occupy Bonn and Kaiserswerth, and preparations for renewed conflict noticeably gathered pace. 'Bring the frontier defences against Germany,' Minister for War, Louvois, wrote to Vauban, 'to the highest pitch of perfection [...] His Majesty wishes that the frontier should be so defended that the Germans would not be able to cross the Rhine without finding a fortress that would stop them.'[1]

In England, meanwhile, King James II had pursued an unwise and highly unpopular policy of forcing Roman Catholics to appointments in the army and the judiciary. He had seen off a rebellion by his young nephew, the Duke of Monmouth, in 1685, but three years later faced a more serious revolt and invasion when the Protestant Wind brought his son-in-law, William of Orange, with Dutch troops, to oblige the King and his Queen and infant son to seek sanctuary in France as an honoured guest of Louis XIV. Subsequent attempts to regain the throne proved unsuccessful, and the inevitable by-product of all this was that the interests and the armed forces of England and Holland were bound tightly together as never before. The French King faced a newly strengthened, and potentially formidable, opponent in the Low Countries.

The result of all this jockeying for position was the opening of renewed conflict in western Europe, in what would become known as the Nine Years War, or sometimes the War of the League of Augsburg. Louis XIV had until then succeeded in extending his territory by short, sharp wars against weaker or less adept adversaries. These campaigns had been attended by a certain degree of 'frightfulness' at times, as in the coldly deliberate devastation of large areas of the Rhineland and the Palatinate in 1674 and 1675. Now the French King was faced with numerous opponents – England, Holland, Spain, the Holy Roman Empire (which was rather waggishly referred to as being neither Holy, Roman or an Empire), Saxony, Swabia, Franconia, the Elector of Bavaria, and the Dukes of Savoy and Lorraine. If these states combined their efforts effectively, France was outmanned and outgunned, even though Denmark and Sweden, for the moment, were not likely to be involved. The powerful and ambitious Elector of Brandenburg hovered in the wings, ready to take an active part in the war on France when the right moment came.

For Louis XIV, there was little prospect of achieving a decisive result whichever way he turned. However, the unexpected recapture of Belgrade by an Ottoman army in October 1690 would divert the Austrian Emperor's attention to the south and east once more, relieving some of the most immediate pressure on the French commanders in the field.

> The Emperor complained that the [French] King broke the Truce that was between them. The King publishes a Manifesto against His Imperial Majesty, wherein he declared to all Europe 'That had not taken up Arms, before he was informed that a Treaty was signed between the Emperor, the Elector [of Bavaria and the Palatinate], and the King of Spain, to make War against him, and to the end His Imperial Majesty only waited to see an end to the War he was engaged in against the Turks, that he might turn all his forces against France. That he had refused to change the late cessation of Arms that was agreed on between them, into a Peace; that the Elector Palatinate had refused to give the Duchesse of Orléans satisfaction for the Fiefs and other Estates that belonged to her by her succession to her Father and Brother [lingering shades here of the causes for the War of Devolution]; that the Emperor had forced the Chapter of Cologne to nominate a Bavarian prince to that Electorate, and used his utmost endeavour to exclude the Cardinal [Louis XIV's nominee].[2]

Vauban had been reviewing the fortifications in Alsace and the Palatinate. Landau having been selected as the most appropriate principal fortress for the defence of the region, his innovative design for the place attracted a great deal of attention. The strong fortress there stood the test of three major sieges between 1702 and 1704, although the garrisons had eventually to submit on each occasion. With a scarce portion of spare time that he enjoyed, Vauban engaged in lively correspondence with General Catinat, an old comrade in arms and friend, discussing points of population statistics, always a subject of keen interest to the Inspector-General of Fortifications. He had come to see that France's military strength, both actual and potential, could be measured in terms of its population, which was not just to be taken as simple numbers with no abstract meaning, but in what they might achieve if properly mustered, trained and directed in the service of the King. One area still of particular concern was the tendency to wasteful dispersion of troops in garrisons for fortresses that were held primarily for matters of prestige, rather than adding anything much to the cohesive defensive structure for France that he had striven so hard to construct. The Fence of Iron was recognizably stronger if it was limited in extent; certain key areas were of strategic importance and gave depth to the defence, and so these had to be held, but other places were retained for wasteful reasons that had little to do with military necessity.

On 24 September 1688, French siege operations began to recover Phillipsburg, on the Rhine between Karlsruhe and Mannheim. The work was overseen by Vauban, who had by then received the long awaited promotion to Lieutenant General. Marshal Duras had command of the field army. The place had previously been made immensely strong by French engineers, and the task was, accordingly, quite formidable. The King's 26-year-old son, the Dauphin, and an array of senior officers and courtiers, including Louvois' eldest son, the Marquis de Barbezieux, were also present. The Royal party arrived on 6 October, so that the heir to the throne could have his share of the glory when the fortress capitulated. It was rather late in the campaign season, but the preparations for draining the wet ground and entrenching commenced on 8 October, with three separate attacks being directed against the Covered Way. The big guns of the siege train were brought up by water on barges, and although the glacis of the fortress was reached without too much difficulty, the weather was miserable and the troops in the trenches suffered badly, with clothing and equipment soaked through with the rain.

The Dauphin was eager to watch the progress of the sappers and their workmen as they inched their way forward, and this naturally caused some anxiety amongst his entourage, and to Vauban, who had to accompany him on his excursions into the entrenchments. An orderly had to be detailed to stand immediately behind the Royal party, ready to throw himself in front of the Dauphin if he was fired on. At last Vauban had to insist that they did not go on; the sapping was being carried out across some marshy ground that was only partly drained, and had they gone on any further, they would all have been floundering up to their knees in mud.[3] As it was, they got forward, despite the best efforts of the nervously solicitous officers who were detailed to keep them out of harm's way, to within only sixty paces of the Covered Way.

Despite the poor weather, the siege operations progressed well and lasted for only three weeks. The Imperial garrison commander in Phillipsburg, General Graf von Stahremberg, capitulated on 28 October 1688 and the fortress was occupied by French troops two days later. Vauban had lost nine engineers killed in the trenches, skilled and reliable men that were hard to replace, while fifteen others had been wounded or injured. In the meantime, Marshal Boufflers had moved on to take Kaiserlauten, and then to lay siege to Coblenz at the confluence of the Moselle river with the Rhine. He drew off for the time being, when confronted by a superior force of Swabian, Bavarian and Franconian troops under command of the Elector of Bavaria, Maximilien-Emmanuel Wittelsbach. The French then turned to the south and moved quickly towards Mannheim, where the town was given up after only two days, with the Governor withdrawing his men into the citadel. The Palatine troops in the garrison proved to be unreliable and ill-disciplined, and this may have been because they had been unpaid for nearly eighteen months. They certainly did not put up a very great resistance, and soldiers of the French Régiment de Picardie had to protect the unfortunate Governor from being manhandled by his own men when the capitulation was agreed on 12 November. Mainz was occupied by French troops soon afterwards, but Coblenz had to be bombarded with mortars, in the face of protests by Vauban at such pointless and un-necessarily needless destruction and expenditure of powder and shot, before it finally submitted in November.

The fortress of Frankentall, sitting at the confluence of the Rhine and Neckar rivers, was captured without great difficulty after only thirty-eight hours, and French troops went on as the frozen months of winter approached, to devastate or strip bare large areas of the Palatinate, 'eating up the country' as it was known, so that no opposing army could quarter itself in the region. The unfortunate population, turned out of their homes in appalling wintry weather, spread tales of the French atrocity far and wide into Germany. Vauban deplored the campaign of destruction, partly no doubt because he disliked waste, and saw little point in hazarding the civilian population, but also for the very practical reason that it prevented French troops too from remaining in the region. The scale of destruction was significant, and towns such as Heidelberg, Worms and Speyer were partially sacked in this ruthless operation. A lady at the Court in Versailles, who was a native of the Palatinate, wrote of her anguish at the devastation of her homeland:

> I am seized with such a horror when I think of it, all that has been
> destroyed, that every night I think myself at Heidelberg or

Mannheim, in the middle of the desolation [. . .] I think of it all as I
once knew it, and as it is now [. . .] I cannot prevent myself weeping.[4]

Claude-Louis-Hector de Villars, a future Marshal of France and one of Louis
XIV's most capable field commanders, was also unconvinced of the wisdom of
this operation. He was concerned that reprisals against France would result, in
time, and wrote, 'It is still unknown by what fatality these atrocious orders
were given, but the Marquis de Louvois, a man of great intelligence, did not
oppose them.'

Rewards continued to flow, in return for Vauban's seemingly unending
efforts. These included a purse of money from the Dauphin for his success
at Phillipsburg, together with the gift of four specially made but almost ornamental small cannon, which were sent to his home at Bazoches as trophies. The
King also sent him another gift of money, and a further gift was made for the
efforts against Mannheim and Frankentall. Of course, the long-awaited,
coveted promotion to Lieutenant General had already been received. Resting
at Bazoches at the end of the year, Vauban was appalled to learn of plans to
further devastate Mannheim, even to the extent of razing the entire city to
the ground, and he wrote to Louvois on 30 December urging restraint. The
destruction wrought by French armies in the Palatinate and elsewhere had
rather inevitably galvanized the energies of Louis XIV's opponents as nothing
had done before. It truly seemed as if the terrible horrors of the Thirty Years
War were set to return, and this could not be borne. The parties to the League
of Augsburg came together with William III, as both King of England and
Stadtholder of Holland, and with Spain, to create the Grand Alliance against
France and what were seen as Louis XIV's intolerable and continuing
ambitions.

The French campaign began to falter in the face of such concerted opposition, and Vauban voiced his concerns at growing successes for the Alliance
along the Rhine. As a result, Louvois wrote to him in rather cutting terms:

I should not have believed that you were capable of believing that
M. de Lorraine could capture the garrison of Mainz; personally I
do not believe, unless an unfortunate accident happens, that the
Germans can make themselves masters of the place.[5]

Despite this rather overblown confidence, Mainz fell to the Allies, and Spanish
cavalry began raiding the environs of Tournai and Lille, where Marshal
d'Humières gave every appearance of fumbling his campaign. French-held
western Flanders appeared to be under threat, and Vauban had once more to
express his anxiety for the security of Paris, where the defences were still
inadequate.

Vauban visited Landau to inspect progress on the new fortress, going on to Strasbourg and Kehl before returning to Flanders, where he gave his attention to the work on improving the defences of Bergues, Dunkirk and Ypres. In the wintry weather he caught another severe chill, which probably turned into pneumonia. The personal cost from his unrelentingly busy schedule was clearly high and now growing, not just in his very lengthy absences from his home in Bazoches. 'I am overwhelmed,' he wrote to Louvois, from his camp tent during one of the siege operations he undertook:

> with work, and it is not possible to visit daily two attacks, where one has to look and look again into I don't know how many different things, to argue, to detail, to give the same orders ten times over, and to spend an hour and a half or two hours every day in reporting everything [...] If all our trenches were put end to end, they would form a straight line of 6 good miles, which I traverse every day more than two-thirds, usually with wet feet, and over 100,000 fascines, which have been used to pave the trenches, and which are about as easy as logs to walk over.[6]

In the course of the entrenching work at Phillipsburg in the autumn of 1688, Vauban refined the use of 'cavaliers', the useful raised firing posts set at intervals along the trenches, that enabled sharpshooters to keep the defenders holding the Covered Way under continuous fire as the sappers drew closer to the glacis of the fortress.

Another technique enlarged on and developed by Vauban was the employment of ricochet artillery fire from the siege batteries. In this way, the guns fired with reduced charges, so that the solid shot were lobbed at a low trajectory into the defences, bounding along and doing damage in the process, rather than burying themselves deep into the glacis or parapet, or otherwise going right over the top of the defences altogether. The reduced charges that were used in such ricochet firing had the additional advantage of lessening the wear on the guns, which had a dangerous tendency to burst after sustained use, and also conserved the stocks of powder. The new technique was, however, not without its critics, particularly artillerymen who did not always appreciate advice from engineers who were, in theory at least, not masters of the art of gunnery, however enquiring a mind they might have. Commanding generals were also rather unconvinced, as it did not seem logical that using less powder in firing could actually produce a better effect, but such really was the case.

Despite this lack of cooperation, Vauban got his way and issued precise instructions for the employment of ricochet fire, particularly when this could

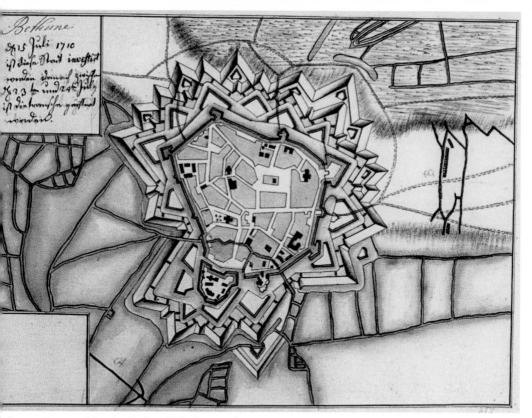

Béthune. Captured by the Duke of Marlborough in 1710.

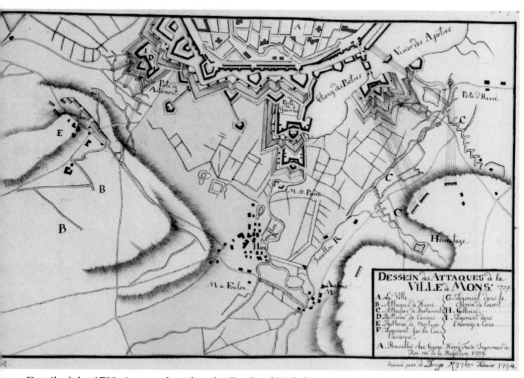

DESSEIN des ATTAQUES de la
VILLE de MONS. 1709.

A. La Ville
B. Attaqués à Havré
C. Attaqués de Bertamont
D. Batteries de Canons
E. Batteries de Mortiers
F. Regiment pour la Con-
    voi esscape
G. Regiment vers le
    chemin de Covret
H. Collines
I. Regiment dans
    l'ouvrage à Come

A. Bruxelles chez Eugene Henry Fricx Imprimeur du
    Roy rue de la Magdelein 1709.

Dessiné par de Denop le 27ᵗᵉⁿ Febuar 1794.

Mons. Detail of the 1709 siegeworks, after the Battle of Malplaquet.

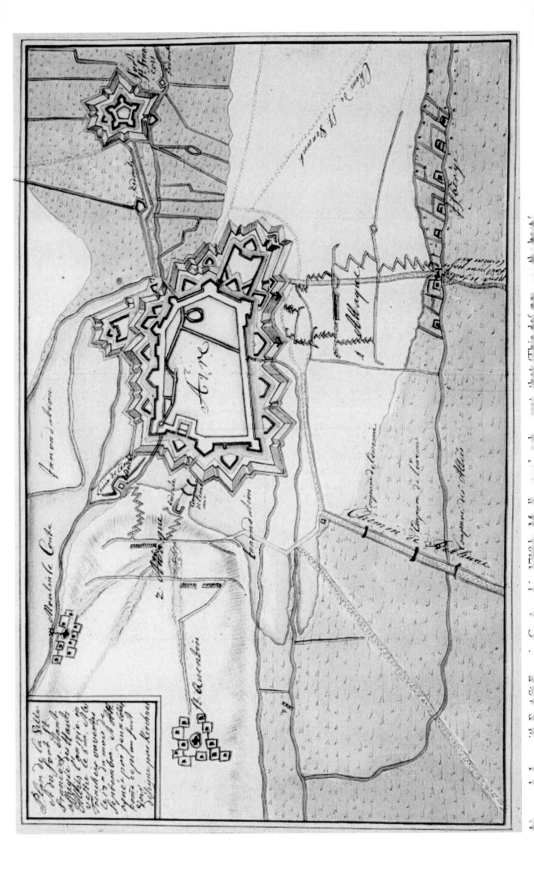

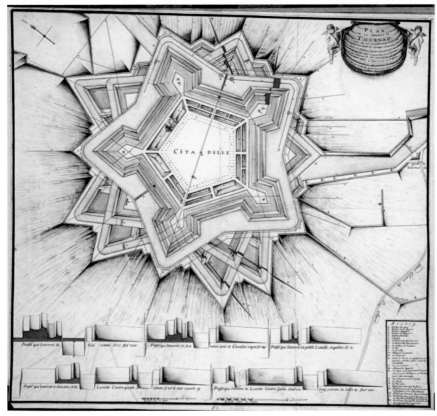

Tournai. The radical Vauban design for the massive new citadel.

Douai. Captured by Marlborough and Eugène in 1710.

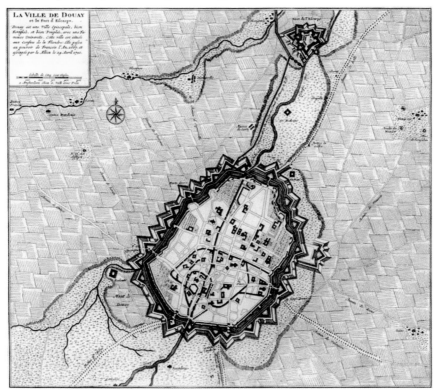

Colmar les Alpes. Fortified sentry post on the defensive ramparts.

Mauberge. The Porte de Mons (2009).

auberge. The defensive ditch with the Porte de Mons in the background (2009).

ons. Louis XIV conducts the brilliantly
ccessful siege of 1691.

Namur. The French siege of 1692. They lost it
to the Allies three years later.

le. The massive gateway into Vauban's new citadel.

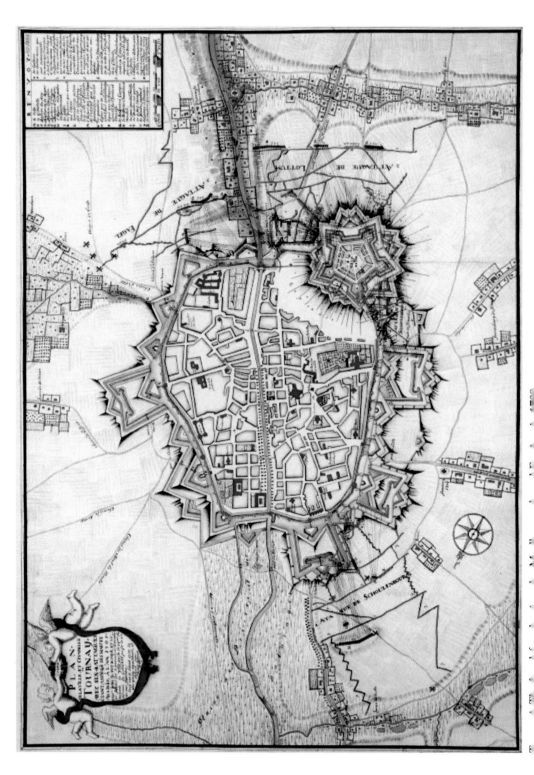

be done from a flank, firing in enfilade as it was known. 'Enfilades from a distance,' he wrote,

> are more dangerous than those close up; projectiles from a distance, being slow and nearly spent, drop and deviate from their flat trajectory, so that interposing traverses, even high ones, cannot stop the projectiles from falling into the trench. On the contrary, it is not difficult to [get] cover against a close enfilade, since the projectile travels with such force that it maintains a flat trajectory [...] Projectiles grazing the top of the trench may not be impeded sufficiently to be halted altogether, but only slowed down and deflected, whereupon they can fall into the sector between the traverse [...] there are few places where a man is really safe.[7]

No matter how complex the design of a fortress might be, and however carefully the approaches were covered by observation and fire, siege batteries would always be found well-placed positions from which the gunners could fire down the length of the defences to one degree or another. This can be clearly seen from the engineer's diagrams that survive from this time. The result was heavy casualties suffered by the garrison, losses which could not readily be made good, and a growing inability to man the Covered Way with enough troops to hold off a determined assault. The early reluctance of the artillerymen to adopt this new method of firing was soon forgotten, and it became the favoured method used to clear the defending musketeers out of a line of defences. Artillery officers started to take particular care, and some pride, in their prowess and skill in the new way of working, so economical in the expenditure of powder and shot, yet so effective in inflicting casualties or forcing troops to take shelter. This all led to one result; once the besiegers were securely in possession of the Covered Way, they would bring forward the breaching batteries to begin their work against the main defences at close range and that, from the point of view of the garrison, was that.

There was still a noticeable divergence of professional opinion, whether it was worthwhile for the gunners of a garrison to attempt to overpower, at least temporarily, the batteries of besieging armies. The garrison always comprised strictly finite resources, men, guns, powder and shot, incapable in all but the most unusual of circumstances of being replenished or replaced from outside. The besiegers, on the other hand, could deploy almost infinite resources, being able to bring forward reinforcements as casualty replacements, and to replenish their magazines and stores. If the defending batteries engaged in an artillery duel too early on in a siege, they might slow, but would probably not stop the entrenching work or the establishing of the breaching batteries. They would, however, have depleted their own stocks of powder beyond what was wise, with no adequate concurrent gain. Accordingly, a technique was developed, as an alternative to outright gunnery duels, to keep guns under cover, and to move them rapidly into position to loose off a few well-placed shots before withdrawing them back behind shelter to avoid counter-battery fire. Mortars, firing at a high angle, did not suffer in the same way, being able to operate from 'dead ground', but these weapons in a fortress would usually find meagre and hard to hit targets in the long snaking approach trenches and parallels of their opponents.

Vauban also refined the methods to be employed in mining and counter-mining during siege operations. This was a highly specialized and particularly dangerous military art, requiring skill and strength, and not a little guile and mental robustness as well on the part of the miners. The use of explosive mines was a technique in which French engineers were repeatedly proven to have more skill than their opponents. These 'infernal machines', as they were quaintly described, could be both offensive and defensive in operation and were routinely used by both attackers and defenders. As the use of gunpowder in mining grew and was refined, the precise measures of powder to be used in each particular type of mine, whether offensive or defensive, was carefully specified. Fortresses often incorporated into their designs preconstructed mine galleries reaching out underneath the glacis, that could be prepared and packed with explosives, once a siege of the place became likely. The attacking force would usually be unaware of their precise location, and at something of a disadvantage, as the Duke of Marlborough and his troops found to their cost at the expensive Siege of Tournai in 1709. These devices took many forms – a 'fougasse', for example, was a directional anti-personnel weapon, packed with stones, while a 'camouflet' was designed to burn out an opponent's mine-workings, along with those of their miners caught in the explosion.

The miners, although highly paid for their labours, either as specialist troops or as volunteers enjoying the bounty offered for their services, laboured and fought their battles in gloom and mud deep underground, in foul air lit by the faint glow of lanterns and candles. They worked with the ever-present threat of tunnel collapse and entombment, flooding and drowning when trapped underground, explosive counter-mining, or with their opponents breaking into the works from galleries of their own, to fight it out with grenades, dagger, pistol, shortened muskets and sharpened spade, at close quarters:

> The Frenchmen let down one of their grenadiers at the end of a rope. He was killed by a pistol shot as soon as he appeared [. . .] Both sides opened fire, and this awful cave resounded with reports of muskets and grenades. This fight would have continued for some time if the smoke, stench and darkness had not imposed a truce.[8]

In practice, the progress that could be made by experienced miners in such dreadful and cramped conditions was surprising, and teams of skilled men were known to progress up to 18 feet in twenty-four hours, even when having to burrow under water-filled defensive ditches. 'The Miners,' John Muller wrote,

> ought to leave no means untried to discover the enemies galleries [...] and use the utmost precautions not to be surprised [...] If the besiegers perceive that their enemies are coming towards them [counter-mining, in effect] a small mine must be made to stifle them.[9]

Vauban's recovery from the chills and fever he caught while working at Ypres took quite some time, but Louvois, driven to press onwards in the interests of the King's service, was not that sympathetic. He wrote from Versailles: 'You speak so casually of the state of your health that I am satisfied [...] the King thinks it well, that as soon as your health allows you to leave home, you should come here.'[10] The period that he had spent in convalescence in Bazoches was an unusual time of relative ease, reflection and respite from the relentlessly punishing schedule placed upon him by Louis XIV and his indefatigable Minister for War. Their concern for Vauban's welfare was somewhat lacking, evident from the correspondence at the time. In May 1690, Louvois wrote to Vauban:

> It is the intention of His Majesty that you should proceed to Guise, where you will assemble all the engineers of Hainault to render an account of the state of their fortresses [...] after which, going through Cambrai, Valenciennes, Condé, Tournai, Lille and Ypres, you can reach Montreuil by way of Béthune and Arras. His Majesty wishes you to remain at Montreuil where the air is good, until the intentions of the Prince of Orange develop, for should he set foot in Flanders, the King wishes you to go to Dunkerque, and should he direct his march in another direction, His Majesty wishes you to go to Sedan.[11]

The demands that flowed from Versailles might vary to a certain degree in their rate, but they rarely, if ever, ceased altogether.

Marshal Luxembourg achieved a notable victory at Fleurus on 1 July 1690, when he defeated the Dutch army commanded by the Prince of Waldeck. Although not yet fully recovered from his ailments, Vauban was sent to inspect the construction work at Charleroi, Philippeville and Mauberge, but, sickening once again, he was forced to return to Lille to rest. At last he found the opportunity at his country home to complete his recovery from illness and by the beginning of 1691 was well restored to good health at last. On 8 January,

Vauban was present at the ceremony in Paris when his 12-year-old daughter, Jeanne-Françoise, was married to M. de Valentinay. This was an unusual appearance by him at a convivial family occasion, although one at which Madame Vauban did not figure, as she did not travel very far from her home in the Morvan.

Louis XIV's hopes for a swift campaign against the Grand Alliance were not met. Attempts in the past to divide his opponents had usually been met with success, but now this could not be had. The French armies were poorly prepared for a long war as a result of this miscalculation, and the King was pushed onto the defensive, having to ruthlessly order that further areas of the Palatinate, Baden and Württemberg be devastated so that enemy armies could not subsist there. In consequence, a number of German states – Brandenburg, Hanover, Saxony, Bavaria and Hesse-Kassel, both those owing allegiance to the Empire and those who did not – were concerned enough to combine their forces to resist any fresh French incursions across the Rhine. There were to be no more easy campaigns of devastation on German soil, whether or not they were thought to be justified militarily.

One of the most notable operations of the renewed hostilities was the siege that the French laid to the Spanish-held town of Mons. The fortress was invested on 14 March 1691, happening with such admirable speed that the 5,000-strong garrison was taken almost entirely by surprise. Vauban presented his plans for the siege works for Louis XIV's approval and this was promptly given, although the Spanish Governor, the Prince de Berghes, sent a rather optimistic if not actually bombastic message to William III, saying that the garrison and the townspeople were in good spirits, and determined to resist until relief came. This happy state of affairs did not last for very long, once ground was broken by French pioneers. The main attack went in against the formidable hornwork covering the Bertamont Gate on the southern side of the defences, and the operations began in earnest on 24 March, once the surrounding inundations and flooded meadows, intended to impede the French operations, had been drained away. The Trouille stream was also dammed and diverted to lower the water level around the fortress. Two days later, a heavy bombardment with eighty-three large guns and mortars was begun by the besiegers.

By the afternoon of 31 March, the approach trenches had progressed so well that an assault on the main hornwork could be made. This effort proved to be premature, and the attempt failed in the face of stout Spanish resistance. A very well-handled counter-attack threw the French stormers back in disarray, with 130 men killed or wounded, a casualty list that included twelve officers and five of Vauban's valued engineers. The attack was resumed the next day, with better artillery support, and this time succeeded in carrying the hornwork, although the garrison managed to flood one of the French battery positions by careful manipulation of the sluice gates that controlled the depleted water defences. The attackers, troops drawn from the Régiment de Roi and flushed with their initial success, then went on too far in their enthusiasm, and while attempting to capture an adjacent demi-lune, were fought to a standstill by the Spanish troops. A truce had to be arranged so that the many French dead and wounded could be recovered, although several of the more lightly wounded men were taken by the garrison into the fortress as prisoners. In the meantime, the breaching batteries had been hard at work, and buildings in the town were receiving heavy damage by their fire, so that the citizenry were eager to avoid more destruction.

It seemed clear that William III, who was still gathering his army together at Brussels, would be unable to relieve Mons, especially as Marshal Luxembourg and his 50,000-strong covering army stood in the way, blocking all roads leading south. The Prince de Berghes prudently acknowledged the hopelessness of his position, and agreed terms for capitulation on 8 April. This inclination to give way was spurred on by a declared threat that the citizenry of the town would be fined 100,000 crowns for each day that resistance was prolonged. These people were mostly French speakers, and their enthusiasm for a fight, if it had existed at all, had now evaporated. The garrison marched out two days later, having suffered heavy losses in the remorseless French bombardment. By contrast, due in the main to Vauban's careful preparations and the layout of his trenches, the French losses were much less, although the fighting, particularly at the hornwork and at the windmill on Hiom Hill, had certainly been severe. Louis XIV was delighted, and rewarded his Engineer with a purse, a 'gratification', of 100,000 livres. There was also an invitation for Vauban to attend the King at a private supper, in itself a most unusual honour, and one that occasioned some surprise and pointedly envious comment from others.

Vauban had again been unwell, but was sent back to Mons to supervise the repairing of the defences of the fortress, as an attempt to accomplish its re-capture was daily expected. On hearing that he had arrived at the town, Louis XIV wrote that now 'he had no fear for the place'.[12] Louvois was his usual hectoring self, however, busily writing to Vauban at the end of May: 'It is seven weeks since Royal Troops entered Mons, and that I have not yet been able to secure your plans; I declare that I cannot observe such extraordinary dilatori-ness without annoyance.' Vauban was in no mood to be lectured, even by the Minister for War, and his reply was measured but contained a distinct barb:

> When you honour me less frequently with your letters, and so give
> me greater leisure for the completion of the plans of Mons, I hope
> that I shall be able to regain my health and give you cause for

satisfaction; otherwise, I perceive that I shall not achieve one or the other.[13]

Despite this success at Mons, Louis XIV's field commanders were losing ground elsewhere and both Kaiserswerth and Bonn fell to troops led by the Duke of Luxembourg and the Elector of Brandenburg. The Grand Alliance, despite a rather faltering start, was growing in strength and improving its strategic posture.

Despite his failing health, Vauban's attention to business did not flag, nor did his concern for the niceties of just how official correspondence should properly be conducted. Although blessed with patience and a tolerant nature, he still deplored irregularity or impudence, and brusquely reproved one of his own engineers, Cladech, who had presumed to write directly to Louvois with critical comments on one of Vauban's designs:

> It is customary amongst decent men of our calling to write to me personally before writing to others, to put their problems to me, and to bring forward any points in need of alteration. You have, in short, mistaken my plans which you have not condescended to discuss, and so badly that what you have done amounts to sentencing someone without wishing to hear the evidence.[14]

Whether the letter sent by the errant junior engineer, who was generally very well-regarded by Vauban, was ever received by the Minister for War is not clear. François-Michel le Tellier, Marquis de Louvois, in so many ways Louis XIV's greatest and most gifted servant, died suddenly on 16 July 1691.

The death of Louvois was a distinct blow for the King, for the energy and capacity for work of the Minister for War was prodigious, as was his formidable intellect. He had been Minister for War since 1666, and in many ways was the architect of the successful French campaigns over the next twenty-five years. It followed soon after suffering a massive stroke, which came on after Louvois had engaged in a furious argument with the King, always a risky thing to undertake, although the subject that was under such heated discussion between the two men is not clear. Almost inevitably, there were some rumours that Louvois had been poisoned, but this kind of idle talk was common in Versailles, where any illness, however mundane, tended to raise such malicious suspicions.

In tones heavy with unmistakeable regret, acknowledging an irreplaceable loss, Louis XIV wrote to Vauban with the doleful news, which had come at a time of escalating war and elusive success, while dangerous opponents gathered around France's borders:

> I do not doubt that you are grieved at the death of the Marquis de Louvois. As he was entrusted with the defences of the fortresses of

my Kingdom, I have thought it to my advantage to appoint someone to that duty as soon as possible, and that I could make no better choice than Sieur le Pelletier, the Inspector of my Finances [...] I rely upon the zeal that you have for my service for your advice to him to the full extent of your ability. And, as the present is generally the preparation of the future, I pray that you, M. de Vauban, are in God's holy and worthy care.[15]

Louvois had, in fact, been an arrogant bully, domineering and impatient. 'Be careful,' Vauban had once written to him, 'harsh measures are a dangerous way of putting a good man right.'[16] He was also acknowledged to be highly capable, energetic and utterly loyal in the Royal service. Of his abilities and diligence there could be no doubt, and he had been a firm supporter of Vauban and his often expensive projects. The French King would find that he could not find material of the same quality with which to replace Louvois; no one was irreplaceable, but the deceased Minister for War came very close.

Louvois' successor as Minister for War was his less gifted son, the Marquis de Barbezieux. This appointment indicated a not altogether healthy degree of nepotism, that was tolerated by Louis XIV in the highest offices of State. Barbezieux had accompanied the Dauphin on his visit to the siege operations at Phillipsburg in 1688, and had not been particularly useful but instead just got in the way. The young man did have an easy charm that his hectoring father either lacked or chose not to show, but was also an effete pleasure-seeker of rather limited abilities. His appointment as Minister for War would prove not to be a success, although he managed to hold on to the post until his own death in 1701 at an early age; a sad fate that was brought on, it was said by the Duc de St Simon, by excessive dissipation:

> He was thirty-three years of age, with a striking and expressive countenance, and much wit and aptitude [...] but his pride and ambition was excessive, and when his fits of ill-temper came, nothing could repress them.[17]

For all his acknowledged shortcomings, however, Barbezieux did what he could to support Vauban, very much in the way that his father had done. The workload of the new Minister was rather less than before; as Louis XIV had explained to Vauban, Louvois' appointment as Director-General of Fortifications, the one that most closely touched on his own professional duties, was now taken by the Minister for Finance, le Pelletier de Souzy.

One project that had not been handed to Vauban, possibly as a belated acknowledgement of the unrelenting pressure of the work he was required to undertake, was the fortification of the small island at the head of the Chapus river, not far from the naval base at Rochefort on the Biscay coast. The work had been entrusted to François Ferry, a budding engineer of great skill, but a really impractical scheme had been devised for a large oval tower with embrasures for artillery, and that project was not progressing very well at all. Shortly after the death of Louvois, the work at Chapus was handed over to Vauban to push forward, and he revised the planned works completely, to both save on cost and to simplify the overly complex design. Construction to the new specification began in 1692, building on what François Ferry had begun, and the work was largely complete just two years later. The result was Fort Chapus, a small but very attractive half-horseshoe-shaped fortification, cut through with embrasures for artillery and backed by a redoubt tower.

French commanders continued to score hard-fought successes on land, although a force led by Marshal d'Humières was mauled at Walcourt by the Prince of Waldeck's Anglo-Dutch army. Marshal Luxembourg then defeated Waldeck's rearguard in a neat cavalry action at Leuze in September 1691, when the Allies were on their way towards their winter quarters. Louis XIV's strategic ability to strike directly at England, by trying to foment unrest with the aid of the exiled King of England, James II and his adherents, was broken, not only by defeat in Ireland at the battles of the Boyne and Aughrim but also by dramatic events on the Channel coast. Between 29 May and 3 June 1692, British and Dutch naval squadrons under Admiral Russell drove Admiral de Tourville's French fleet to defeat and destruction in the surf during the five-day battles of Barfleur and La Hogue. These defeats were of enormous significance and the loss in men, ships and expertise could not easily or quickly be made good. James II, who had intended to try to reclaim his throne by getting his troops, and those loaned to him by Louis XIV, across the Channel on de Tourville's ships, watched the defeat and the wreck of his own hopes. Despite the efforts of the French cavalry who rode into the shallows to try to drive off the English and Dutch longboat crews, twenty French vessels were beached and burned. The depredations of French privateers in the Channel and the Western Approaches would go on, but strategically Louis XIV had little choice but to turn his attention back to his land campaigns.

The summer campaign pressed onwards in the Southern Netherlands that year. Despite his years, Louis XIV was again present with the army, although Marshal Luxembourg was also given an independent command. One rather caustic commentator wrote, with very clear and rather prim disapproval, that the King was now 'Accompanied by musicians, dancers, opera-singers, and all the voluptuous Ministers of Luxury.'[18] This may have been so, but the aging King was used to his comforts and could hardly be expected to live in a tent. He took the opportunity to review his army at Gevries on 20 May 1692: 'It was certainly the greatest spectacle anyone had seen [...] I cannot recall that the

Romans saw anything comparable [. . .] There were 120,000 men assembled in four lines, it took two hours to go from one end of a line to the other.'[19] A formidable force, seemingly incapable of anything but success, but it would have to be seen whether the doughty, if occasionally uninspired, performance of the Dutch and their allies could not hold the French in check. As it was, William III and his commanders hesitated too long and the French managed to hold on to the initiative.

Matters were certainly on the move, and two days after the great review of the army at Gevries, the key fortress and citadel of Namur was invested by Marshal Luxembourg's cavalry. The Governor of the now strengthened fortress was the Prince of Brabançon, and he had the immediate assistance of Meinheer van Coehorn, the renowned Dutch military engineer. The defences of Namur were in good order, the well-drilled garrison comprised some 6,000 Dutch, Walloon, German and Spanish troops, and the magazines and store-houses were amply stocked with provisions of every kind. The task was, on the face of things, formidable. Preparations for the siege began immediately, with Vauban commanding the troops in the trenches under Louis XIV's watchful eye, while Luxembourg drew off with his army to cover the operations from any attempt at interference by the Allies. Some 20,000 peasants were recruited, or impressed, to dig the entrenchments, and the main attack was made against Fort Saint Nicholas. The King took a keen interest in the progress of the operations, adding to Vauban's concerns by once more making visits to the trenches to see what was going on, and to offer a few words of advice. There, on one memorable and heart-stopping occasion, a chance musket-shot from the garrison struck a gabion close to the King's head and while ricocheting, slightly wounded an attendant.

Such chance, unnecessary incidents made life fraught for the senior officers, who were trying as they were to push the siege forward at the best possible pace. Vauban and his chief engineers also showed a measure of coolness, behaviour bordering perhaps on the reckless, while conducting a close reconnaissance of the town's defences:

> Walking, like townspeople do, with our hands behind our backs, so
> that I am quite certain that everyone we met, including the sentries,
> took us for citizens out for a stroll [. . .] Sometimes we lay down as if
> tired, that was when we drew up our plans, making sure that the
> maps were concealed.[20]

Work on the approach trenches progressed well, and the Covered Way was reached without great difficulty, so that work could begin filling in the 60-foot-wide defensive ditch. By 5 June, the main defensive wall had begun to show signs of a developing breach, suffering under the impact of the well-directed French bombardment. So the city was evacuated by Brabançon's troops, and he and his troops were permitted to withdraw into the citadel of Château-Neuf during an agreed lull in the hostilities. Fighting began again on 7 June, once the truce had expired, and the poet Racine wrote:

> M. de Vauban, with his cannon and bombs, was alone responsible for the enterprise. He secured heights on either side of the Meuse, on which he placed his batteries [. . .] In three days he had advanced his works as far as the brook which runs at the foot of the counterscarp, and from there in less than sixteen hours, he carried the whole of the Covered Way.[21]

It had been agreed that the city would not be bombarded from the citadel, nor would the French site their batteries amongst the houses, and so the civilian population were, to a limited degree, spared the worst trials of the siege, as counter-battery fire from the citadel would not be directed at them or their families.

The renewed French attack went in across the line of the Sambre river, with Louis XIV, although now suffering the agonies of gout, an eager spectator. Unseasonably bad weather set in, and the soldiers in the trenches were sometimes ankle- and even calf-deep in water. Progress slowed, and rations grew short as the supply convoys could not easily make their way along the rutted and muddy roads from Mons, Dinant, Mauberge and Philippeville. Vauban was in low spirits: 'I have seen him,' Catinat wrote, 'bursting with anxiety.'[22] Progress was slower than anticipated, but an important outwork, stirringly named Fort William, capitulated, along with the wounded Meinheer van Coehorn, who had been supervising its defence. The Dutch Engineer and Vauban met on the glacis of the fort and engaged in courteous conversation for some time, discussing as professional men might, the progress of the operations so far against the city and fortress.

Van Coehorn commented sharply on Vauban's tactic of having parallel trenches dug and laid out to encircle the defences, in a way so to give no clear indication of just where the main French effort would be made. Had a more direct method been taken, in the old style (which van Coehorn appeared to think more acceptable), he was sure that the garrison of Fort William would have been enabled to hold out for a further fortnight at least. Well, if that were so, the value of Vauban's technique seemed to be very well proven. The garrison were permitted to march away to Ghent without giving their parole, and French attention could then turn to the surviving troops in the citadel. Despite the massive strength of the place, after another thirty days and the breaching batteries having done their work, the Governor agreed to a capitulation. Once again, the survivors of the citadel garrison, reduced now to only 2,500 men and having done their best, were accorded the honours of war and were permitted to march out on 1 July.

The success at Namur was a considerable achievement, but obtained at a similarly considerable price. Some 5,500 French troops had been killed or wounded, and of Vauban's mere sixty trained engineers, no fewer than thirty-eight had become casualties. The French batteries had fired over 50,000 round-shot and the mortars some 11,000 explosive bombs. Expenditure in munitions, food and fodder had simply been huge, and the French commanders had been increasingly concerned at a lack of supplies and forage in a war-ravaged region, while the weather had remained foul and depressing. Had William III found it possible to challenge the siege operations, interdicting the French lines of supply and communication instead of just observing Marshal Luxembourg's covering army across the marshes of the Mehaigne stream, not far from the watershed of Brabant at Ramillies, then he would very probably not have lost Namur. This mistaken calculation, and lack of action, was a gift to the French.

Vauban was again handsomely rewarded by the King for his success in the capture of Namur. He received a huge purse of 120,000 livres, reflecting both the strength of the fortress and the prestige that had been gained by its sub-mission. Vauban was then directed to supervise the repairs to the fortifications, made necessary by the heavy French bombardment, and he added in the process a line of outworks to add a degree of depth to the defences. It was acknowledged that gaining possession of Namur had improved the French strategic position significantly: 'The strength of their armies have made it possible for the King [Louis XIV] to attack them with prudence and the loss of the town of Namur have given the French the advantage.'[23] By this success, the French held the initiative in the campaign, and this advantage was largely the work of Vauban's efforts. William III did attempt to surprise Mons as a means to offset the loss of Namur, but the plan failed when poor security gave the French warning of his intentions.

Once work on repairing and strengthening Namur had reached a satisfactory point, Vauban was sent on another round of inspections of the fortifications in south-eastern France. Fresh plans had to be made for the defence of the Dauphine region, which included the construction of a new fortress at Mont-Dauphin, high in the mountains to the south of Briançon. He then went on to Nice, which had been captured from Savoy by Marshal Catinat just the previous year. The first draft proposed for the refortification of the place was not approved, as it was considered to be too elaborate and expensive. The signs of financial stringency were becoming more evident as the ruinous costs of war went on. Still, the intention did not change, and the King was reassuring in tone in his letters to Vauban:

> Continue to write to me; do not be disappointed if I do not always adopt your suggestions, and if I do not answer your letter very regularly [...] I assure you that no one could have a higher opinion of, or more esteem and friendship for, another than I have for you.[24]

It was as well to be on the alert, for France's opponents were learning from their errors, slowly it is true, but surely. Marshal Luxembourg, frail and unwell, but certainly the King's best field commander at the time, put his army into a strong camp to the south-west of the town of Enghien. He did not expect there to be any more significant moves in the campaign that year.

Luxembourg's right flank rested on the small and marshy Senne stream, while the open farmland to the north offered good country in which to deploy the French cavalry if it became necessary. All appeared to be quiet, but this was an illusion. On 3 August 1692, at the hamlet of Steinkirk between Halle and Soignies, William III's Anglo-Dutch army suddenly struck at the French right flank. A bloody infantry battle broke out in the close and wooded country. At length, the attack bogged down and Marshal Luxembourg was just able to recover his army's composure. After hours of heavy fighting, William III had to draw off, having suffered about 7,000 men killed or wounded in what was, by common consent, a drawn battle and certainly a missed rare opportunity to rout a French army in the field. For Luxembourg, whose own losses were much the same, it had been a very close call, and disaster was only narrowly averted by the valour and bravery of his troops at all levels. The dashing young men at the Court in Versailles, most of whom would never ever hear a shot fired in anger, soon took to wearing their neck-cloths carelessly knotted, as the French officers had done as they scrambled out of their tents on the day of battle to meet the sudden attack. This rather raffish style, carefully casual as it seemed, was known as to dress 'à la Steinkirk'.

The province of Dauphine had come under attack by Savoyard troops in July 1692, with Marshal Catinat being obliged to pull back and leave exposed the towns of Gap, Embrun and Briançon. Vauban had been undertaking another extensive tour of the fortresses in the north and east, but he was now despatched southwards once more to supervise the strengthening of Briançon's defences. The instruction was politely worded, acknowledging the constant demands on Vauban's time and energy, but was still insistent. What he found on arrival was not encouraging: 'I venture to tell you,' he wrote to Barbezieux,

> Most of the land is burned up, where the enemy has foraged and devastated the harvest, and where little or no sowing has been done. Of all the miseries which I have seen in my life, none has touched me

as deeply as this. It is necessary to build a frontier in the province, and it was a great mistake to believe that none other than the Alps was required for they can be crossed at all points at certain times, and are as much in favour of the enemy as of us [...] All of this frontier is of such irregular contour that I have had to devise a new system of fortification to take advantage of it.[25]

By 22 November 1692, Vauban had drawn up 'A project of work to be carried out on the town and castle of Briançon – a small town [...] protected by two surrounding walls, one old and one new, but we can hardly rely on the old one, which is in ruins.'[26] The plans were duly approved in Versailles, a budget for the project agreed after a little hesitation at the simply enormous cost, and the work commenced.

Vauban's almost continual round of inspections of the fortresses girdling France was bearing fruit, as the Fence of Iron that he sought to establish gradually took shape. The cost was great, and Vauban still warned against pushing France's defences so far forward that they could not be held, other than with extraordinary and unproductive effort. As an example, such seemingly well-sited places as Casale and Pignerole on the Italian side of the Alps did not really serve as forward breastworks for a cohesive defensive scheme, but were a wasteful distraction that added little to the whole. If anything, because of their cost in money and men, they were a weakness. Vauban wrote rather acerbically that:

If, instead of chasing butterflies beyond the Alps, they [Louis XIV and his Ministers] had taken care to defend the frontier properly, we should have been secure now, and the King's mind would be at rest, instead of which two or three years of anxiety lie before.[27]

Taken up with schemes to improve the defences on the frontier with Savoy, whose rulers were proving to be such inconstant allies to France, Vauban had plans drawn up for Sisteron overlooking the Durance valley, at Gap, Seyne les Alpes, Saint Vincent, Colmar, Digne, Château Queyras, Embrun, Entrevaux, and, of course, at Mont-Dauphin and Briançon, which was almost completely rebuilt. These were all set in difficult mountainous country, taxing to the utmost his ingenuity to produce designs that were effective, practical and not least affordable. 'It is difficult to imagine,' he once wrote, 'anything less even, with mountains which touch the sky and valleys which plunge to the depth [...] extremely awkward for those attacking and those defending.'[28] So formidable were the difficulties at a place like Château Queyras, occupying a dramatically elevated position some 4,500 feet above sea level, and made very strong by nature. All that Vauban undertook was some limited strengthening and augmentation of the existing structures, but the result was still a defensive masterpiece, demonstrating economy and inventiveness, that can be seen today.

In February 1693, a French attack on Rheinfels in the Moselle valley was an abject failure. This enabled the Allies to claim, somewhat speciously, that a great victory had been achieved. Vauban learned of the setback, which appeared to lay bare the Moselle as an avenue of invasion into France, and of the ineptitude shown during the operations, with exasperation: 'Most discreditable for France and harmful to the troops.'[29] His illness from the time of his stay in Ypres had recurred, and he was now suffering from chronic bronchitis which prevented him from being as active as he liked, and no doubt did little for either his temper or patience. An example of this change in his manner can be seen in advice offered to the King over the enlisting into regimental service use of Cadets. Vauban, who had been a Cadet in the Régiment de Condé in his youth, now advised that they had become so ill-disciplined, and militarily irrelevant, that they should be disbanded. They were, he wrote in his usual atrocious handwriting, 'The worst subjects of His Majesty'.[30]

Things looked rather brighter on 9 May 1693, when Vauban was made a member of the newly-instituted Order of St Louis. Any officer who had served with distinction for ten years was eligible for admission to the Order, whether nobly born or not, but only eight Grand Crosses were bestowed. With Vauban as one of the recipients, this was an undoubted honour of the very highest degree, a mark it might seem of his position at the very top of his profession and circle. As yet, he was not to be made a Marshal of France with the right to be addressed by the King as 'My Cousin', and this was an undeniable gap in the ranks of the Marshalate, given his services and the high regard in which he was held. Vauban's background as a provincial was no real bar to this advancement, but his being just an engineer may well have delayed things. Not only was that professional calling still felt to be rather humble, but the King may also well have thought that it would not be possible to employ him, if a Marshal of France, on relatively mundane duties such as the kind at which Vauban had repeatedly proved himself to be a master, and not to be easily replaced. In effect, the higher he rose, the less easy it was to use him.

The French had seized Huy on the Meuse, severing direct links between the Spanish Netherlands and Luxembourg, and then moved on to threaten Liège. William III moved his army into position to cover the city, and an attempt by Marshal Luxembourg to surprise and overwhelm the Anglo–Dutch army at Landen (Neerwinden) on 29 July 1693 narrowly failed after the bitterest fighting and severe casualties to both sides. William III's regiments just managed to hold their own, fighting with their backs to the marshy banks of the Gheete stream, and only the most gallant conduct prevented a complete disaster. 'I write to you from a Field of Battle,' Luxembourg's report to the King in Versailles began, 'full of dead and dying men [...] the Victory is ours [...] the courage and bravery of our troops at last surmounted every obstacle.'[31] It had cost both armies very heavily in killed and wounded that day, and the French success was rather limited. Some commentators even felt that the scale of casualties was such that a few more such victories would put paid to the French army as a fighting force for good. Still, the outcome was that Luxembourg was left free to go on to lay siege to Charleroi, relatively untroubled.

The fortress of Charleroi on the River Sambre was well-provisioned and strongly garrisoned with 3,500 veteran Spanish troops under command of the Marquis de Villadarias. 'Your presence is absolutely necessary,' the King wrote in a letter that summoned Vauban to the siege.[32] He hurried northwards from a tour of inspection of the fortresses in the Savoyard Alps. Vauban knew the layout of Charleroi and its fortifications very well, having designed most of them, and he made his preparations for the siege with particular care. Jean-Martin De La Colonie, a distinguished French infantry officer, wrote that:

> The trenches were begun before Charleroi during the night of September 8 1693, and I was ordered as engineer to mark out the angles and distances for the attack [...] This is always an extremely risky piece of work, although conducted at night, for the noise made by the picks and tools is certain to draw the fire of the enemy.[33]

Vauban soon had cause, all the same, to complain at a lack of trained engineers, and the apparent incompetence of the gunners: 'I have had to put up with a lot,' he remarked, 'due to the ignorance of the artillerymen.'[34] Despite these problems, the bombardment by the siege batteries got under way on 15 September, inflicting heavy damage to the outer defences and losses amongst the garrison.

Good progress was made despite heavy fire from the fortress, and Vauban had one parallel trench constructed hard up against the glacis. This was actually beyond a water obstacle, but he knew the layout of the defences by heart, and that the demi-lune here was a vulnerable point. 'M. de Vauban passed about this time,' Jean-Martin De La Colonie remembered, 'and assured us with a confident air, that we should make short work of the half-moon battery.'[35] The garrison were prevented from dominating the glacis by the concentrated fire of the French batteries confronting a redoubt near to the Brussels Gate, and the Governor prudently decided to capitulate after thirty-two days, which proved to be twice as long a resistance than Vauban had rather optimistically predicted at the start of operations. If the Marquis de Villadarias had set out to delay the French campaign, he had succeeded.

By this time, only 1,300 of the garrison were fit enough to stand at their posts, but their good conduct was recognized and they were permitted to march away to Brussels with all the honours of war. Vauban's careful arrangements and the calmly measured but clearly effective conduct of the siege attracted some criticism from young French cavalry officers who had found themselves with little to do, there being no opportunity for glory and reputation, and they complained that their men had only been employed in fetching and carrying bundles of fascines cut from nearby woods for use in the entrenchments. Vauban's tart response was that if they had been asked to stand in the rain and the mud of the trenches, as the sappers and engineers had to do, they would have had just cause for complaint. Even so, the Marquis de Villadarias had done his best, and 4,000 French casualties had been inflicted during the siege.

> The officers who had volunteered for the siege as engineers received through M. de Vauban a small gratuity of fifty pistols each – not a very great burden on the government, as very few of us were left to receive it.[36]

With this success, Louis XIV now held the line of the River Sambre from Mauberge to Namur and the Meuse up to Maastricht, an important and strong strategic posture, and one which would be difficult to challenge with any real degree of success.

In the high summer of 1693, French naval squadrons intercepted the valuable Anglo-Dutch Smyrna Convoy, outward bound to the Levant and carrying in their hulls the fortunes of so many merchants in London and The Hague. Serious loss was inflicted in ships and cargoes, and there was outrage and uproar in both England and Holland. Stern demands were made that Brest, in particular, from which de Tourville's squadron operated, should be destroyed as a naval base. The attention of some members of the Grand Alliance now turned, in part, to naval affairs. For a variety of reasons, this was an open secret.

Louis XIV had been alerted to the likely threat to his naval bases by an abortive fire-ship raid on the port of St-Malo. The English vessel, packed with explosives and combustibles, had blown up prematurely and the only casualty was a cat, which lingered too long on the shore and was struck by flying debris. The King wrote:

> I have had information from different quarters which all tends to make me believe that the plan of the Prince of Orange is to try with

the combined English and Dutch fleets to burn the ships at Brest, and with a force of 6,000 to 7,000 men to make himself master of that place.[37]

The information was accurate, and speculation continues as to its sources, with hints that some highly-placed Englishmen were indulging in indiscreet correspondence with the exiled James II at St-Germaine. On the other hand, it may, of course, simply have been good calculation, after seeing the St-Malo attack, of what the Dutch and British might attempt next.

Vauban was sent to command the King's troops in Brittany, and instructed to improve the defences of that region in case of a seaborne attack. As he grew older, he had taken to travelling less frequently on horseback and made use instead of a carriage of his own design, with two mules in traces in front and behind, an inelegant but eminently practical mode of conveyance. While on the move, he was thus enabled to keep busy with his drawings and plans for new fortifications, or in dictating letters to his long-suffering secretary. Approaching his new task in the west with typical zeal, Vauban reorganized the generally ineffective militia, improving both their recruiting and training. Louis XIV had given him wide discretion to act as he saw fit, as Brittany was ill-served with overland communications, and remained a rather lawless place, only just acknowledging Royal control. Vauban was given the honorary title of Lieutenant General of Marine, by virtue of his appointment to command in the region, and the King wrote to him:

> The importance of Brest is such that I do not wish to reproach myself for not having done everything in my power to prevent the enemy succeeding [. . .] I have chosen you to command both the troops and the town [. . .] Place troops wherever you think it advisable [. . .] The responsibility with which I entrust you is one of the most important from the point of view of the good of my service, and of my kingdom, and for this reason I do not doubt that you will be pleased that I have entrusted it to you, and you will give me signs of your zeal and capabilities as you do on every occasion.[38]

Vauban was being sent to the right place, as William III certainly planned to attack French naval bases, commenting on 'the impossibility of blocking up their fleets for any considerable time [. . .] the only way to conquer the fleets of France was in their own harbours'.[39] Vauban arrived in Brest on 23 March 1694, and he calculated with a neat degree of accuracy just what the Allies would do, if they tried to attack Brest or St-Malo. He made a judicious choice, assessing with neat judgement what was to come, and concentrated what reliable troops he had under command on the Quelern Peninsula and at

Camaret Bay. A French squadron under de Tourville left Brest in April to raid Allied shipping in the Mediterranean, and the port was, on the face of things, left exposed. Vauban made his arrangements, and expressed outward confidence that the port was in no real danger: 'His Majesty need be under no apprehension [...] all Troops were in good order.'[40]

On 18 June the Allies made their attempt, with an amphibious landing of some 6,000 troops at Camaret Bay, just as Vauban had foreseen. The whole enterprise quickly turned into a disaster, in the face of a vigorous French counter-attack. One of the ships transporting the Allied troops, the Dutch vessel *Weesp*, was boarded by French infantry and seized as it ran aground in the dark and the confusion. The Allied commander, General Thomas Talmash (Tollemache) was mortally wounded at the water's edge, on a sandspit that became known as 'the English Death'. He was carried back on board his flagship to die. Another casualty, amongst more than 400 Allied troops killed or wounded in addition to prisoners taken, was Captain De La Motte. The young engineer, who Vauban had found so useful in the trenches at the Siege of Mainz, had left France in accordance with the dictates of his conscience, and with the revocation of the Edict of Nantes:

> La Motte was a refugee, a French Protestant, who had served in the King's armies [...] The King has been informed that M. de la Motte, Captain of Miners, after having rendered excellent service at the Siege of Mainz, took it into his head to say, as he left, that his conscience would no longer permit him to serve without complying with the demands of his religion.[41]

The young Frenchman lay dead in the surf, having taken service with France's opponents.

Vauban's report to the Minister for War, Barbezieux, which was written that very same evening, gave an account of the fine conduct of his men. Whether Regulars and Militia, they had not suffered severely in the action, taking fewer than fifty casualties. He was generously at pains to explain that he had not been present during the actual fighting, and wished to ensure that those junior officers who had been involved should get the just credit for the success.

This was a success, a task well accomplished, but Vauban found time to again submit a detailed memorandum for the King's attention. The paper outlined those fortresses which were of only secondary importance to the defence of France, and were a wasteful diversion of troops, effort and money that could be better used elsewhere. No fewer than twenty-three fortresses or fortified posts were listed as being in this category, with Vauban estimating that a saving of the cost of maintaining eighty-two battalions of garrison troops could be had. Perhaps not surprisingly, the King was reluctant to accept all that was suggested, for territory once seized had a certain attractiveness and charm, and was difficult to give up. Still, much had subsequently to be relinquished as the price necessary for negotiated peace at the Treaty of Ryswick in 1697, and at a time of even greater distress for France, at the Treaty of Utrecht, sixteen years later.

While Vauban was engaged in the west, Dixmude in Flanders had been lost to the Allies. The fortress of Huy, well placed and high above the Meuse, had also been recaptured by William III's troops, in a very neat operation that took only nine days of siege. For a time the Allies had the initiative, and on 2 July 1695, the army jointly commanded by the Earl of Athlone and the Elector of Brandenburg invested Namur. Vauban had warned that this attack might happen, and advised that an entrenched camp might be constructed near to the city, from which a French field army could operate to support the garrison. No notice seemed to have been taken of this warning.

The 13,000-strong garrison in Namur was commanded by the veteran, Louis-François de Boufflers, while the Marquis de Villeroi had command of the French field army. Boufflers managed to reinforce the garrison, just before the investment was complete, with seven regiments of dragoons adding another 2,000 valuable bayonets to his strength. The Prince of Vaudamont led the Allied covering army, observing Villeroi and manoeuvring to prevent any attempt at a relief of the garrison. The Marquis was a capable, if rather uninspired soldier, on quite easy terms with the King as they had been boyhood friends, but he was really more comfortable in the courtly circles at Versailles than in the field. Finding no opportunity to lift the Allied siege, Villeroi moved instead against Dixmude and Deynse, and overwhelmed the Allied garrisons there. He then went on to threaten Brussels, in an attempt to relieve the pressure on Namur.[42] 'Villeroy', wrote an English officer who was in the city:

> entered into the resolution of bombarding Brussels [...] he caused to be planted thirty mortars, and raised a battery of ten guns to shoot hot bullets [heated round-shot] into the place [...] Five days the bombardment continued; and with such fury that the centre of that noble city was quite laid in rubbish. Most of the time of bombarding I was upon the counterscarp where I could best see and distinguish; and I have often counted in the air, at one time, more than twenty bombs; for they shot whole volleys out of their mortars all together [...] But after they had almost destroyed that late noble city, Villeroy, finding that he could not raise the Siege of Namur by that vigorous attack upon Brussels, decamped at last, and put his army on the march [to Namur].[43]

All this proved to be fruitless. Van Coehorn commanded the Allied siege operations which proceeded without delays. The approach to the fortress had to be made from the southern side, as the outer defences had been strengthened on Vauban's instructions over the previous two years, with lunettes constructed on the Heights of Bouge, to the north-east of the town. Soldiers under van Salisch stormed the outworks on the night of 17/18 July 1695, but the last of these, at the Balard lunette, did not fall until eight days later after prolonged and costly fighting. The next day, 27 July, William III was present to oversee the capture of the outer Covered Way, but that night the Governor of the Bank of England, the unfortunate Michael Godfrey, who was visiting the army and rather rashly decided to accompany the King to watch the progress, was decapitated by a French round-shot as he stood at his side. On 4 August, the French garrison gave up possession of the town, and Boufflers withdrew with his 8,000 surviving troops into the newly-strengthened citadel. An English soldier who was present at the time, Sergeant John Wilson, wrote:

> All things being in a readiness for a general storm, Count Guiscard [the French Governor of Namur] came and satt upon the Demi Bastion where he ord'd Chamade to be beat [. . .] their affairs were not so much to oblige them to capitulate, yett for the preservation of the town, they were willing to give it up upon hon'ble terms [. . .] Upon the 3rd day following, a body of the troops in the town marched into the citadel and joined the troops under the command of Marshal Boufflers.[44]

So far, the Allied siege batteries had failed to subdue the guns in the town and citadel, and the casualties in the headlong infantry attacks, which van Coehorn seemed to favour, had been severe. Vauban's own comments when told of the employment of this blunt technique, which he deplored for the wasteful loss of life, was that he hoped the Allies would continue to go on in this foolish way, as it would ruin their army and could only be to France's benefit.

At van Coehorn's insistence, the breaching batteries were concentrated to better effect against the easternmost branches of the citadel, at the Terra Nova and Fort William. The results of the newly-directed bombardment were dramatic and on 30 August, when five breaches had begun to be made, John, Lord Cutts, the 'Salamander', led his English troops into a storm of the now very battered defences of the Terra Nova. There was hand-to-hand fighting and casualties were again heavy. George Carleton who took part in the affair wrote, 'We marched up to the breach with the greatest intrepidity; receiving, all the way we advanced, the full fire of the Coehorn fort.'[45] A truly daunting toll of 18,000 casualties would be suffered amongst the besiegers, while of Boufflers' garrison in the town and the citadel, some 8,000 were killed or wounded throughout the siege. This was far higher than when Vauban had conducted the siege in 1692 when a relatively minor 2,600 French casualties were suffered, although the circumstances were rather different:

> The Besiegers having lodged in the Breach at the salient angle of the Bastion, were blown up by a mine and the Breach destroyed, so as to render it impracticable to repair. They made another Breach near the angle of the shoulder, and when they had lodged in it, were blown up as before [...] the flower of the army was destroyed.[46]

Terms for the capitulation of Namur were signed on 1 September, and Marshal Boufflers was permitted to send his surviving troops away, having been granted the honours of war. There was, however, then a bitter dispute over the actual terms of the capitulation, and Boufflers was apprehended by Allied troopers, when he attempted to accompany his men:

> M. Dijkveldt begged him to go aside a trifle as he had something to impart, but he replied three times that he was marching at the head of the garrison so that he could not comply, and that he could impart anything he desired there and then. My Lord Portland [Bentinck] then approached and besought him also, so that he at last sent off an aide de camp to the Elector [of Brandenburg] to complain that we were breaking the convention in respect of his person.[47]

The problem stemmed from the reported ill-usage of the Allied garrisons at Deynse and Dixmude, who had been taken into captivity as prisoners of war, despite being granted good terms by the French when those places fell to Villeroi earlier in the campaign. The garrisons in the two forts had submitted much sooner than might have been expected, and their commanders were under a distinct cloud. Such was the disgrace that one, a Danish officer named Ekenberger, was executed at Ghent for dereliction of duty, while the other, marginally more fortunate, was cashiered after a court martial. Colonel Ekenberger's lacklustre conduct was a real mystery, as he had a good combat record.[48]

There is at least a hint that an example had been made of the unfortunate Danish officer, 'to encourage the others' as Voltaire would one day remark. As for Marshal Boufflers, detained on the road out of Namur, and fuming with indignation:

> Seeing that it was all to no avail, he drew aside, biting his lip. He demanded with heat to know if it was thus that we treated a man of his rank, one of the first men in all France, who was more important than we knew, and he claimed that all Europe would cry out against

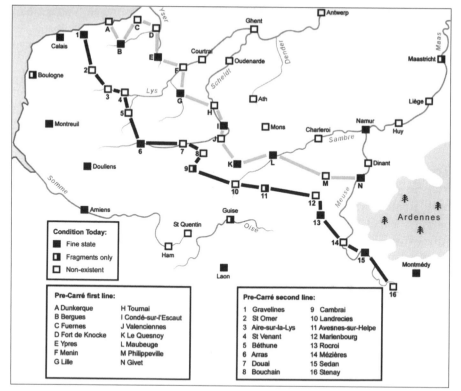

Map 4. Vauban's Fence of Iron, the 'Pre-Carré'.

the affront now being made to him, and that the Allies would be able to boast with cause that it was the first advantage they had ever gained over him, for never before had a Marshal of France been seen in the breach, personally repelling an assault.[49]

He certainly had a point, for Boufflers' own conduct at the siege had been exemplary and he had displayed great courage. The conventions of siege warfare, which worked by and large to the benefit of all sides and certainly made campaign life simpler and to a certain degree more civilized than might otherwise be the case, were put at risk by such an apparently flagrant breach of etiquette.

However, the Marshal was also engaging in bluff and bluster as the garrisons from Deynse and Dixmude were certainly being held against the terms agreed at their capitulation. Boufflers, normally an urbane and composed man, was now in a towering rage by this point, but was told bluntly that King William:

Was distressed to have been brought to this extremity [but] that he was only countenancing it because he was forced to it [...] we were generous enough to offer him the chance of leaving on parole providing he would send back our troops [from Deynse and Dixmude]. This he refused, saying that he could not undertake a thing that was not in his power, and so he is still here in Namur without guards, the town being his prison.[50]

Boufflers wrote indignantly to the Minister for War with an account of his treatment: 'As I am arrested under pretence that the garrisons of Deynse and Dixmude have not been released [...] employ your good offices with His Majesty, to induce him to procure me my liberty as soon as possible.'[51] As was probably expected, Boufflers had not long to kick his heels in comfortable idleness, as the Allied troops were released shortly afterwards, and as a result so too was he, although bristling with outraged dignity, but being at last permitted to go with his baggage and servants to Dinant.

Van Coehorn's reputation was greatly enhanced by his conduct of the Siege of Namur, despite the heavy casualty toll, to the degree that he was accorded the rank of Baron by Spain, and made Director-General of Fortifications for Holland by William III. For Vauban, on the other hand, the submission of the fortress was sobering. Namur was a place of the first importance, and the massively strengthened citadel, a prime example of his own particular design, had succumbed after a relatively short time. Vauban's rather sour comment on hearing of the Allied success in taking the fortress was to take heart in the heavy losses that had been suffered, and that 'I see it as one of the most stupid mistakes that has ever been seen in siege warfare. We should be very fortunate if God put it into the heads of our enemies to keep on attacking us in this way.'[52] On the other hand, he attempted to excuse Boufflers' inability to hold out longer: 'Perhaps the garrison was exhausted and ruined in the process of defending bad positions at the beginning of the siege; perhaps some essential prerequisites were lacking.'

Vauban, although casting about to make excuses, had concentrated on William III's losses, not an insignificant consideration. Others were also less than impressed by the Allied success, as the cost of the war in blood and treasure was certainly heavy, taxation was increasing, and English and Dutch trade on the high seas was increasingly interrupted by the activities of French privateers operating out of Dunkirk. Vauban's newly-constructed, but as yet incomplete, fortifications were proving more than a match for the Anglo-Dutch warships that, from time to time, ineffectively bombarded the place. In a comment that would be echoed in 1704 after the ghastly battle at the Schellenberg in Bavaria, the English diarist John Evelyn wrote of the loss of trade and the attacks on Brussels and Namur, that 'The losses of this sort to the nation [in trade] have been immense [...] infinitely more of concern than bombarding and ruining two or three paltry towns.'[53]

Vauban had gone back to Bazoches to complete his recuperation, and he was using his free time to ponder over the wretched state of the ordinary French people. He had seen this as he crossed France on his many journeys on the King's business, while Louis XIV, and his Ministers in Versailles, did not do so. Heavy taxation, an inevitable product of the almost constant state of war, was plainly grinding the population down. Yet, those few who had power and influence were permitted to avoid the heaviest burdens of tax-gathering: 'The direct taxation of this country has become so corrupted that the angels in heaven could not find a means of rectifying it or preventing the poor from always being oppressed.'[54] Vauban was also concerned that, on the one hand, the war was now being prolonged for its own ends, almost as a quarrel without real purpose or meaning but pursued for its own wicked sake, but that simultaneously unwise concessions to France's bitter opponents were being considered. He wrote to a friend on 11 September 1696, that 'France has brought herself close to ruin and expended a great many men to free herself and establish a frontier [. . .] I have no language in which to discuss such incredible behaviour.'[55]

Active campaigning in the Low Countries now consisted of a series of manoeuvres, some skilful but mostly clumsy, with few major engagements. British warships attempted amphibious assaults at various places along France's coastline, at such places that had been strengthened by Vauban as Belle-Île and Saint Martin de Ré, but they met with little success. Recruiting officers strained to keep depleted ranks filled, and a series of bad harvests progressively weakened France's ability to support a major war effort, an effort that was plainly not going too well. Peace terms had been arranged with Victor-Amadeus, the Duke of Savoy (whose daughter would in due course become the mother of the future Louis XV). Savoy formally abandoned the Alliance and concluded a separate peace with France in August 1696, and would regain the towns of Casale, Nice and Pignerole in the process. The troops of Victor-Amadeus, with remarkable promptness, marched to join the French forces under the command of Marshal Catinat in attacking towns in the Milanese.

The war was almost at a standstill, with neither opponent in a strong position to force a decisive result, having become a dreary 'Mixture of pacifick negotiations and military expeditions'.[56] With the Alliance ranged against France thus weakened, William III concluded that, for the time being, there was nothing more to be gained from fighting on. Peace was not yet at hand, however, and manoeuvring for position and advantage continued. In May 1697, Louis XIV ordered an attack on the eight-bastioned fortress of Ath on the Dender river in the Spanish Netherlands. As much as anything, the aim was to maintain pressure and secure advantageous terms for peace, but the seizure of the place would also expose Brussels to attack, while offering a measure of protection to French-held fortresses such as Tournai and Mons. The 45,000-strong French army was commanded by Catinat, newly-returned from successes in the south of France and northern Italy, with his good friend Vauban, as usual, conducting the siege operations. The 3,700-strong garrison in Ath, commanded by the Prince of Anhalt, was insufficient to hold out for very long, and Vauban had the distinct advantage of knowing every inch of the defences as he had overseen their repair and improvement in the early 1670s. He had also managed to evade instructions from Louvois to slight the works when the place was handed back to Spain, although this oversight may well have seemed to the French troops to be something of a mixed blessing, twenty-three years later.

Rather than ruin the defences that he had taken such pains to design and construct, Vauban had in 1673 drawn up detailed and confidential plans of the fortress, that set out just how best and at least cost Ath could be attacked and taken, if it should ever again be necessary to do so. 'The spots by which we can make our re-entry into these places, by making good plans and schemes [. . .] which if they are followed some day, will be half the work done, and will lead us safely to their capture.'[57] Amongst the innovative defensive arrangements of the fortress were the planting of rows of lime trees, placed so that round-shot fired by breaching batteries would not bounce and rebound along the defences and into the town.

Ath was invested on 15 May 1697, and the ground was broken and entrenchments started just seven days later. The two main attacks were aimed at the Bastion de Namur and the Bastion de Limbourg, both of which covered the Porte de Bruxelles. These works were dominated by nearby Mont-Ferron, the very same feature that Vauban had planned to level when redesigning the fortress, and which had caused such consternation in Versailles when the likely cost became known. Little apparent effort was made by the Allies to relieve the garrison, although a simultaneous French attempt to seize Brussels was neatly thwarted by William III's commanders.

While inspecting the siege works from a rather forward position, Vauban was wounded on the left shoulder by a spent musket ball fired from the garrison, but this was 'Nothing but a bruise,' he insisted, although 'in a bad place, but it is not sufficient to make me relax for a instant'.[58] Vauban's bluff good nature and natural energy were not diminished, and he was up early, enquiring, inspecting, encouraging and supervising everything, and only went to his camp bed late 'with a cheerful and lively countenance, I took great care to show myself next day in the trenches'. The incident was of course promptly reported to Versailles, and the King was not at all pleased with what he heard. 'I am sorry to hear of the wound you have received,' he wrote,

> but at the same time I am relieved to know that it is not dangerous, and that there is every hope you will so be restored to health [...] continue to tell me how the siege is progressing, but as you have every day more to do, instruct your secretary to do this in a simple memorandum.[59]

Ricochet fire from the French batteries, placed only some 300 paces from the Covered Way, was employed to particularly good effect and inflicting heavy loss on the defenders. 'I observe with delight,' Vauban wrote, 'that I know their fortress better than they do.'[60] Vauban also directed that the mortar batteries should fire at and disable the sluice gates, which regulated the level of the water-defences of the town:

> The rivers Dender and Lense covered several of its fronts with inundations, and formed reservoirs by the aid of which the besieged could direct artificial torrents into the ditches of the place, and even against the bridges of the lines of contravallation. The besieged had not made themselves acquainted with the properties of the sluices, and had neglected to form the inundations of the Lense; but that of the Dender afforded a more copious reservoir of water [...] Vauban ascertained that the sluice which formed this inundation was badly defended, and that it might be crushed by shells of large calibre [...] A shell of 500 pounds weight fell on the head of the sluice and destroyed it wholly. A part of the waters rushed into the city, inundated the cellars, rose to a height of 4 feet in the square and in the principal streets.[61]

The loss of the obstacle that was achieved in this way greatly impaired the ability of the garrison to resist for long.

The siege went on very well and French casualties were light, as Vauban was allowed to proceed in the careful and measured way that he had long advocated. Observers were convinced that the operation might just have been a kind of field day, a simple demonstration of how these things should be done in the best of circumstances. Vauban found no need to create a third parallel, and the saps went forward to the Covered Way from the second parallel. By 3 June the big guns were established on the counter-scarp, and the demolition of the nearby bastions began. The next day, the Prince of Anhalt asked for terms, and these were promptly granted. Vauban wrote to the Minister for War:

> Monsieur le Marshal de Catinat and myself were at the time on the bridgehead. Some of their chief men came down through the

breaches to speak to us. They were much pleased with their defence, having regard, they said, to the terrible way in which they had been attacked [...] and so Ath was surrendered.[62]

The garrison had done their best in impossible circumstances, and were allowed to march out with their arms and colours, drums beating bravely, and allowed fifty wagons for their equipment, sick and wounded. Their artillery was, however, forfeited and to be left as trophies for the victors.

Vauban wrote with understandable pride that 'I do not believe that there was ever a regular siege such as this, in which so excellent a place as that which we have just taken has been reduced so quickly and with so little loss.'[63] There were those who thought this was overstating things a little, however, and that with Vauban's detailed knowledge of the layout of the defences, the relatively swift success should have come as no great surprise. However, as the French casualty toll was less than 200 and Ath was certainly an important place to hold, such sentiments may be seen as rather ungenerous. In fact, the fortress was too far north to be held permanently by the French without disproportionate effort, but Louis XIV had gained an additional, and very useful, bargaining counter in the negotiations for an acceptable peace that lay just ahead.

The Nine Years War, the War of the League of Augsburg, came to a tired end in October 1697 with the Treaty of Ryswick, negotiated between Marshal Boufflers on the one side for France, and William Bentinck, Earl of Portland, on the other for the Alliance. The King of Sweden played a useful mediating role between the parties. Louis XIV was well aware that the odds against France were, for the time being, too great, and he was eager to achieve an adequate peace. The King's confidential instructions to Boufflers were that he should be cautious and moderate, and not to 'Boast of France's strength, as that will only bring a new coalition against us'.[64]

During this period, Vauban prepared a fresh memorandum for the King to consider, setting out those fortified places that might be given up as of only marginal importance to an overall defence structure for France, or those requiring too much effort to hold. It was clear that a peace settlement should be readily secured, but not at the risk of losing security that had been so hard won. Louis XIV could, in this way, appear to be reasonable and accommodating towards his late opponents. Casale on the Po river in northern Italy, with its massive citadel, was clearly too far advanced to be sustained without enormous effort, and should be handed over permanently to Savoy. The fortifications at Pignerole, Nice, Montmerail and Chambery could all be demolished without serious or lasting harm to French interests. This would, coincidentally, prevent Savoy from establishing in future too robust a defence. On the Rhine, Freibourg and Alt-Brisach could be given up, although Strasbourg should be retained if at all possible, but Kehl just across on the far bank would go too. The fine fortresses of Mont-Royal and Trier in the Moselle valley were too far forward to be of real value, again without great effort, even though they neatly shut the door on that route into the heart of France very nicely, and they were to be relinquished. In all, Vauban's outline proposals were judicious, and would save men and treasure, able resources to be concentrated to better effect, and assuage France's opponents with evidence of Louis XIV's earnest desire for peace while handing over fortresses and territory that were of only secondary importance to the cherished Fence of Iron. The defensible borders of France would be left intact, strengthened even, with the added advantage of a prolonged period of peace lying ahead.

To Vauban's dismay, the King was apparently prepared to go much further, and he expressed his concern at what was to be given up in the course of the negotiations, protesting at the excessive and unnecessary loss, as he saw it, both of prestige and territory:

> I will not speak of the other fortresses we are to give up. What is certain is that those who have advised the King in this sense are doing no disservice to our enemies [...] it is certain that no power would have been able to drive us out [...] With them we lose for ever the chance of making the Rhine our frontier, for we shall never return there [...] If we had lost five or six battles in succession and a large area of our territory, if the State was in imminent danger, which could not be averted except by peace, there would still be reason to complain of a peace such as that now contemplated.[65]

This was no blind or ill-informed warmongering; Vauban was in essence a most humane and practical man, but he had a clear idea of what it was best to hold and what could be given up. He was also very pragmatic, and regretted letting go so much that had both taken so much effort to obtain and still had lasting value for the security of France. Although he had often warned against overstretching French resources in holding on to territory and fortresses of only secondary importance, he felt that to give up so much and so easily was a military disaster not seen since the bad old times of King Henry II. Nonetheless, Louis XIV had determined to make more concessions to secure a peace, and he responded rather tartly to such protests: 'I shall do what I believe to be for my own good, for that of my kingdom, and my subjects [...] If peace is made it will be honourable to the nation; if the war continues we are in a condition to carry it on.'[66]

Louis XIV held on to Strasbourg, that strong bastion for France, but agreed to give up a number of those fortresses seized by his armies in the Southern Netherlands. These included Charleroi, Courtrai, Ath and Mons, all, arguably, of secondary importance and forming only a modest part of Vauban's planned Fence of Iron. Mont-Royal, on the Moselle, was to be demolished by the French garrison before they left, and possession of Trier relinquished. Casale, Nice and Pignerole had already been handed over to Savoy, exposing Briançon and necessitating further enlargement and strengthening of the defences there. The long-standing but quite unrealistic French claim to Barcelona was given up for ever. Luxembourg, Landau, Kehl, Freibourg and Alt-Brisach on the Upper Rhine were also to be handed over. So, too, was a strategically important island, the Ville Neuve opposite Alt-Brisach, but the vital crossing-point over the great river still had to be guarded. Accordingly, the existing fortress was demolished, and Neuf-Brisach, an entirely new 'model' fortified town, designed and built under Vauban's supervision, took its place on the left bank of the Rhine, although the work was not completed until 1708, a year after the Engineer's death. The displaced French inhabitants of Alt-Brisach and Ville Neuve were offered financial inducements to cross the river and settle in the new town.[67]

On the other side of the negotiating table, much had been achieved. William III was acknowledged by France as King of England, and the lost cause of James II's restoration was abandoned, at least outwardly. Still, the French would long make the Jacobite cause their own if it inconvenienced Great Britain, and did not require too much effort or expense on their own part. The Dutch also had some cause for satisfaction, as they had strengthened their own security by gaining the possession of a series of strategically located Barrier Towns, such as Namur, Oudenarde, Dendermonde and Ypres, but the French King's inclination to regain what he had at one time thought it necessary to negotiate away would lead him into making a serious strategic error within a few years.

A sustained period of peace was welcome to all, but it was apparent to some that it would not last. The burning question all across western Europe had become that of the troubled succession to the throne in Madrid. This grew more acute, as it was almost certain by now that King Carlos II, invalid, ineffectual and childless, had not long to live. The prize was potentially enormous with the huge Spanish Empire stretching across much of the western Mediterranean and Italy, huge parts of the Americas, and the Philippines. Enormous, too, was the likelihood of serious trouble between the various parties who had claims, of varying worth, to the succession. Arrangements for an orderly solution to the thorny problem of who would succeed Carlos II all fell to pieces when the young Bavarian prince, chosen by Versailles and Vienna as acceptable to both, suddenly died of smallpox early in 1699. Louis XIV was initially circumspect over the issue, given the financially ruinous war of recent years, but if he was to secure French interests in Spain, then he needed allies.

In time he would find one in the Elector of Bavaria who saw a chance to gain from Vienna's weakness, but in the meantime the King had, surprisingly, apparently found an ally in his old adversary, William III. Marshal Boufflers wrote to the King with a detailed account of the lengthy negotiations he had conducted with the Earl of Portland to bring the recent conflict to an end, and he ended with the comment:

> Perhaps, when peace was once more concluded, and the agitation of people's minds calmed, Your Majesty would not be sorry to have an ally like the Prince of Orange, and that you would find him as faithful and conscientious in favouring the interests of Your Majesty, as he has hitherto been opposed to them.[68]

There were many good intentions, and mostly genuine efforts, to avert a new war, but there was a certain sad inevitability in what took place.

As the century came to a close, Vauban was instructed to undertake yet another extensive tour of France's borders, and to report on the condition of the fortresses that guarded them. Work at the building of Neuf-Brisach was to receive his particular attention, as Lille had done thirty-three years earlier. Plans were also laid for the construction of a military canal in Alsace, for the ready movement of troops and guns from one place to another as a threat developed. By the middle of 1700, he was in the south of France once more, inspecting works in Dauphine and Provence and the seaward defences at Marseilles. Despite his concern at what had needed to be given up to achieve peace, a peace that he recognized France needed, Vauban was apparently now confident that what had been achieved and had been retained was enough. He wrote to le Pelletier in October 1697 concerning the defence arrangements in the north-east:

> The projected line of Stenay, Montmédy, Longwy, Thionville and Saarlouis separates Lorraine well enough from Luxembourg, so there is no need to do anything else there. Besides, Metz, where the fortifications are well advanced and in very good order, give us a strong reserve in the middle of the Duke of Lorraine's territory.[69]

Amongst the fresh honours that now came to Vauban was his elevation to the Académie des Françaises, as an honorary member. His interest in statistics, both military and civil, fitted him well to this new accolade. However, the old soldier's health was clearly beginning to falter, and his coughing was persistent and tiring. All the same, his energy in the service of the King seemed to be undiminished, despite his lengthening years. His standing amongst the military men of the day, and professional reputation, had become so high that the important role of the military engineer in all phases of operations, not just those closely associated with the siege, was increasingly regarded with respect and interest. Men sought to learn from him and to emulate his efforts. Much thought was, of course, also given to his innovative fortress designs, with fresh interest shown in devising ways to re-establish the old advantages of the formal defence over the well-organized attack.

In this, military men were to a certain degree chasing shadows, as much of Vauban's own efforts were still devoted to devising efficient ways to overcome those same defences without disproportionate cost. Also, the old unavoidable truth remained good that, however well prepared for a defence they might be, all fortresses would have to submit in the end to any besieging commander who would devote enough time, skill and effort to the task.

Chapter 8

The Long Campaign

The War of the Spanish Succession was outwardly fought to determine just who would sit on the throne in Madrid once King Carlos II was in his grave. The opposing parties were France, understandably supporting the French claimant to the throne, together with those many Spaniards who stood by him; and on the other side of the argument was the Grand Alliance, whose main parties were still England, Holland and Imperial Austria, joined latterly by Portugal and Savoy, together with the Habsburg-inclined party in Spain. The conflict was waged on many fronts – Italy, Spain, Germany, in North America and in the West Indies, and on the High Seas. The Allies sought to limit the seemingly ever-growing power of France, and most importantly to achieve a division, on broadly equitable terms between the interests of France and Austria, of the vast and militarily moribund but still wealthy Spanish Empire. This latter aspiration was shared by Louis XIV, who with a Treasury badly depleted by the seemingly endless wars of the closing years of the seventeenth century wished to avoid a renewed conflict. For all that, war it had to be, ruinously expensive and with an end result that satisfied no one, yet seemingly impossible to avoid. Miscalculation and misjudgement were in play, and astute diplomacy came to nothing. Nowhere was the campaigning more crucial than in the Spanish, or Southern, Netherlands, and this was most sensitive territory for France, now sprinkled with fortresses of Vauban's innovative design.

It had been agreed in 1698 by France, England, Austria and Holland that the Spanish throne, when it became vacant, should be taken by a young son of the Elector of Bavaria, a prince who was an acceptable choice and a neat solution to a difficult problem. Sadly, he suddenly succumbed to smallpox and this threw everything into doubt once again. When the moment came, Louis XIV felt that he must allow his youngest grandson Philippe, Duc d'Anjou, to accept the offer in the late King Carlos' will of the vacant throne in Madrid. Despite the pomp and grand ceremony that attended the announcement, the French King had his doubts about the wisdom of this inviting course, and he wrote to Camille d'Hostun, Duc de Tallard, his adroit Ambassador in London, that 'I know how alarmed all Europe would be to see my power raised to a greater height than that of Austria.'[1] He was faced, however, with an un-doubted dilemma, for if Anjou refused the offer, it would immediately be made instead to Archduke Charles of Austria, youngest son of Emperor Leopold. This possibility, opening up the old fear of Habsburg encirclement of France, could not be borne in Versailles.

The Spanish Netherlands remained a rich and prosperous region, providing Madrid with desperately needed tax revenue. As a consequence, whoever controlled the territory gained an advantage in terms both of prestige and tax-raising possibilities. At the same time, France's long northern border was kept in relative security by having the region in friendly, or at least neutral, hands, and this strategic position would be imperilled if a hostile army was able to operate there. Louis XIV had extended his realm by conquest, northwards into Artois, and parts of Hainault, Brabant and Flanders. In the process he took possession of such strong places as Lille, and, anxious to make his new acquisitions more secure, had given the Inspector-General of Fortifications, Sébastien le Prestre de Vauban, the task to fortify the region. This had been accomplished with energy, imagination and skill, and the dilapidated and obsolete fortifications of the region, half-ruined by war and bombardment as they were, had been transformed, at huge effort and expense, into a stout fortified belt of modern design and construction – the Fence of Iron.

The region also remained of great importance to the Dutch as a major element of their own security. Louis XIV's armies had made a practice in the past of marching over parts of the Spanish Netherlands when advancing to attack Holland. Carefully crafted treaties to bring to a close the seemingly interminable French and Dutch wars in the closing years of the previous century had secured for Holland the 'Barrier', a series of fortified towns in Spanish territory that would be garrisoned by their own troops, to serve as a bulwark against any future French aggression. A major cause of the eventual outbreak of the war for Spain, quite apart from the question of whether it was more desirable to have a French or an Austrian prince on the throne in Madrid, was the unwise seizure of these same 'Barrier Towns' by French troops, as Louis XIV sought to secure his own grandson's recently-acquired possessions in the area.

This gave great offence to the Dutch, who had to ask that their interned garrisons be released by the French (except at Maastricht where the Governor had stoutly refused the summons to submit). Louis XIV had, it appeared, quickly annexed the Spanish Netherlands without a shot being fired. William III, King of England, was also the Dutch Stadtholder, and so the interests of these two participants in the Grand Alliance against the renewed French threat were welded closely together without too much difficulty. 'For twenty years,' he wrote, 'I have toiled unceasingly to preserve this barrier for the State [of Holland] and now I have to watch it swallowed up in one day without a single blow being struck.'[2] The King also addressed the House of Commons in London in plain and uncompromising terms:

> By the French King placing his grandson on the throne of Spain, he is in a condition to oppress the rest of Europe, unless speedy and effectual measures be taken [...] If you do not hold on this occasion, you have no reason to hope for another.[3]

Despite such high-flown sentiments, both England and Holland had been prepared to abandon the cause of the Austrian claimant, as long as their own interests were kept secure. Louis XIV's miscalculation over the whole question spoiled all this, and was an unusual and serious error of judgement.

Louis XIV had met the young John Churchill when he was serving with an English regiment loaned into French service by Charles II. Perhaps Vauban also made his acquaintance at this time, when he was serving as a junior officer busily engaged in siege operations. Marlborough, as the Englishman became known, certainly fought at the French Siege of Maastricht, but he and Vauban never faced one another as opponents across a battlefield or palisade. When active hostilities between France and Spain (in the form of Philip V – the Duc d'Anjou), and the Grand Alliance began once more in May 1702, Marlborough was appointed to be the Captain-General of the Anglo-Dutch armies. Fighting had already broken out in northern Italy where Marshal Catinat and the Duke of Savoy were busily engaged with Imperial Austrian forces. Louis XIV's more immediate aim, though, was to ensure the security of his northern border and that of the Spanish Netherlands, and in the process to drive Holland out of the war with an early strike against their fortresses on the Lower Rhine. In this endeavour the French commanders failed, largely because of the astute handling of the Anglo-Dutch forces by Marlborough. Dutch caution, however, prevented the Earl from making the most of his successes. Something approaching a stalemate was soon reached in the north, while campaigns large and small flared up elsewhere, in Spain, northern Italy and southern Germany. For the time being, French armies clearly had the better of things over their less inspired opponents.

At this point in the war there was not a lot of active employment for Vauban, who had for some time been frustrated by the seemingly measured progress of his promotion. He took the opportunity, early in 1702, to write to the King and remind him, perhaps a little too pointedly, that he was amongst the most senior of the General officers, and that his elevation to Marshal might well be thought to be long overdue, given the distinguished service that he had rendered over the years:

> Sire, the rumours current in Paris, at Versailles and throughout the army of impending promotions to Marshals of France, lead me to

represent to Your Majesty that my position as Lieutenant General is one of greater seniority than most of those likely to claim promotion. My services, of which I wish for no better witness than Your Majesty, have been more deserving than theirs and give me grounds for hoping that Your Majesty will not deem me unworthy of this promotion.[4]

The letter appears to have gone unanswered, but the request can hardly have gone unnoticed by the King. Such matters, of course, had a certain measured pace of their own and were not to be hastened.

Out on campaign, Marlborough had manoeuvred the French away from the reaches of the Lower Rhine, out of Dutch territory, and back into Liège and Brabant. French-held fortresses such as Bonn, Ruremonde, Liège, Geldern and Huy were secured in the process. The tactics of Marlborough's commanders were effective, but at times they disregarded heavy losses in order to overwhelm their opponents by outright assault, while the French commanders, in turn, seemed to be at something of a loss as to how to combat the Duke's methods. At this time Vauban, having been called on to advise on improvements to the defences of Antwerp, was entrusted with the command of French forces on the Channel coast around Ostend and Nieuport, but the main focus of the fighting was elsewhere. Marlborough found that his plans for decisive action, confronting the French field army in the open, were brought to nothing, in part due to the continuing cautious attitude of his Dutch allies. In almost equal measure, it was evident that the French commanders could manoeuvre around the strong fortress belt in the region, avoiding engagements in the open and eating up the few precious campaign months of summer rather well.

On 14 January 1703, Vauban was at last made a Marshal of France. 'The King said nothing of this until after dinner,' St Simon wrote, 'when he suddenly announced his decision.'[5] This was certainly a signal honour for a man of such relatively humble beginnings, and whose career, by and large, had rested on the once poorly regarded tasks associated with siege warfare and military engineering. Moreover, this was a man who had never had command of a victorious army in the field, the skirmish at Camaret Bay some years earlier not quite falling into that category.[6] The typical look of a soldier, in St Simon's rather cutting phrase, had plainly done Vauban no harm in the end, and 'All congratulated him on this access of honour, to which no other of his kind had risen before him or has risen since.'[7] That the advancement was well merited, and overdue, was not in doubt.

As a Marshal of France, however, it was not thought appropriate that Vauban should actively engage in siege operations – not that the fortunes of war permitted France very many opportunities to undertake these at this stage. When a siege of Kehl, just across the Rhine from Strasbourg, was proposed, Louis XIV gently reproved Vauban for the enthusiasm with which he volunteered for the task of supervising the operations: 'Do you not think such employment beneath your dignity?' To which the Marshal replied, 'Sire, the question is to serve you [...] I will leave my Marshal's baton behind.'[8] The King was not persuaded; the dignity of a Marshal of France could not be put down and picked up at will, and Vauban was no longer readily given the kind of task that suited his talents and experience so well.

It was soon evident that such talents could not be left idle, however. Late in the summer of 1703, Vauban was recalled from his post on the Channel coast and engaged in his last major formal siege, that of Alt-Brisach. Such a task was still thought by some to ill befit the dignity of a newly-elevated Marshal of France, but he accompanied the Duke of Burgundy, eldest grandson of Louis XIV and thus heir to the throne of France. Accordingly, the arrangement was apparently sufficiently lofty, with a Prince of the Blood present before the fortress for the scruples against the Marshal engaging in mere siege to be set aside.

The King was naturally concerned that his grandson should receive most of the credit for the confidently expected success at the siege, stressing that the orders should be issued in the young Prince's name. Louis XIV wrote to Michel de Chamillart, the Minister for War now that Barbezieux had died, with very precise details of how the siege and the covering operations were to be conducted:

> Marshal de Vauban has told me that he proposes to do no more with the army of the Duke of Burgundy than he has done with me at all the fortresses I have taken, when he only concerned himself with the trenches and the assault [...] The Duke of Burgundy can depend in everything upon Marshal de Vauban as upon Marshal de Tallard, but of operations beyond the trenches, Marshal de Tallard will be in charge, and will issue all orders under the authority of the Duke of Burgundy.[9]

The defences of the fortress had been partly remodelled by Vauban before it had to be returned to Imperial control at the Treaty of Ryswick in 1697, and Burgundy teased him good-naturedly as to how he would overcome his own designs. Vauban replied, with an equally good-natured challenge, 'Monsignor, we shall see how you contrive to take the fortress I have built.'[10] The siege began on 23 August, and, despite his advanced years and the onset of foul weather, the old soldier was as active as ever. 'I have found some very favourable sites there for reverse and ricochet batteries,' he wrote, 'which, please

God, I shall take advantage of.'[11] Burgundy was conducted around the siege-works by Vauban, who wrote to the Minister for War three days later:

> I took Monseigneur to the trenches, almost against my will, because the besieged maintained a heavy gunfire, which I would have preferred to have silenced before exposing him to risk. But, he was so desirous to go, that I let him [. . .] he came back so tired that he could hardly put one foot in front of the other.[12]

As it was, the siege was concluded, despite the unseasonably bad weather, in a little more than two weeks; in part because much of the defences of the town were flooded by the rapidly rising waters of the Rhine. 'His Majesty is greatly pleased,' Chamillart wrote to Vauban, late in September, to which the slightly weary and pointed comment in reply was then 'Let us thank God, and not give it up again.'[13] After the success at Alt-Brisach, Vauban sought another command but the response from Versailles was not encouraging, and in this it seems that an appreciation of his years and visibly failing health, as much as anything else, and no lack of faith in his abilities, played their part.

Vauban had an enquiring mind, and he continued to write on many subjects other than those in the strictly military sphere – farming, forestry, recruiting for the army, colonization, pig-breeding – little seemed to escape his notice. With particular regard to his career as a military engineer, he produced three major works which were intended for the education of French Princes of the Blood and the Marshals of France. Soon after the conclusion of the operations to take Alt-Brisach, Vauban published his influential work *Traité de l'Attacque de Places*, dedicated to the Duke of Burgundy. Erudite and highly informative, packed with detailed information and closely-argued advice, and beautifully illustrated with minutely observed and often quite charming coloured scenes of the different phases to be undertaken during an attack, the work became the essential text book to be consulted by military engineers for generations to come. Copies of these works were always few in number and they are now very scarce and valuable indeed, but this author was privileged to have the loan of a very well-preserved copy of *Traité de l'Attacque de Places*, for an all-too-short afternoon, courtesy of one of the major auction houses in London, while preparing this book. *Traité de la Defense de Places* was published in 1706, and *Traité des Mines* in 1707, although earlier drafts were prepared some years earlier. These works were all intended to be confidential, almost secret, so as not to alert France's adversaries to his techniques, but there was too much interest in their contents, and almost inevitably copies were soon produced and translated and sold abroad, where they found a ready market.

French commanders, struggling to keep pace with the Allied campaign in the north, resorted to preparing long lines of defence behind which their armies could manoeuvre, shielded from sudden attack. These lines were a mixture of field works – redoubts and gun positions, fortified farmhouses and villages and flooded meadows, all ready to be occupied in strength when any particular sector came under threat. Nothing wrong there, and in a way they were rather similar to the Lines of Contravallation and Circumvallation routinely constructed by besieging armies ever since the long-ago days when Julius Caesar conquered Gaul with his Roman legions. Vauban approved of these measures, as defensive grand tactics which conserved the strength of the army but at relatively modest cost, although at the outlay of considerable back-breaking effort on the part of the troops and those conscripted peasants who could not find ways to avoid the work. The lines of defence added materially to the strength of France's borders and were therefore a good thing, so long as Louis XIV's Marshals did not become too defensively-minded as a result. That the construction was out of necessity, as French commanders were out-generalled by Marlborough, did not detract from their effectiveness or value of the field defences, or lessen the difficulties that they imposed upon his freedom of action.

Early in 1704, Marlborough, who had been made a Duke in recognition of his successes in the Low Countries, received permission from Queen Anne (who in 1702 had succeeded her Dutch brother-in-law on the throne in London), to take those troops in English pay to campaign in southern Germany. There, he would unite with the Imperial armies under Prince Eugène of Savoy and move to defeat a French and Bavarian attempt to attack Vienna. This was the renowned campaign that led to the great victory at Blenheim (Höchstädt) on 13 August 1704, establishing for ever Marlborough's place as one of the great Captains in history.

French war plans lay in ruins after the battle. One of Louis XIV's field armies was wrecked, and another was in flight along with his Bavarian allies. Marlborough and his victorious troops closed up to cross the Rhine, and laid siege to Landau, taken by the French the previous year, and to Trarbach in the Moselle valley. Both fortresses fell to the Duke in the closing weeks of the year. The difficulties encountered in preventing a siege are well illustrated by the comments of the Comte de Merode-Westerloo, a Walloon officer in the service, at the time, of King Philip V of Spain (the French claimant to the throne):

> The enemy arrived to besiege Landau [24 October 1704], the Emperor himself hurrying post-haste to be present at the event. M. de Villeroi called up all his men in Alsace, including the garrison troops, and posted himself on the little River Queiche in an attempt to daunt the enemy. His announced plan was to cover Landau, pre-vent the siege, and even fight a battle. But, the moment they heard

from a sure source that the enemy would without fail attack our position the next day, the army fell back the very same night [...] The confusion and consternation that accompanied this manoeuvre had to be seen to be believed.[14]

Things were not always straightforward, and Louis XIV congratulated Marshal Villeroi on his cautious moves, agreeing that to risk what was left of the army in the region, after such a dreadful defeat at Blenheim, would be too rash. It was always regrettable to lose a fortress, even more so to lose two, but the French field armies had to be preserved from further damage.

The Governor of Landau had been killed by a round-shot early in the operations. His deputy, the Marquis de Laubanie, although blinded by stones throne up by an exploding shell, continued valiantly to conduct the defence of the place, organizing sorties, counter-approaches and defensive mining. The Marquis held on gamely and with devoted determination, defying Vauban's model timetable for a siege and extending the defence to over seventy days. The task was made the more difficult as improvements to strengthen the defences were incomplete, some of the mortar used was faulty, and in other parts it had yet to set properly and was visibly crumbling. Laubanie still felt obliged to dictate a rather moving letter to Louis XIV, to explain the need to submit, when he gave up the fortress on 25 November 1704:

I ask pardon of Your Majesty, Sire, for having lost the town of Landau. I employed all the means at my disposal to keep it, but they were unavailing. I can assure Your Majesty, as a most honourable man, that from the first day of the siege to the last, though blinded and dangerously wounded, I did not cease to give the necessary orders in the attempt to hold it, but the weakness of the garrison and the shortage of warlike matériel did not permit me to hold out longer lest it should be carried by storm, and we be taken prisoners. Several officers distinguished themselves during the siege, and are worthy of Your Majesty's favour [...] I shall continue my service [to you] by my prayers, and I shall ever be mindful of the favour Your Majesty has shown me.[15]

The Marquis had done his best, in appalling circumstances, unable any longer to see and groping about the defences to measure the widening breaches in the defences by hand, and reliant upon the verbal reports of his subordinates. His defence of Landau was a notable and very creditable operation, and the surviving 3,400 members of the garrison were permitted to march out with all the honours of war. Marlborough's army had paid a stiff price for their success, having lost 9,322 killed and wounded in the siege.

The effect of this siege, and that at Trarbach which submitted on 20 December, was that the Allied campaign to follow up the triumph at Blenheim had been slowed to a virtual crawl. These valiant defensive efforts, together with other well-conducted rearguard actions, did much to blunt the success that Marlborough and Prince Eugène had so daringly won by battle that August. For all the trouble, effort and expense that was entailed in Vauban's designs and programme of construction, the defence of places such as Landau in 1704 and the drag it imposed on Marlborough's campaigns, illustrated very well the value of such formal defences, when the efforts of commanders and their armies in the field could be, to a large degree, frustrated and brought almost to nothing. Wars were not won by such defensive methods, but the beaten field armies and their commanders were able to gather themselves in relative security, regroup and replenish their ranks, and get ready for the rigours of campaigns yet to come.

The disaster to Marshal Tallard's army at Blenheim was a deep shock for Louis XIV and his entire circle, but honours were awarded, where they reasonably could be given at a time of such adversity, and promotions conferred. A signal honour was certainly bestowed on Vauban by the King in January 1705, when he was made a Knight of the Order of the Holy Spirit. The Order was highly exclusive, limited to 100 members only, and required strict proof of nobility. The Duc de St Simon, in typically caustic fashion, expressed his surprise that so exalted a mark of honour should be bestowed on a mere engineer, and a provincial at that.

Victor-Amadeus II, Duke of Savoy, courted or neglected in turn by Louis XIV as he chose, had abandoned France's cause and joined the Grand Alliance in 1704. The following February, Vauban advised against an attack on Turin as being unlikely to succeed, but expressed to the Minister for War his concerns for the security of Marseilles and the great naval base at Toulon: 'What would become of the fleet? [...] The very thought is frightful, and nothing short of the fall of Paris could be more serious than that of Marseilles.'[16] The war was going badly, but it would be shown that Louis XIV and his generals were remarkably resilient. During 1705, Marlborough was once more obliged to pursue a campaign in the less promising confines of the Spanish Netherlands. This he did with his usual skill and vigour, but Dutch reluctance to engage the French field army under Villeroi once more frustrated the Duke's efforts. He did achieve a success at the Battle of Elixheim in July 1705, and recaptured the fortress of Huy on the Meuse, the seizure of which by Villeroi had obliged the Duke to abandon an apparently promising advance into France through the Moselle valley. Marlborough was then prevented from mauling a large part of the French army on the River Yssche to the south of Brussels, when the Dutch commanders again refused to accept any risk, even where there was the promise of great advantages. With such frustrations, the results of the year's campaign for the Grand Alliance were a disappointment.

Jeanne, Madame de Vauban, died on 18 June 1705 at her home in the countryside at Bazoches. The interment was attended by some 2,000 people, including many local worthies, indicating the high regard in which she and her family were held. Vauban remained in Paris. The long forty-five years that they had been married had been marked by frequent absences as her husband pursued the King's interests, both in times of war and of peace, across the length and breadth of France. Madame Vauban, a true countrywoman who never travelled outside of Burgundy, was noticeably protective of her husband's own interests in the Morvan, and had proved to be a very good manager. Rather inevitably, Vauban had strayed as a man, after the custom of the time, and he certainly made provision in his will for several natural children born to various women with whom he had clearly had liaisons over the years. There is no particular reason to suppose that otherwise, and subject to the voracious demands on his time from his Royal master in Versailles, Vauban was anything other than an affectionate husband, after his own fashion.

Vauban was in semi-retirement now, becoming rather deaf and with a persistent chronic cough, without active appointment or command but planning a military canal to run from Lille to Gravelines, a project that never came about. It is perhaps a measure of his declining influence that little attention was paid to his warnings – Turin was attacked by the French in 1706, and Vauban offered his advice which was pointedly ignored and the campaign ended in a major defeat. Vauban also sent advice to James Fitzjames, Duke of Berwick, 'the great English devil', in his successful operations to capture Nice from Savoy.

Several times Vauban requested to be given a more active command, but this may have been more for the sake of form as much as anything, for his health was plainly failing. Also, at a time of growing crisis for France, with hostile armies gathering on the borders ready for a fresh campaign in 1706, Vauban had fallen into disfavour with the King that he had served so long and so well. He was accustomed to speaking his mind, and had often been encouraged to do so: 'The King, who, I am proud to say, knows me thoroughly,' he once wrote, 'is used to all my freedom of speech, and were I to cease to be free, he would take me for a man turned courtier, and would no longer have confidence in my words.'[17] That may have been so, but he would soon find that the King's forbearance had distinct limits. Vauban had been concerned for some time at the escalating cost to the common people of the taxation required to fund the war that raged from one year to another:

> It is a constant that the greatness of Kings is measured by the
> number of their subjects; in this consists their welfare, their happi-
> ness, their wealth, their strength, their fortune, and all the consider-
> ation they have in the world.[18]

In effect, his quite radical argument ran, that the more a monarch had a
numerous and well-contented people, then the more real strength was had; the
more oppressed that the common man became, the more precarious was the
King's position in proportion.

Vauban declared as illogical and pernicious the many concessions and privileges by which the wealthy and the well-connected at the Court in Versailles
were able to avoid much taxation. The common tradesman, farmer, soldier,
shopkeeper or labourer could not do so. Vauban had calculated that one tenth
of the population were in beggary, half the population teetered on the edge of
penury, and three-tenths were in debt at least partly because of heavy taxation.
The remaining fortunate tenth of the population, who escaped the worst of the
taxes, comprised the nobility, the clergy, and the wealthy merchant class.
Vauban wrote:

> The causes of the misery of the people of this kingdom are well
> known, I will however give a general view of the most considerable of
> them, but it would be a thing of great use and importance to find
> some substantial remedy for this evil.[19]

Strong words, which certainly did not commend themselves to much of his
likely audience by listing in elaborate detail those classes of persons, from the
King and his immediate family downwards, who were exempt from much
taxation and who, by implication, would have to start to pay more if his ideas
were adopted.[20]

Vauban went into print, preparing a well-argued proposal that would intro-
duce a single rate of tax for all, with no exemptions, which would be both
simpler and fairer than the confused mass of petty taxes then in force. The
lavish spending on war, a feature of the reign of Louis XIV, had its inevitable
effect in depleting the Treasury and keeping it so despite heavy taxation, and
the cost of Vauban's programme of fortress-building had, of course, been a significant part of this expenditure. Military spending was also unevenly applied,
as with the massive purses of money that Vauban received for his successes at
siege warfare, and he was by no means alone in this, for this was the way the
King rewarded his principal servants. This lack of balance had been noticed by
Marshal Tesse, who drew attention to the increasingly threadbare, even gaunt,
appearance of the French soldiers he led. The money for fresh equipment and
supplies was simply not to be had, while bread and water was the routine

ration, with meat only issued occasionally, contrary to regulations on what the soldiers should receive.

Official censorship was commonplace, and a risk had been run by the old soldier with the publication of his proposition without Royal permission, but the intention was plainly honest. 'This folly,' Vauban wrote, 'of which I am both father and godfather, is called "A proposal for the conversion of the taille, the aides and the provincial customs, capitulation, special levies, octrois, commissions, gaugings, and several other duties onerous and mostly arbitrary, into a Royal Tythe."' He went on that the Tythe, or Tithe, would be:

> Apportioned from time to time by the necessities of the State, which would be imposed upon all who have an income of any kind whatsoever without distinction of small or great [...] by which means the State, sick and languishing though it be, would find itself in good condition again. Call me foolish as much as you please, I have experienced such abuse and worse, but it has not prevented me from surviving it.[21]

Vauban added the simple and pious hope, one that unfortunately would fall on deaf ears, that:

> What remains is to offer up my fervent prayers to God, that it may be received as kindly and impartially as I have writ it with an Honest and sincere Intent; and without any other passion or design, than that of serving my Prince, and endeavouring the Quiet and Happiness of my Fellow-Subjects.[22]

In the main, the taxes that then existed were the Taille, the aides, and the Gabelle. The Taille was a levy upon the value of property; the aides were supplementary taxes imposed in time of war or national emergency; while the Gabelle was an ingenious tax on salt. To add to the burden of the Gabelle (embezzlement of which was widespread), all adults were required by law to purchase a set amount of salt each week and thus evasion of the tax was almost impossible. However, a favoured few, nobles and certain officials, were permitted an exemption from some, or indeed all, taxes; a situation that gave rise to understandable resentment and encouraged tax evasion where it could be had. 'The Dime Royal, or Project for a Royal Tythe', setting out Vauban's proposal on taxation, was printed and 300 copies got ready for distribution privately by February 1706. It was not intended for general sale:

> I feel myself constrained by honour and conscience to represent to His Majesty that it has seemed to me that at no time has enough

regard been paid to the poorer classes [...] The most ruined and most miserable class in the kingdom, although the most considerable number [...] they it is who furnish all the soldiers and sailors.[23]

Whether or not what was proposed could really be put into practice, or indeed was all that original or groundbreaking, was not particularly important. The effect was immediate, and the reaction that Vauban met was fierce, as it touched on the privileges and fortunes of an army of bureaucrats and placemen who administered the existing wide range of taxes and tithes, and those influential few who were able to avoid paying many of the taxes. 'Vauban's book,' wrote the Duc de St Simon from Versailles,

> made a great stir [...] Popular with the public, censured and loathed by the financiers, hated by the Ministers [...] Even Chamillart [the War Minister] forgot his usual politeness and moderation [...] It had a grand fault. It described a course which, if followed, would have ruined an army of financiers, of clerks, of functionaries of all kinds; it would have forced them to live at their own expense.[24]

Whether Louis XIV ever read Vauban's proposal with any great attention is uncertain, although he was sent two advance copies to which a lofty regal disdain was shown, and he chose not to acknowledge them. It was enough that the King's Engineer had presumed to stray into such sensitive territory that was deemed to be none of his affair, or of which it was probably thought he could have no real understanding.

The Council in Versailles met on 14 February 1706 to consider Vauban's publication and disapproval was expressed, but this was tempered with respect for him and his reputation. A month later, as further copies were produced, the Council considered the matter again, and this time their disapproval was less qualified. From now on, a cold shoulder would be shown by the King to the old soldier. Vauban's letters to Louis XIV tended to go unanswered, but Michel de Chamillart wrote confidentially to offer assurance that the King would not abandon him; in effect he had not fallen into most serious disfavour. Outwardly, at least, he would continue in the Royal service. Vauban's concerns and effort, and his courting of such displeasure, were all in vain as the Duc de St Simon wrote:

> Some time after, instead of following the system of Vauban, and reducing the imposts fresh ones were added. Who would have said to the Marshal that all his labours for the relief of the people of France would lead to new imposts, more harsh, more permanent, and more heavy than he protested against?[25]

Despite this, it does not seem very certain that Vauban's proposal, in fact, led to higher taxes, as it is more likely that the voracious demands of continuous war demanded them.

The Duke of Marlborough took the field in 1706, with more optimism than the year before. He had made it plain to the States-General in The Hague that he would no longer campaign under such restrictions as he had met the previous year. The Dutch quickly transferred the more awkward of their generals and the civilian Field Deputies that accompanied the army elsewhere. The Duke was concerned that the French commander, Marshal Villeroi, would avoid battle once more, using the river lines of Brabant to shield his army's movements. What became apparent was that Louis XIV, concerned to bring the Allies to the negotiating table ready to agree terms for a good peace, had issued instructions to his field commanders to go on the offensive every-where. They were to show his opponents that the martial vigour of France was undiminished. As a result, on Sunday 23 May 1706, Marlborough found that Villeroi's freshly reinforced army was deploying for battle across his own line of march on the low ridge line at Ramillies to the south-east of Brussels. Neither commander had a significant superiority in numbers, but in the space of a short afternoon and evening Marlborough smashed the French army and their Bavarian allies to pieces, and sent the survivors fleeing for their lives, abandoning all their guns and gear. The fine French army was no longer a military formation but a mob, and the Marshal, although graciously received by Louis XIV on his return to Versailles, never held a field command again. 'We have now,' Marlborough wrote, 'the whole summer before us, and with the blessing of God, I shall make the best use of it.'[26]

The Duke's rapid pursuit of the French soon brought under his control such important towns as Louvain, Malines, Brussels, Oudenarde and Courtrai, almost without another shot being fired. The privileges of the 'Joyous Entry of Brabant', granted by Philip II of Spain during the Dutch War of Inde-pendence, was reaffirmed by Marlborough to reassure the citizenry of these regions that their interests would be protected. Antwerp, hugely important as a port and financial centre, submitted after only a token show of resistance by the Spanish Governor, the Marquis of Tarazena, who soon saw where his own interests lay in the new circumstances after the recent battle. The port and town of Ostend proved to be a more formidable task, and had to be ruined by bombardment before the garrison surrendered.

The pace that Marlborough set in this astonishingly successful campaign is indicated by the speed with which most of the fortresses were taken. In Louvain, Brussels and Malines bewilderment at the outcome of the battle was the key factor. In the case of Antwerp it was the Governor's lack of spirit that ensured rapid success, but at Ostend the Duke's troops suffered casualties at a rate that could probably have been avoided, had it been seen as desirable to adopt the more measured approach preferred by enlightened engineers such as Vauban. These are often hard decisions, and Marlborough certainly did not treat the lives of his men lightly, but the military objective was always the key factor. He had a golden opportunity to seize the Spanish Netherlands from the French, and would not waste a day in making the most of it. The Duke's soldiers stood on the very border of northern France in the autumn, an extraordinary situation, with little to hold them back except those troops who had been hastily scraped together to begin to rebuild the French army in the region. The morale of these troops, in the circumstances, was a little fragile. Of rather more effectiveness for France's security was Vauban's thick fortress belt, prepared with such care over the previous thirty-five years, and now called into service under the most severe and testing conditions. If Vauban's handiwork held in the face of Marlborough's victorious army, then so would France.

The Duc de Vendôme, an uncouth but bruisingly confident commander, was brought from northern Italy to try to restore French fortunes in the Low Countries. He manoeuvred with the depleted forces at his disposal to try to save Menin, but Louis XIV urged caution when dealing with Marlborough: 'The Duke,' the King wrote, 'only attacks places to entice you thither.'[27] This was not quite so, as the capture of French-held fortresses would provide valuable prizes on their own account. The capture of a fortress like Menin or Ath was a significant military achievement, and Marlborough could not lightly think of moving on towards the French border, however tempting that prospect would be, while powerful garrisons were left behind to threaten his own lines of communications and supply reaching back into southern Holland. On the other hand, if the French army commander could be tempted far enough forward to try to save the threatened fortresses, Marlborough might be able to force another catastrophic defeat, this time on Vendôme, a defeat from which France could hardly hope to recover. Much as he regretted the loss of the fortresses, Louis XIV knew that the threadbare field army that had been hastily assembled after the recent defeat, and whose confidence was now so fragile, was irreplaceable. Vendôme was to manoeuvre to cover France's border, but he was not to accept battle.

The French defeat at Ramillies was not the only concern, dreadful though it was. The performance of Louis XIV's commanders had been noticeably lacking for some time, and the victorious age of the great men – Turenne, Luxembourg and Condé – was clearly long past. The quality of the French infantry gave increasing concern also. Their bravery was seldom in doubt; although morale might be shaky there were plenty of examples of valour and selfless courage to be found, even in dire defeat. The constant state of warfare, a state that was increasingly unfunded as it went along, had its effect as did the frequent misemployment of trained soldiers as labourers and pioneers. There was malpractice in the recruitment methods necessary to fill depleted ranks, and often this was no better than simply impressing men from the locally-raised militia:

> These were unmarried youths from each parish [. . .] You have never seen greater sorrow in the parishes given the treatment that is meted out to them on the march. They are bound and chained like veritable animals and treated even more shamefully [. . .] It is this which empties the parishes of young men and which makes cultivation difficult.[28]

Vauban wrote an essay on 'Means to Improve our Troops and to Establish a Perpetual and Very Excellent Infantry. France is a country as exhausted in terms of men as of money, to a point of being in real danger [. . .] the soldiers of today being badly organized and undisciplined. They are all pressed men.'[29] He went on to say that the ranks were kept filled only by deceit and bad practice: 'What sense of duty can one expect of soldiers collected from any-where with nothing in their hearts except the vexation resulting from being forced into a life for which they have no inclination?' Vauban was clearly struck by the slack attitude and conduct of many officers: 'Each waits for his duty to come to him, and no one puts himself forward, nor is there any urge to excel.' He was, of course, yearning for the old days of professional soldiering, of times when men volunteered for service in the ranks, with the valid search in the profession of arms for valour and personal reputation; the age in which he had learned his trade and established his own reputation and the grounds for his fortune. This was now remote from the implacable demands of constant and unwinnable war, with ruthless methods having to be employed to maintain armies on a huge and constant scale.

A widower now, bowed with age and increasingly unwell and out of Royal favour, Marshal Vauban was nonetheless given the task, with a modest detach-ment of troops, to secure the Channel coast around the fortified places of Nieuport, Dunkirk, Bergues, Calais and Gravelines. This was a distinctly secondary, but not unimportant task that he performed rather well: 'Your name alone,' Michel de Chamillart wrote in a charming if overly effusive letter, 'will impress the enemy.'[30] In the extreme distress in which France was placed after the disaster at Ramillies, Vauban was a safe pair of hands, providing a measure of security for the left flank of the French posture in the Southern Netherlands; he had, however, been relegated to a sideshow and would receive little support, as everything else for France in the Low Countries fell to pieces. In the event, it proved that Marlborough's attentions, for the time being, were elsewhere which was perhaps just as well.

Vauban had tried to hamper the Allied operations against Ostend by constructing an entrenched camp near to Dunkirk, and the presence of French troops there was certainly a distraction for the Allied commanders. Plans to create the entrenched camp, to guard at relatively little cost against an Allied thrust along the line of the coast, were prepared by Vauban, but Versailles was frustratingly slow to approve them:

> I have suggested [...] that to put the entrenched camp in a defensible state, ready for occupation by troops this autumn or next, we take part of the money allotted to complete the jetties, money which cannot be spent this year [...] I get no kind of answers at all.[31]

Approval came through at last, and Vauban again applied his failing strength with devotion. So well made was the camp that the surviving earthworks were even employed to good effect by French infantry during the Revolutionary War of the 1790s. Short of supplies and munitions for his troops, Vauban inspected the defences in the coastal region, and considered opening the sluice gates in order to create a water-obstacle to counter any Allied advance along the coast. The Duc de Vendôme would do so two years later, in a belated effort to halt the Siege of Lille. On this occasion in 1706 they were left undamaged, in part to protect the valuable crops that would otherwise be ruined before they could be harvested, but also because it was felt that the local peasants would try to sabotage the work anyway.

Meanwhile, Marlborough's triumphant campaign sped onwards. Menin was an important fortress that had been redesigned by Vauban with great care and at considerable expense. The 6,000-strong garrison was commanded by Comte Pierre de Caraman, a capable soldier and one of Vauban's pupils in the arts of military engineering and siegecraft. Entrenching began on 4 August 1706, and two weeks later the counter-scarp at the Porte d'Ypres was reached. A mine was blown, and breaching batteries established at close range. On 22 August Caraman agreed to a capitulation, and was permitted to march out with his troops, having been granted the honours of war. The Allies turned against Dendermonde, which at last fell despite extensive inundations, and this enabled the Allied supplies to come up by water along the River Dender so that the fortress of Ath was captured soon afterwards.

The Duc de Vendôme, despite great odds, had pulled together a defence of sorts for the French border. In poor health, Vauban was ailing, but just about able to hold secure the line of the coast, with little expression of encouragement and appreciation, in what remnants of the Spanish Netherlands were left in French hands. This was the last service that Vauban was able to do for his King, and he wearily wrote:

> I can do no more here, and the chills begin to attack me fiercely [...]
> I certainly did not seek this employment which I shall be well out of,
> old and infirm as I am. I have nevertheless performed my small
> duties as well as I could, and I scarcely think that anyone else would
> have done better.'[32]

Vauban doubted he was now able to carry out his duties adequately and he felt that others thought the same, but were hesitant to say so. Perhaps because of this, he would not be employed at the Siege of Turin, which failed disastrously in the autumn of 1706, under the inept command of Marshal la Feuillade, Michel de Chamillart's son-in-law, and Marshal Marsin (who was mortally wounded in the battle). Vauban did send notes of advice on the importance of strong and well-sited Lines of Circumvallation and Contravallation, but these seem to have been ignored. De Chamillart admitted to Vauban afterwards that his presence at the siege would have been invaluable and that his advice should have been taken, but by then it was all too late. Of course, it was widely known that the old soldier was out of favour, and his words carried less weight now and went unheeded. Vauban felt that it was necessary to dictate to his Secretary a summary of his services:

> I am now in the seventy-third year of my age, bearing the load of
> fifty-two years of service, and the extra load of fifty important sieges,
> and nearly forty years of incessant journeys to examine fortresses on
> the frontier which have cost me much suffering and fatigue, both of
> my mind and body, for winter and summer have been alike to me.[33]

On 6 November 1706, his request to be allowed to resign his command and retire from active service was granted, and he went to Paris to rest. Vauban wrote to an old friend, looking forward to happier times: 'You will doubtless do me the honour of coming to see me; I will do my best to welcome you as a good neighbour and as a comrade from the wars; and you may count on drinking your share of the best wine I have.'[34] Such a happy and convivial occasion proved to be too elusive.

A giant of the age, a man of well-established merit and with a fine reputation acknowledged by military men across Europe, Vauban passed from the active scene. A Decree of Council formally suppressed publication of the 'Proposal for a Dime Royal or Royal Tythe' on 24 March 1707, and Vauban took to his sickbed at his home in Paris the following day. On 27 March, he had revived a little and gave his confession, which was heard by a Dominican Friar who received a copy of the controversial book as a remembrance and keepsake. The King, on hearing the news of his ill health, relented the outwardly stern attitude towards his faltering servant, and sent his personal physician, Boudin, to attend at the sickbed, as if going to that of an old and valued retainer: 'The King ordered him to go at once, and spoke of M. de Vauban with much esteem and friendship.'[35]

Despite this rather grudging and belated care, Sébastien le Prestre, Seigneur de Vauban, Inspector-General of Fortifications, Marshal of France, died of pneumonia in his town house in the Rue St Vincent at 1.45am, on Wednesday 30 March 1707. Just his son-in-law, Jacques de Mesrigny, was at his bedside. Louis XIV undoubtedly seemed, at the end, to regret the recent neglect of his old and indefatigable servant, writing of the death of Vauban that 'I have lost a man very devoted to my person and to the state.'[36] Still, there was to be no great funeral, no grand oration read by a Marshal of France, no parade to mark the passing of the soldier whose services for his country demanded so much notice. Just a small private affair was held, with representatives from neither the Court nor the army present. Embroiled in a war it could not win, France was on the rack, but this official neglect was astonishing. After a simple absolution in the Church of Saint Roche, Vauban's body was taken back home to Bazoches and laid to rest on 16 April in the family vault in the chapel of St Sébastien, in the church of Saint-Léger-de-Foucheret, where he had been christened seventy years before. In contrast to the official indifference, many hundreds of local people thronged the church and the churchyard to be present at the interment of this great man.

The passing of so great a soldier of France was not to go entirely unnoticed, however, for the Academy of Sciences in Paris held a Mass, said for the repose of Vauban's soul, and which was attended by eighty-six eminent men of letters. The distinguished writer, Bovier de Fontenelle, the Secretary of the Academy, produced a nicely-measured eulogy. By instinct a man of considerable personal reserve, even aloofness, Fontenelle did not hold back when speaking of Vauban:

> His nature was like a happy instinct, so prompt that it forestalled argument. He despised that superficial politeness, which pleases the world and which often hides so much harshness, but his kindness, his humanity, his liberality made for him another and rarer politeness which was entirely of his heart.[37]

Louis XIV had lost yet one more of that great rank of servants who had served him so well over the years, men on whom he placed such reliance, and on whose efforts much of his long run of successes had been built. Vauban was dead, but he left behind him the fortress belt, the Fence of Iron, on which he had lavished such time, attention and care, to fight his battles *in absentia*. That his efforts had been worthwhile and would repay his Royal master's trust and phenomenal outlay of money many times over, would soon be seen.

Chapter 9

The Greatest of His Services

Marshal Vauban had died, and his like would not be seen again. Equally, he would not see his own monumental work, the fortified defence of France's northern border, succeed in unmistakeable fashion against the best and most sustained efforts of the leading military commanders of the generation. Darker times lay ahead for France and for Louis XIV, whose resources would at last run dry – the King had overreached himself and the capabilities, if not the courage, of his resilient people and was now facing defeat. The old Engineer was not there, but Louis XIV depended upon what Vauban had achieved now more than ever.

The campaign in 1707, by comparison with the glorious year for the Grand Alliance that had seen French defeat at both Ramillies and Turin, was a disappointing affair. Fleetingly, everything had appeared to be possible, and there was nothing that would be demanded which Louis XIV could refuse. This was a miscalculation of enormous proportions. The resources that France could deploy, while not inexhaustible, were deep both morally and physically, and the King and his field commanders showed resolve and resilience, despite such adversity. A campaign of manoeuvre in 1707, in a period of unseasonably bad weather in the Low Countries, saw Marlborough unable to pin down the French army long enough to bring on a general action. Their commander, the Duc de Vendôme, was like a fox, formidable when cornered and showing his teeth, but then slipping away.

On the Rhine and, most significantly, in Spain, the Allied commanders lost ground to their French opponents, and Marshal Villars took his cavalry on a grand raid, delving into those same German principalities that provided such excellent troops for the Grand Alliance. An attempt by Prince Eugène to capture the great naval base at Toulon in southern France miscarried badly, although the need to divert troops to the defence of the port prevented the French from making the most of their recent victory at Almanza in Spain. The Allied cause in that country never really recovered however, although the French were forced to beach or burn at anchor their Mediterranean Fleet in Toulon harbour to avoid its capture by Eugène.

To all parties involved, the cost of the war was increasingly burdensome. Many wondered whether it was capable at all of being won, for all the heartening successes of Marlborough and Eugène in battle, if Louis XIV and his grandson, Philip V, could not be brought to submit. In actual fact, the Grand Alliance had been found to have no plan in place to take full advantage of the victorious conquests of the Ramillies summer. Made greedy by success, the Allies carelessly added demand to demand to what they expected of the French King in return for peace. In this negligent way they made attaining that peace all but impossible, unless France should first be ruined. The Dutch, in particular, flushed with the apparent victory, demanded and were rather rashly promised by their partners in the Alliance a greatly enlarged barrier of fortress towns, which included such places as Ypres, Mauberge, Menin, Condé-sur-Escaut and even the citadel of Lille.

The Duc de Vendôme had built up the strength of his army along the border with the Spanish Netherlands to some 100,000 troops by the time of the opening of the spring campaign in 1708. The resources that France could still muster were evident, as was the resolve of Louis XIV and his generals when faced with apparently insurmountable difficulties. Marlborough by comparison could only deploy about 85,000 men, while his close friend and colleague, Prince Eugène, had 40,000 Imperial Austrian and German troops in the Moselle valley, facing a French army commanded by the Duke of Berwick. The Allied commanders had prepared a fresh plan which, in essence, was for Eugène to march north to combine forces with Marlborough, and to then over-whelm Vendôme's army before Berwick could arrive with his own reinforcements. The plan was rather obvious, and certainly not a secret to the French, but Berwick could not move to support Vendôme before Eugène set off for fear that the French position in the Moselle valley would be exposed. Eugène took rather longer than had been intended, but while preparations for all this were in progress, Vendôme moved forward from near to Mons to appear to threaten Brussels and Louvain. Marlborough manoeuvred to cover the two cities, and early in June Vendôme came to a halt near to Braine l'Alleude, as if foiled in his intentions. Both armies settled down to watch each other; the generals on each side taking the opportunity to review their troops while waiting for reinforcements to come from the Moselle, and there was a period of several weeks of relative and uneasy inaction.

The French commander, as it happened, had a promising plan of his own in mind, fully hatched and about to be put into dramatic effect. It had become known that the inhabitants of the Spanish Netherlands were resentful of oppressive Dutch taxation, which was in itself a product of the need for Holland to pay its now ruinous expenses in the war. Marlborough had been warned by the Comte de Merode-Westerloo that Ghent and Bruges were seething with popular discontent, and were accordingly at risk. The Duke instructed his garrison commanders throughout northern Flanders to be on the alert, but he appears not to have given enough weight to the warning received.

Early in July, the French army threw off its inaction and began to march to the westwards. Flying columns of hard-riding cavalry spurred to Ghent and Bruges, summoning the citizenry to return to their true allegiance to Philip V of Spain. The civic dignitaries in these towns did so with remarkable promptness, indicating a high degree of prior collusion, and the small Allied garrisons in both places were unable to prevent their occupation by the French. At a stroke, Marlborough had lost control of this important region; his conquests of 1706 had, at least in part, been swept away, and his communications through Ostend to southern England were put in peril. So too, in a very public way, was his carefully nurtured reputation also imperilled. The Duke had clearly been caught out by Vendôme, who had pulled off a very creditable coup in seizing the two towns. Marlborough, suffering with a migraine headache and a fever, was cast into a state of near despondency and took to his tent.

Prince Eugène, whose troops were now at last hurrying along the roads from the Moselle, arrived in Marlborough's camp just to the west of Brussels on 6 July 1708. He declared himself unmoved or downhearted by the supposed importance of Ghent and Bruges, insisting that what was most important was to bring the French field army to battle and defeat. With that accomplished, everything would fall into place once more. The Duke's spirits lifted under Eugène's invigorating energy, and by noon on 11 July, William Cadogan, Marlborough's Quartermaster-General was looking down from the high ground at Eename, near to Oudenarde. He had with him the 15,000-strong advance guard of the Allied army that was now hurrying along the roads to the battle. Just a few miles away, Vendôme's army was making its unhurried way across the River Scheldt at the small village of Gavre, preparing to take up a defensive position behind the wide water-obstacle from which they could both defy the Allies and cover their own fresh conquests in northern Flanders. Unaware until it was too late that Marlborough and Eugène were bearing down on him, Vendôme allowed his army that afternoon to drift into an unplanned infantry battle in close country alongside the Scheldt, and he suffered a heavy and humiliating defeat. All that could be done was to gather the battered remnants of the army behind the comforting protection of the Ghent-Bruges canal. From there Marlborough's supply lines could perhaps be interdicted and reinforcements be summoned, while Marshal Berwick brought his own troops northwards from the Moselle.

Marlborough, reinvigorated with his recent success, now prepared and put before his generals an audacious plan to advance on Paris and Versailles, leaving behind the dense fortress belt along France's northern border. This was thought to be too risky, and Prince Eugène, usually the most intrepid and audacious of commanders, thought the Duke's plan to be impractical, at least until Lille and perhaps also Ypres were safely in Allied hands. In this, he was probably right. Those fortresses were not mere stone piles to be ignored; each contained a garrison of seasoned troops commanded by officers of skill and bravery, and they could be counted on to wreak havoc in the rear areas and the supply lines and communication of the Allied armies, once they had plunged deep into northern France. These fortresses had to be occupied before any major advance forward from the border region was attempted. As this was so, Vauban's strategic plan created to defend France and impose a real delay on any attack from this quarter came into play. He had left the scene, and would not see his creation fulfil its intended role, but his Fence of Iron was, for the first and only time, to be put to a real and prolonged test at the hands of such peerless commanders as Marlborough and Eugène. If it held firm, then so too would France, and that was Vauban's most obvious and enduring legacy.

For all the dazzling moves of Marlborough, Eugène and their generals, and their skill in open battle, the 1708 campaign was brought to a halt while the huge siege train of the Allied army was brought forward to Lille from their depots around Brussels and Antwerp. All this mass of matériel, involving transport on hundreds of wagons and carts, had to be brought across the poor roads of the day before the siege operations could commence. Vendôme's position in northern Flanders, despite the enfeebled state of his army after the dramatic defeat at Oudenarde, maintained a firm grip on the valuable waterways in the region that would otherwise have been so useful in bringing these stores to the trenches in front of Lille. Vendôme and Berwick were not, however, able to prevent the gathering of vast quantity of stores and matériel ready for the siege, or intercept the huge convoys in which they were transported, despite several rather ill-coordinated attempts to do so.

The fortress of Lille was, however, not to be given up lightly. Elderly Marshal Boufflers, vigorous still and a close confidante of the King, was sent to take command of the garrison in the fortress, and the veteran soldier performed the arduous task with great skill. He had the valuable assistance of Puy de Vauban, who followed in his late uncle's footsteps as a skilled military engineer, and the Marquis de la Frequelière, the master exponent of aggressive artillery tactics. It was soon evident that Marlborough and Eugène had underestimated both the strength of the Lille defences, and the determination of Boufflers and his garrison to hold out: 'All of which made the Duke of Vendôme say that he did not think so wise a Captain as Prince Eugène would venture upon such an enterprise.'[1] Vendôme and Berwick (together with the Duke of Burgundy – the King's grandson and, nominally at least, the army commander in the Southern Netherlands), prowled around the besieging army, looking for but failing to find a weak spot at which they might strike.

Eugène commanded the operations in the trenches, and undertook a series of poorly prepared assaults that cost the Allied troops heavily for little gain. When Eugène's soldiers made an attack on the evening of 7 September, Boufflers's chief of artillery, de la Frequelière, defied conventional wisdom (and one of Vauban's own strictures), and packed the Covered Way with men closely supported by batteries that would usually have been pulled back to avoid capture if the attack had proved to be successful:

> There was a mistaken opinion abroad in the army, to the effect that once a covered way was assaulted it was bound to fall. Boufflers was even presented with a memorandum of the late Marshal Vauban concerning the defence of fortresses, from which it appears that he was in favour of abandoning the salient angles of the covered way, and retaining the troops only in the re-entrant place of arms, where they would be afforded more protection.[2]

Boufflers, remembering the Siege of Namur thirteen years before and the casualties that had been inflicted on the attackers, held on to the Covered Way as long as he could. In the event, the attack went in and was a complete and dreadful failure for Eugène, with hundreds of his stormers killed and wounded and left strewn thickly all over the glacis.

Only when Eugène was wounded in the forehead by a musket ball in one of these ill-prepared attempts, of a kind that would certainly have been roundly condemned by Vauban, did Marlborough have to take a hand in the actual siege operations. Eugène was fortunate that the stiffened brim of his hat took the main force of the ball, but he was concussed and had to take to his bed. The Duke was alarmed to find that the stocks of ammunition for the battering guns were too low for sustained firing and much of the powder was of inferior quality. Also, the breaching batteries were poorly sited, being at too great a distance for real effect, and the engineers had seriously underestimated the strength of the defences. Marlborough applied his usual energy to putting matters right, but his campaign was becoming bogged down, while the French field army had been allowed a breathing space in which to recover to some measure both in morale and in strength of numbers.

Vendôme turned his attention to Marlborough's lines of supply, and moved his army into position to blockade the crossings of the River Scheldt, cutting the Allied troops off from Brussels and southern Holland. Marlborough switched his main line of supply northwards to Ostend, and despite French efforts to flood the region by opening the sluice gates along the rivers and canals, the vital supply convoys were forced through in the teeth of fierce opposition. At Wynendale, late in September 1708, Comte de la Motte, the French commander in Bruges tried and failed, with heavy casualties, to intercept the laden wagons as they hurried south to supply the Allied guns in the breaching batteries before Lille.

Boufflers had withdrawn his troops into the citadel of Lille once a breach was made in the main defences of the city, but all attempts at relief having failed, he had to submit on 9 December 1708. His defence of the city had tied Marlborough and Eugène down for over three precious months and was recognized as a significant achievement. Even though the loss of such an important place was greatly regretted in Versailles, Louis XIV was aware what had been achieved by such a defence, and he wrote with warm praise for the Marshal on his conduct:

> I cannot sufficiently praise your vigour, and the pertinacity of the troops under your command. To the very end they have backed up your courage and zeal. I have given the senior officers special proofs of my satisfaction with the manner in which they have defended the town. You are to assure them, and the whole of the garrison, that I have every reason to be satisfied with them. You are to report to me as soon as you have made the necessary arrangements for the troops. I hope these will not detain you, and that I shall have the satisfaction of telling you myself that this latest proof you have given of your devotion to my service strengthens the sentiments of respect and friendship which I have for you.[3]

With Lille city and citadel safely in his hands, Marlborough moved quickly northwards to retake Ghent and Bruges. Despite deteriorating weather, the Ghent-Bruges canal was forced and the recapture of the two towns soon accomplished. By the turn of the year, the French had withdrawn all their garrisons from northern Flanders. What Marlborough had achieved after Ramillies in 1706, and had two years later seemed lost, had in large part been recovered. The Duke could look forward to his next campaign, and to breaking even deeper into the French fortress belt, and onwards to the open fields beyond.

Negotiations for peace had been in progress for some time, and almost succeeded, with a general expectation emerging that the war was over. The talks irretrievably broke down over important details, and the fighting had to go on. Due to this and the delay in closing the previous year's campaign, the opposing armies took to the field rather later in 1709 than would usually have been the case. So, in midsummer, Marlborough and Eugène moved forward with their combined armies to challenge their opponents once more. The French field army was now under command of the very able Claude-Louis-Hector, Marshal Villars; Vendôme having been removed from command once his mishandling of the battle at Oudenarde became fully known in Versailles. He was packed off to campaign in Spain, where he did rather well before dying of food poisoning in 1711.

France was in great difficulties after eight years of ruinous and largely unsuccessful war. The previous winter had been particularly severe, and the nation's fortunes were at a low ebb. Louis XIV's Treasury was empty, the harvest had failed again, and there was near starvation with bread riots in some districts. The French armies were threadbare, the soldiers could hardly be fed, let alone clothed, paid and equipped; they had been fought to a standstill in the north, and only in Spain had some significant and lasting success been achieved. The main peril for France remained in the north, laid open to attack by Marlborough and Eugène. Vauban's fortress belt, the only real and viable defence left, had to continue to take and withstand their repeated blows. 'Let us show our enemies,' Louis XIV wrote to his provincial Governors, having to explain why the war with all its privations was to continue, 'that we are still not sunk so low, but that we can force upon them such a peace, that shall be consistent with our honour and with the good of Europe.'[4]

Given the poor state of his troops and with clear instructions not to risk an open battle, Marshal Villars had little choice but to hold firmly to the defensive. He manoeuvred with the protection of the fortress belt to shield his lack of strength, but was particularly concerned that his opponents would move against his left flank, possibly towards Aire and St-Venant on the Lys river, and then towards the Channel ports. Villars moved troops that way, but this was a misjudgement as the Allies laid siege to Tournai instead. So mistaken had Villars been, that he had actually drawn troops out of the garrison in Tournai to reinforce his field army, just before Prince Eugène appeared before the fortress on 27 June. Louis XIV wrote to the Marshal with congratulations that, after all their successes of the previous year, the Allied commanders had been tied down to conducting just a single siege. This had a rather hollow ring, for Villars had without doubt been outwitted by Marlborough at this stage of the campaign. In any case, Tournai was an undeniably important place, the loss of which would open up extensive parts of the second line of the 'Fence of Iron' – Bouchain, Cambrai, Douai – to attack.

Marlborough wrote, with what proved to be rather rash optimism, that he hoped the Siege of Tournai would not detain his army for long: 'They expected our going to another place, so that they have not half the troops in the town they should have to defend themselves well.'[5] The Duke was sadly mistaken in this, for the fortress was of the most formidable and modern design, with a large citadel, constructed under the supervision of one of Vauban's most adept pupils. The garrison, commanded by the Marquis de Surville-Hautfois, although at 7,000-strong rather lacking in numbers after Villars had taken so many away to bolster the strength of his army, was composed of well-trained veterans. They soon proved to have a particular skill at the techniques of mining and counter-mining. It was clear that their opponents lacked such skills; the siege operations edged forward slowly in gruelling conditions, and Marlborough's engineers appeared to be fumbling in unfamiliar and daunting conditions.

The Allied soldiers in the trenches, suffering from bad weather and flooding, had a particular horror of the deadly miners and their subterranean activities. 'Of a sudden they sprang a mine,' an Allied soldier wrote, 'which made the earth tremble under us [...] which stifled great numbers of our men.'[6] Strenuous efforts were made to curtail the French operations underground, with countermines being dug and hand-to-hand fighting erupting in the dark and wet tunnels whenever the opposing sides came upon each other. Sharpened spades were the weapons of choice; useful for digging or hacking as occasion demanded, handier than a sword and more effective in the damp air than a pistol. 'We are preparing,' Marlborough wrote wearily in one of his dispatches to London, 'to roll bombs into these galleries to dislodge them.'[7]

The town of Tournai was given up on 27 July, and the Marquis de Surville-Hautfois withdrew the surviving troops of his garrison into the citadel, a massively strong structure with five bastions. The French soldiers referred to the fighting as an infernal labyrinth as the mining and counter-mining operations grew in scale, but they were gradually worn down, although imposing a suitably heavy cost. Captain Robert Parker wrote that, 'Our approaches against this citadel were carried out mostly underground [...] in them our men and the enemy frequently met and fought it out with sword and pistol.'[8] At last, on 31 August, Marlborough could write: 'We were agreeably surprised at six o'clock this morning by the enemy's beating the chamade and desiring to capitulate.'[9] Over 3,000 of the French garrison had become casualties, while the success had cost Marlborough and Eugène some 5,000 killed and wounded. This gruelling effort, severe enough in itself, was followed almost immediately afterwards by the grim battle in the woods at Malplaquet on 11 September 1709.

As soon as the capitulation of the Tournai citadel was certain, the Allied army had moved quickly to screen the small French garrison of St-Ghislain, and the more substantial nearby fortress of Mons. Marshal Villars was now urged by Louis XIV to save the place: 'Should Mons follow on the fate of Tournai our case is undone, [...] the cost is not to be considered, the salvation of France is at stake.'[10] This was a clear and very different instruction for Villars; he was to go out and give battle, and this suited his aggressive inclinations very well. In a day of heavy fighting and ghastly casualties in tangled close country and wooded copses at Malplaquet, the French army was driven from the field of battle. Villars got his troops away in fairly good order, although he was gravely wounded in the process and lost thirty-six guns. Louis XIV was assured that a victory had been achieved in the woods that day, but this was not so, as the Allied Siege of Mons went on almost without missing a beat. The exhausted French field army could do no more than stand by, manoeuvre ineffectively to threaten the Allied lines of supply, and watch events unfold. Some French reinforcements did manage to slip into the fortress, and Mons was well-garrisoned under the able command of the Marquis de Grimaldi. Nonetheless, the place fell to Marlborough and Eugène six weeks later. So confident were the Allied commanders of the relative impotency of the French army, that the troops were not even put to the trouble of constructing the usual Lines of Circumvallation and Contravallation.

The year 1710 found France weakened, but still resolute. Louis XIV's field commanders, aware of the risk of confronting the Allies in open battle, prudently kept within their defensive lines, which still added significant strength to the formal fortresses of Vauban's 'Fence of Iron'. Not only had the Allied commanders the task to capture those fortresses, but they had also to try to entice the French field army into a position to be confronted and defeated. The French commanders were made cautious by experience and on the whole they were able to read Marlborough's intentions very well. They would give up fortresses as necessary, but at a coldly measured pace, and without seriously challenging the Duke's army in open battle. Louis XIV would not allow the field army to be risked at any cost, so the French garrisons were required to do their duty; they were intended to be expendable, each fulfilling their purpose by extracting a suitable price for their eventual submission.

The Duke of Marlborough, spurred on by the need to demonstrate the vitality of the Allied war effort and to confound his own critics and opponents, continued to drive his army at Vauban's fortress belt during 1710. His tactical successes in this hard and gruelling campaign were numerous, with important places such as Aire and St-Venant on the Lys river being taken, but only after hard fighting. Béthune was captured, after the garrison put up a stiff resistance. Vauban's nephew, Lieutenant General Puy de Vauban, was the Governor of Béthune, although the garrison was commanded by an Irish officer, Major General Michael Roth. Douai also fell, 'In which was a garrison of 10,000 troops [...] the works were strong, and a great many of them, and well stored with all manner of necessaries.'[11] Each submission gradually but certainly eroded France's defences. This success was only had, however, with heavy casualties. At Aire in particular, in appallingly wet weather, Marlborough's soldiers suffered badly in the trenches as the French garrison commander, the Marquis de Goesbriand, grimly held out. This defence was the best, as the Duke admitted with grudging admiration for the conduct of the French garrison, adding that as the siege guns could not be dragged out of their muddy battery positions, they may as well go on firing. When Aire capitulated on 9 November and the campaign for the year came to a close, Marlborough could count his losses at nearly 20,000 killed or wounded, with many more languishing sick in hospital, compared with the French total of casualties at just over 6,000. A truly terrible toll had been paid for limited gains, demonstrating plainly the ability of well-handled defences to inflict disproportionately heavy casualties upon an attacker who had not the patience, aptitude or available time to reduce fortifications with true and careful method. Had Vauban been there, it seems certain that he would not have approved of the Duke's tactics at this point in the war.

Marlborough embarked upon his final campaign in 1711 with no very high hopes. Enmeshed in the 'Fence of Iron', his army had struggled for two years to break free and get into the open country beyond. The Duke's influence was failing in London, and few now thought that he could succeed in winning the war for the throne in Madrid by battering his way through the fortified belt along France's northern border. Marshal Villars, on the other hand, could afford to bide his time, stay carefully within lines of defences, and wait for Marlborough's tenure as commander of the Allied field armies to slowly but certainly come to an end. Prince Eugène was away on the Rhine with the Imperial troops, while the succession to the throne in Vienna was settled, and Marlborough once more lacked superiority in numbers. Nonetheless, the Duke formed an imaginative plan to seize the strong French fortress of Bouchain, sitting at the confluence of the Escaut and Sensée rivers. Success there should, with good fortune, lay open the road to Cambrai and beyond.

Marshal Villars, deploying superior strength now that Eugène's troops were elsewhere, could manoeuvre fairly comfortably to foil Marlborough's moves, wherever he might choose to strike. One potentially weak spot, however, was at Arleux on the Sensée river, where the causeway leading from Douai southwards crossed the river. The crossing-point was defended by a small French-held fort and in July 1711, Marlborough sent a strong detachment to seize the place. This was accomplished without very much fighting, but the Duke then left the captured fort in the hands of an inadequate garrison. This may have been done on purpose, although Marlborough's inclination would not be to needlessly imperil the lives of his men. Villars promptly counter-attacked and retook the weakly-held post, and then had the fort demolished, not wanting further wasteful skirmishing and distractions well away from the main area of threat. The Allied army was gathering to the west, apparently readying itself for a major assault on the French lines near to Arras, so that all attention was on that quarter.

Early on 4 August, having drawn his opponents' attention away to the west, Marlborough set his troops marching quickly eastwards through the summer night, towards the now undefended crossing-place at Arleux. Villars spotted the deception soon enough and also had his regiments on the road, but however much he pushed his men he was an hour too late, and by early afternoon on 5 August, the Allied army was in place south of the river and preparing to invest Bouchain. Villars took up a position in Bourlon Wood, and could do little more than to stand by with his army and watch, and manoeuvre without a great deal of success as it proved, to drive Marlborough away from the fortress.

Marlborough's Siege of Bouchain was an epic operation carried out with great skill. The Duke held off the numerically superior French army, which was actually in close communication with the garrison along a muddy farm-track known as the 'cow-path'. Villars put his troops into a secure entrenched camp, of a kind greatly favoured by Vauban for such occasions. He even managed to establish batteries with which to bombard a part of the Allied siege works, but this was all in vain. The very close proximity of a strong opposing army should normally have made any siege a broken-backed affair, but the Marshal was unable to raise the siege or save the fortress, and the garrison surrendered on 14 September. The Governor of Bouchain, the Marquis de Ravignan, wrote with some considerable bitterness at the failure of Villars to relieve the place. The Marshal had, de Ravignan claimed, 'Stood looking on with an army much superior to that of the Allies, and yet could suffer him to be drove to these dishonourable terms.'[12] The terms were that the garrison had to surrender as prisoners of war, 'at discretion', and accordingly were not eligible for parole unless it suited their captors. It did not suit Marlborough, and attempts by the French to claim, quite wrongly, they had been granted better terms and could march away with the honours of war were brushed aside.

The Duke of Marlborough's success at Bouchain, startling as it was, proved insufficient to save him, and on 31 December 1711 he was dismissed from all official posts. He was held responsible for the failure of the Grand Alliance to decisively win the war for the throne of Spain, and for being unable to dictate whatever extreme terms it chose to put to the French King. Additional charges of maladministration and financial peculation were levelled against the Duke, but these proved to be groundless and malicious. Everything had seemed possible after the resounding successes of the summer of 1706, yet real victory had eluded the Grand Alliance. In part, this failure was due to the resilience of Louis XIV and his generals and armies, but also, and rather more evidently, it was because Marlborough, for all his tactical brilliance, had been unable to force his way through Vauban's thick fortress belt along France's northern border. The Fence of Iron had held firm, when little else had done so. The subsequent successes for reinvigorated French armies in the two years following Marlborough's dismissal were such that under the inspired leadership of the now lame Marshal Villars, many of the Vauban-designed fortresses that had been lost to the Allies in the years since Ramillies were retaken.

Two years after Marlborough's dismissal, the war that had been fought to see who would be King of Spain came to a tired end. A French prince sat in some security on the throne in Madrid, although Spain had lost her possessions in Italy and the southern Netherlands, which went to Austria. In the process, France's northern border was, arguably, made less secure than before the war began, and Vauban's fortresses assumed renewed importance. France was also weakened by the incessant demands of constant and lengthy wars on Louis XIV's Treasury, which inevitably translated into higher taxation. On the other hand, the southern border along the Pyrenees at least had the protection of a friendly power, Spain, across which any invaders must make their laborious way before French territory could be invaded.

Chapter 10

Engraved on the Soil

More than any other military man, Marshal Vauban laid the foundation stones, almost literally, for the shape of how the French would defend their heartland until well into the twentieth century. The concern to establish and maintain security, particularly in the north, was obvious. In the late seventeenth century, Louis XIV had been determined to do what was possible to put an end to the potential menace from the north, and to a degree this endeavour was successful, once Vauban's massive belt of strengthened fortresses was in place. Still, it had proved to be a close thing, in the awful years for France immediately after the victories achieved by the Duke of Marlborough at Ramillies and Oudenarde. The Fence of Iron created by Vauban had held, but had been under great strain. Paris, in particular, remained vulnerable, as the events of 1814, 1870, 1914 and 1940 would repeatedly demonstrate in dramatic fashion.

The comparative vulnerability of north-eastern France, along the winding border with the Southern (Spanish or Austrian) Netherlands, or Belgium as it became, dictated that formal defensive arrangements, on a huge scale, had to be put in place. This work by Vauban quite naturally attracts the most attention. Elsewhere, on the Atlantic and Mediterranean coasts the sea was the protector, but the French were never able to establish and maintain naval supremacy for long. In consequence France was always vulnerable to a naval or amphibious strike, and Vauban left a number of small, but very attractively designed maritime forts dotting the French coastline, many of which still exist in various stages of repair today. In the south and east of France massive mountain ranges served as comforting natural obstacles, together with wide areas of broken country. The passes and defiles through these barriers had to be guarded too, and innovative designs for hard to access places were required. Accordingly, on the line of the Pyrenees border with Spain, in the mountainous Alps to the south-east, and along the course of the difficult country of the Upper and Middle Rhine, it was necessary to fortify many places. The natural obstacles, while formidable in comparison with those on the comparatively open border with the Southern Netherlands, were not adequate on their own account to deter a resolute invader.

War came again to many of Vauban's fortresses throughout the eighteenth century, most evidently along the French border with the Austrian Netherlands. Dutch-held Menin, Knokke and Furnes in West Flanders were overwhelmed by the French in 1744, while the Battle of Fontenoy was fought the following year in a futile attempt to raise the French Siege of Tournai. The engagement at Laffeldt in July 1747 led to a failed French attempt to seize Maastricht, although they succeeded the next year. Most of the fortresses in the Austrian Netherlands were 'slighted', or ruined, to render them militarily useless during 1781–1783, once they were vacated by the Dutch troops who had been holding them as part of their cherished Barrier against French aggression. The work of slighting was done on the orders of the Austrian Emperor Joseph II, who wished to avoid giving the impression of being an oppressor, but their loss was regretted on the outbreak of a civil insurrection later in that decade, once the local privileges and rights enjoyed under the terms of the 'Joyous Entry of Brabant' (confirmed after the Duke of Marlborough's victory at Ramillies in 1706), were carelessly repudiated by Vienna. The fortresses ruined in this way would have had an undoubted value, also, during the confused campaigning of the French Revolutionary Wars. At the same time, the vulnerable new French republic of the 1790s, beset by enemies on several fronts, largely survived because of the robustness of the surviving fortress belt along the border with the Austrian Netherlands. All but forgotten cavalry battles at places like Beaumont (on the site of the August 1914 Le Cateau battle), and Willems were fought in 1794 to try to secure possession of fortresses such as Cambrai and Tournai.[1]

Many of those fortresses designed, built, repaired and improved during Vauban's prolific career subsequently fell victim to town planning, industrial and residential development, and the demands of motor traffic management. Some of his works, mostly the smaller forts, have unsurprisingly gone altogether. Calais, Dunkirk, Verdun, Lille and many other places would come to bear little resemblance to what Vauban had envisaged. It is hardly surprising that many of his fortresses, where they have not been demolished or built over, are no longer in the state that the great military engineer intended. Some were enlarged and modernized to cope with improved weaponry and proved their worth to one degree or another in succeeding wars, while others were even demolished in Vauban's own lifetime, as either too expensive to maintain or no longer required for the cohesive defence of France. Pressure of expanding urban population is nothing new, and even in Vauban's day towns would spread themselves out over formal fortifications if the Governor was not strict about such things. Those suburbs would routinely have to be levelled in the event that a besieging army approached.

It is fortunate that a good number of Vauban's works still remain, some in remarkably fine condition such as the fortresses of Mont-Louis, Château Queyras, Briançon, Neuf-Brisach, Besançon and Le Quesnoy, while others survive in part at Lille, Arras, Calais and Gravelines for example. The sturdy fortress of Mauberge on the Sambre river lasted until 1958, when all but the northern portion was demolished. The rot had actually set in some years before, and Reginald Blomfield, architect designer of the Menin Gate, wrote of his dismay when he visited the town in the 1930s and found that workmen were busily knocking gaps in the walls to make way for a ring road. Traffic congestion is plainly not a new problem. However, that portion of the defences at Mauberge that remains does give a good indication of the sheer majesty of Vauban's work there, with a wide ditch and commanding flanking bastions. The massive Mons Gate, luckily, still stands intact.

International interest in the state of repair of Vauban fortifications is considerable, and in 2008 twelve of his fortresses, or the surviving parts in some cases, were listed as UNESCO World Heritage Sites – Arras citadel, Besançon in the great horseshoe-shaped loop of the River Doubs, Blaye, lofty Briançon, Camaret sur Mer, Longwy, Mont-Dauphin with its bastions of the curious locally-quarried pink stone, Mont-Louis, symmetrical Neuf-Brisach, Saint Martin de Ré, Saint Vaast la Hogue and Villefranche de Conflent. UNESCO declared that:

> The work of Vauban constitutes a major contribution to universal military architecture. It crystallizes earlier strategic theories into a rational system of fortifications based on a concrete relationship to territory [...] Vauban's work bears witness to the peak of classic bastioned fortifications [...] Vauban's work illustrates a significant period in human history. It is the work of the mind applied to military strategy, architecture and construction.[2]

Allowing for the slightly overblown language, the safe future of these places, at least, should be secure, and there is every hope that the list of sites, adding to the preservation and protection already increasingly provided by the French themselves, will be extended in time.

The fine city of Lille has spread its suburbs wide over the centuries, and most of Vauban's fortifications, which defied the Duke of Marlborough and Prince Eugène so well in 1708, were demolished in the process. However, the huge citadel is still intact, and may not have been listed as a World Heritage Site as it is still in daily use as a military base, although the same could also be said of Mont-Louis. The Lille citadel gives us a glimpse of the scale and might of Vauban's plans for the defence of the place, which took six years of hard work to accomplish between 1668–1674. The Paris Gate, designed and constructed under the supervision of Simon Vollant, also survives, but it is the massive citadel that catches and holds the attention. This structure covers some 300 acres of ground, and took 60,000,000 bricks in its construction. Six substantial bastions are protected by ravelins and a wide moat encircles the whole; although this is mostly dried up now, it was originally fed by the waters of the River Deule (Dyle). The main gateway into the citadel is surmounted by the carved Arms of France, and gives access to the interior, aptly named the Quartier Boufflers after the valiant defender of 1708. As it is still in military use, access to the general public is restricted to pre-arranged guided tours.

The charming small town of Le Quesnoy, between the Escaut and Sambre rivers not far from Valenciennes and Cambrai, has Vauban-built fortifications that have survived almost intact. Captured for France by Marshal Turenne in 1654, the town formally became a French possession five years later. Vauban, given the task to repair and improve the existing damaged fortifications, based his work upon eight substantial bastions (stirringly named Caesar, Royal, Imperial, Green, Soyez, Guard, Castle and Saint Martin). Water defences were added by damming the nearby Rhônelle stream, to form the Horse-shoe Lake and the Red-Bridge Lake. However, when war resumed in 1673, a part of the new fortifications between the Caesar and Royal bastions collapsed into the ditch, and it was fortunate for the garrison that the Spanish besiegers were not in a position to take advantage of the accident. The contractor responsible for the faulty work was quite rightly ordered to make good the damage at his own expense.[3]

Le Quesnoy was spared many of the horrors of war over the years, partly no doubt due to the strength of the town's defences, although it was obliged by circumstances to submit on several occasions. It was only on 4 November 1918 that the town was taken 'sword in hand' when two battalions of the New Zealand Division, part of General Byng's 3rd British Army, stormed the town in a general assault using scaling ladders placed between the Guard and Saint Martin bastions:

> Le Quesnoy was completely isolated, but its ancient walls and gateways were strongly defended by all modern devices [...] the enemy refused to surrender [...] a forlorn hope of New Zealanders then approached with scaling ladders in the good old style and swarmed up the walls. There was only one ladder and three successive walls, but in some miraculous fashion the whole of the 4th New Zealanders battalion reached the top of the rampart with the loss of one man.[4]

An extraordinary military exploit, achieved at slight cost, and very much in the old style even when faced with machine guns. The morale of the German garrison was, however, decidedly shaky by this time, and this no doubt played a part in the affair.

Well to the east, on the River Rhine, the city of Strasbourg, the 'strongest barrier for France', had been captured in 1681, and Vauban completely re-designed the fortress and citadel. The whole of the old town was encircled by a new Trace, featuring bastions and two crown-works, with outer-works and flooded obstacle defences. Fort Kehl, facing Strasbourg from across the river, was also rebuilt with four massive bastions and a huge hornwork, but this was given up by France under treaty terms. The Vauban fortifications at Stras-bourg were largely destroyed in the Franco-Prussian War of 1870 and 1871, and those that remained, and those at Metz, were extensively redesigned and rebuilt by the Germans in the years leading up to 1914.

The defences of Verdun had been remodelled by Vauban, although the full extent of his plans were not put into effect until many years after his death. Shielded by other fortresses (Neuf-Brisach, Sedan, Montmédy and Metz), Verdun seemed to take second place when it came to finding the funds for building works. The eventually rebuilt fortress had a powerful citadel and extensive bastions. Captured by the Prussians in 1792, it was evacuated by them after the French success at the Battle of Valmy. During the Franco-Prussian War, Verdun had the distinction of being the last French-held for-tress in the north-east to submit. Despite shell damage during the First World War, many of the Vauban-designed fortifications remain today in generally good condition, although those to the north-east of the town have largely been lost to urban sprawl.

Vauban's reach was wide, and in the south-west his fortress at Bayonne occupied Wellington's attention, being blockaded for some weeks in 1814 as preparations were made to invade southern France. It was also the scene of a famous and bloody sortie by the French garrison. In the north, Péronne, standing on the River Cologne and improved by Vauban in the 1680s, was stormed by the light companies of Wellington's Foot Guards on 26 June 1815, as the Duke's army advanced on Paris after the Allied victory at Waterloo. The fortress fared rather better in 1870 when it held out during thirteen days of Prussian bombardment. The last formal siege of a fortress of Vauban's design was probably that of Antwerp in 1832, when the Dutch had to submit to a French siege in the fighting that led to the establishment of Belgium's inde-pendence from Holland.

As time passed, methods also moved on, and the intricacies of Vauban's designs inevitably underwent changes in the face of the accelerating pace of military and technological innovation. Improved gunnery, in particular, proved to be the significant factor:

> On all sides, in fact, bastions and curtains [walls] hornworks and
> half-moons, are passing out of use, and out of existence. A few green

mounds on the hill-tops to right and left are all that meets the eye of the traveller [...] The revolution which has taken place in artillery has give the chief stimulus to these changes in fortification [...] The perfection to which Vauban brought the art of attack, and the consequent abridgement of sieges, had left many men in the eighteenth century to cast about for some fresh means of restoring the balance between besieged and besieger.[5]

The city of Paris would get its own system of defence in time. The distinguished engineer Baron François-Nicholas-Benoit Haxo had fresh and supposedly more radical ideas on what was required or demanded by military innovations. A system of forts to defend Paris, a cherished project of Vauban but not one that found favour with Louis XIV, was put into effect in the 1840s, but sadly proved to be not that effective when put to the test. That such a defensive ring should have been so delayed in the making, given that France was one of the most politically centralized countries in Europe at the time, is surprising.

Baron Haxo, who had enjoyed a successful career as an engineer officer in Napoleon's army, laid out the defences for Paris during the Waterloo campaign, but the Emperor was sent on his way to St-Helena and they were not tested. Haxo's services were retained after the Bourbon restoration, and he was made Inspector-General of Fortifications. In this capacity he rebuilt or added to a number of Vauban-designed fortresses, including those at Belfort, Grenoble, Besançon and Saint Omer, in order to give the defences greater depth and to keep an attacker at arm's length. One difficulty was the sheer numbers of artillery pieces that were required to equip the enlarged forts being constructed, but this demand was met by the mass production of cheap iron guns rather than the more expensive bronze models. This expedient had originally been suggested by Vauban in the late seventeenth century, when drawing up his own plans to fortify Paris.

French officers took the field in 1870 provided with maps of Germany, but not of France, so great was their misplaced confidence of early success. Instead, the German armies sliced through the fortified belt to elbow one French army into the illusory security of the fortress of Metz, while trapping another army around Sedan. The ailing Emperor Napoleon III was taken prisoner and the Germans came to the environs of Paris, where the ring of defences were enough in the face of explosive shellfire to prevent a swift capitulation, but the French politicians and their generals proved to be less robust. This German success did not, however, seriously dent the perceived value of formal defences. The war was rightly recognized to have been lost due to lack of preparation, insufficient numbers, and overconfident but lacklustre French generalship when faced with more dynamic opponents who could mobilize more quickly and efficiently. When that opponent was armed with superior modern artillery, as the Prussians and their allies undeniably were, even brave infantry armed with the wickedly deadly French Chassepot rifle could not prevail.

The fortress of Belfort, completed to Vauban's design in 1700, had been progressively extended and improved, with a number of judiciously placed outworks to keep any attacker at a safe distance. Baron Haxo added a series of detached forts – la Justice, la Miotte, and du Vallon – between 1818 and 1830, and these proved their worth in 1870, when the garrison of the fortress under the command of Colonel Deufort-Rochereau successfully resisted a Prussian attack despite a heavy and prolonged bombardment:

> The long and successful resistance of Belfort was mainly due to the bold maintenance of outlying positions, the favouring of an active defence, the occupation of valuable sites [...] rifled guns had made it all important to enlarge the circle of defences.[6]

To address the perceived command shortcomings, and perhaps to expunge the deeply-felt shame of the calamity of 1870 and 1871, the French espoused the aggressive tactical doctrine of 'Offense a Outrance', known as Plan XVII. At the same time, the fortification belt in north and eastern France was greatly enhanced in the years leading up to the First World War. The Secretary to the French Committee of Defence was General Raymond Serre de Rivière, an engineer by training. He developed a scheme that would revise and correct, as he saw it, the main flaw in the designs of Vauban and Haxo, which had been fit for their time, but by the late nineteenth century could not face the added power of modern weaponry. In particular, he would develop Haxo's theme of extending the detached works outwards to distance enemy guns from the heart of any fortress. De Rivière, in practice, copied much from Vauban's 'Fence of Iron' to produce what the Germans in turn dubbed a 'Barrier of Fire'. He drew up a vast plan, which was indeed put into effect, for four groups of major fortresses all constructed to a modern plan and design – Group Jura was based on Besançon, Group Vosges based on Belfort and Épinal, Group Meuse based on Verdun and Toul, and Group North based on Montmédy but stretching to the Channel coast at Dunkirk, and taking in Mauberge and Lille.

An astonishing total of 166 forts was constructed under de Rivière's ambitious plans, with forty-three smaller works. Notable amongst these in military history were Fort Douamont and Fort Vaux, just to the north of Verdun, where they would play a role in the long and grinding battle fought there in 1916. Fort Douamont was noticeably of a polygonal plan that would have been instantly recognized by Vauban. De Rivière also laid a trap for any unwary invader, by leaving relatively unguarded a gap some 40 miles wide between Épinal and Toul on the Moselle. Any army that ventured into this 'Troue de Charmes' would find itself attacked and enveloped by mobile French forces operating against their exposed flanks; at least, that was the plan, but it never came to be put into effect.

This philosophy for formal systems of defence, fit for modern times, was mirrored in Belgium. Notwithstanding the pious hopes reposed in that country's guarantee of neutrality, strong and well-designed fortresses were constructed around Liège and Namur, and at Antwerp. These places proved their worth and put up a tough defence in 1914, barring the path of the advancing German armies who were instructed to respect Dutch neutrality, and in consequence had to advance on a narrowed front between the border of Holland at Maastricht in the north, and the wooded country of the Ardennes.

The unexpectedly effective defence by the Belgian garrisons slowed the German advance and bought precious time for the French and British armies which, having advanced into Belgium, found themselves in danger of being enveloped. They had to withdraw by forced marches to find ground on which to make a proper stand; in this case it would be well to the south on the Marne river, and so to regain their tactical poise. It is almost certain that, without the benefit afforded by the French defence of Mauberge, Cambrai (where French Territorials put in a gallant delaying action on 26 August in support of Smith-Dorrien's corps at Le Cateau), and other places, this withdrawal from contact would not have succeeded, with incalculable consequences for the subsequent course of the war. The commander of the German 1st Army, General von Kluck, hoped at one point to elbow the British Expeditionary Force into the beckoning shelter of the defences of the formidable fortress of Mauberge, where they could be corralled and isolated: 'The place loomed out of the fog of war like a safe and welcome haven.'[7] To his great credit, the British commander, Field Marshal Sir John French, resisted the temptation to take this beguilingly prudent course, and kept his tired troops in the field, where they could play their part in throwing the Germans back and away from the outskirts of Paris.

The garrison in Mauberge actually held out against the attack of the German IX Corps for a very creditable twelve days (Vauban had captured the place in less), until 7 September 1914. The Vauban-designed fortress at Longwy did just as well, resisting for a fortnight, while the French garrison in Montmédy, yet another of his works, attempted a desperate breakout after a most resolute defence, but were caught and overwhelmed piecemeal on the road.

The fact remained that the fortress belt constructed at such enormous effort and cost under de Rivière's plans did not secure France's northern and eastern border regions from invasion and occupation. Salvation for the Allies in 1914 came from mobile field armies manoeuvring for position – even though that position proved to be the long line of trenches of the Western Front. Still, had de Rivière replicated Vauban's 'Fence of Iron' with a stout belt of modern fortresses stretching along the length of the Belgian border, everything might have been so different, with a German advance into northern France either impossible or of a more limited nature. As they would discover at Verdun, the large German howitzers and mighty mortars would strain to reduce modern cupolas comprising belts of steel with layers of sand interspersed between to absorb the impact of the projectiles.[8]

As von Moltke's flawed and cropped version of the ambitious Schlieffen Plan swept through Belgium that baking hot summer of 1914, the remnant of King Albert's Belgian army fell back from their defence of Antwerp. His engineers opened up the sluices at Nieuport and Dixmude, which had been constructed by Vauban, and so flooding wide areas of the surrounding country-side to impede the German advance: 'The engineers of 1914 made use of the sluices built by the engineers of 1680.'[9] In just the same way, Vauban had considered this step in 1706 after Ramillies, and the Duc de Vendôme's troops had actually opened these same devices in 1708, when attempting to interrupt the supply lines from Ostend leading southwards to the Duke of Marl-borough's army in the trenches before Lille.

The terrible grinding Battle of Verdun in 1916, with the German and French army commanders each attempting to annihilate their opponent's army with artillery, understandably became the stuff of legend in France. Verdun was held, at great cost, and the enduring power of formal defences even when confronted by modern artillery appeared to have been restated. Lessons were learned, and the art of manoeuvre was neglected, particularly so when the Nivelle offensive of the following year, a much-heralded attempt to regain the initiative with a sudden breakthrough and resumption of a war of movement, failed so disastrously. The subsequent British 'all-arms' advances late in 1918, with French and American support, as the war drew to a close, offered a new lesson on how to conduct these things. If those lessons were learned, it was apparent that it was the German General Staff that did so.

The appalling casualties suffered between 1914 and 1918 had an inevitable effect on all the participants during the post-war period. For France, with huge numbers of men killed, missing and mutilated, a constant and corrosive reminder of the danger that might one day come again from across the Rhine, there was a powerful desire to ensure that such a national calamity could never happen again. 'The waves of shock produced by the war losses went beyond the 1,040,000 disabled, the 630,000 widows, and the 719,000 orphans [. . .] The 1,400,000 dead constituted only a part of the population loss.'[10] This was both understandable and logical, as France was demographically weakened, and the current birth rate would not replenish the population. The percipient and principal concern for the French was that Germany would recover more quickly and to a greater degree, and become a threat once more.

In the 1920s the decision was taken to entrust the defence of France's eastern border to a massive newly-fortified line, on a far greater and more complex scale than those fortresses that had existed previously, and one that would forever shelter France and her weakened and wearied people. It was almost as if Vauban's dusty old files had been extracted from the archives, brushed off, and brought into life in modern form as a kind of twentieth-century 'Fence of Iron'. On this occasion, unlike in the late seventeenth century, iron, or at least steel, really would be used in the construction of French defences, rather than just earth, brick and stone. These modern works became known as the Maginot Line, being named after the French Minister of War at the time, Andre Maginot, himself a veteran of the Great War. After the calamity of 1940 this would become a term that was synonymous with defeat and defeatism, an apparently futile attempt to wage defensive war in the old static way, failing when faced with the aggressive type of mobile warfare developed by the Germans. Static defences were held to have failed and the concept was therefore considered flawed, but this point of view was only valid if it were assumed that a defence would always hold out, no matter what should occur. Military engineers like Vauban always knew that this was not so. Fixed defences supported mobile field armies, and in turn they had to be supported by field armies, or they would both be lost.

There had been a natural desire amongst French politicians to limit costs, and they were apparently blind to the lack of protection for France that the neutral territory of Belgium and Luxembourg offered, despite the obvious and presumably fairly fresh lessons of 1914. The designers and builders of the Maginot Line stopped short when they could have continued their work both into the woodlands of the Ardennes, and along the Meuse, Escaut and Lys rivers to the beaches of the Channel coast. This would, of course, have risked souring relations between Paris and Brussels, as the Belgians would have been left on the wrong, exposed, side of the line. Marshal Ferdinand Foch's own plan for joint Franco-Belgian action to counter any renewed German aggression had come to nothing: 'The Belgians refused to commit themselves to joint action in response to every violation of the Versailles Treaty.'[11] Whether such offence to Belgian sensibilities would have been a greater evil that what actually befell in May 1940, with the Maginot Line left massive but bypassed, is hard to judge.

Between 1936 and 1940, defences of a basic and infinitely second-rate nature were constructed to partially close the gap along the Belgian border, but when put to the test they proved inadequate. As a result, the Maginot Line failed in its role, not by having inferior installations or feeble-hearted garrisons, for that was far from the case where it had been constructed properly, but because it was a fixed obstacle that could be avoided with just a little imagination and daring. German armies thrusting confidently through the woods of the Ardennes, ground that was deemed to be unsuitable for the movement of armour, were not foreseen or catered for. They then moved on across the River Meuse into the Low Countries, using dynamic command and control procedures that left their opponents, French, Belgian and British, at a standstill, and with their makeshift defences overwhelmed or disregarded.

On those occasions when the Germans actually attacked the more formidable installations in the Maginot Line, they failed, with just one notable exception. That was not all, for the Vauban-designed citadel at Lille defied German attacks, both on land and from the air, from 28 May to 1 June. The doughty garrison, drawn from the 1st French Army, were eventually permitted to submit and evacuate the place with the full honours of war, and were saluted by their German opponents for their valour, in an echo of older, possibly more gracious if no less deadly times.[12] Time was bought in this way for the establishment of the Dunkirk perimeter, while the grim defence of the citadel of Calais by British and French units that same month is a well-known epic, gaining yet more valuable time for the evacuation.

Formal defences, massive and static, acquired a certain air of quaintness throughout much of the twentieth century, a time of brilliant technical innovation and rapid movement both on land and in the air. However, the ability of French and British armies to fight on the Marne and so save Paris in 1914, rested in large part upon the delay imposed on the Germans by a stout defence of the Belgian defences on the Meuse. Vauban fortresses such as Mauberge, Montmédy and Longwy also played their part. Twenty-six years later, had the defenders of Lille and Calais in 1940 been less resolute, and the Anglo-French evacuation from the beaches at Dunkirk not succeeded, the likely impact on the future of Europe would have been dire. As always, fortresses could not hold indefinitely, but invaluably, they bought time for others, the classic role for which they were intended.

It is understandable that Marshal Vauban should best be remembered as the designer and builder of fortresses, in what became an instantly recognizable mould. Generations of engineers and military students and theorists studied his life, works and reputation as a prime example of all that was best and most logical in the complex art of military engineering. It is easy to see why this was so, for his range of fortress construction was visible and strikingly impressive, and remains so. The most urgent peril always lay in the north and north-east, and to the task of establishing a proper defence there, Louis XIV summoned the energies and the genius of Vauban. His imprint on the physical fabric of

France, that which is 'engraved on the soil', is unmatched and to be found in the numerous fortresses he designed and built, many of which still remain to be seen and enjoyed.

The Fence of Iron created by Vauban in the north was only once put to a real test. Between 1706 and 1711, the Duke of Marlborough led huge armies in a sustained campaign to penetrate the fortress belt, and break through into the open fields of France. The formal defence established by Vauban played a key role in saving France from defeat at the hands of Marlborough and his colleagues in those incredible years of peril. The Fence of Iron was, therefore, just as effective as it was always intended to be. This was a significant achievement, perhaps the greatest of all, although Vauban did not live to see it, having died in 1707, at a moment of low ebb for France's fortunes, and just before his life's work would be tested. At that moment, even the most ardent optimist in Versailles, or pessimist elsewhere, could have foreseen the overall satisfactory result which was achieved by France at the Treaty of Utrecht in 1713.

For all that, it should be remembered that Vauban devoted at least as much thought and attention to the most effective way to attack fortresses without incurring heavy casualties. His concern for the life and wellbeing of the common soldier was evident throughout his career. The model timetable he devised for a formal siege of a fortress, giving forty-eight days for the conduct of such operations, allowing for a certain element of lost time, was a fine example of logic and reason itself. It was, however, intended as a guide; not an instruction to be followed slavishly.

Much, of course, would depend upon the ready supply and maintenance of the besieging army, but any competent commanding general should be able to ensure this, otherwise the operation was foolhardy and not to be attempted at all. The almost inevitable effect of this model timetable, however, was that it could be followed too closely. A cautious besieging commander had a reason not to push the pace too fast but to follow the timetable, regardless of wider considerations; the garrison commander, having lasted the forty-eight days set down, had a sound reason, if not actually an excuse, to give up without further ado, honour having been seen to be satisfied. Both commanders, it could be argued, would have achieved their objective – the defender had bought time, irreplaceable and precious, while the attacker had secured a valuable fortress – good reputations could be secured in this way. Clearly not all sieges went to the model timetable, and garrisons could be surprised, or besiegers foiled and forced to give up the attempt. Impetuous and ill-prepared assaults and grim last-stand defences to the death were not unknown, with all the associated horrors of corpse-strewn defences, sacked towns, and butchered garrisons and civilians that would ensue. Such excesses were greatly deplored by Vauban and, mercifully, they had become the exception rather than the rule by the close of the seventeenth century.

Vauban was certainly an innovator in the method to be employed in attacking fortresses, and his teachings on the subject were, and are, valued and studied. This study is repaid, as the Engineer's concern to protect the common soldier from needless slaughter in ill-prepared attacks is very clear. Still, this is not how he is best remembered. There have been few soldiers quite like Sébastien le Prestre, Seigneur de Vauban. He was, of course, a man of his own time, acknowledging his own place in a layered society, just a provincial nobody able to wield little family influence. He rose by his own efforts to enjoy the patronage, almost the friendship, of the Sun King and the powerful men he used as Ministers for War. By virtue of his many abilities, energy and diligence, Vauban also became a man of influence, rank and reputation, addressed by Louis XIV as 'Cousin', as were all Marshals of France. Vauban also had a keen sense of duty, both to his King and to the State, but also to the soldiers he led, for his concern for their welfare was noticeable. He had sound judgement, and a keen sense of human value and weakness; he was ambitious also, of course, and no worse for that, for his ambition led to the better security of France at a crucial time. Of perhaps most significance for one who is engraved on the soil of his homeland, no one held John Churchill, 1st Duke of Marlborough, more in check when he was in his dangerous prime and so very close to bringing France low, than the late Marshal Vauban, and that says a very great deal.

Appendix I

Vauban's Siege Operations

Vauban would not have command of the covering army in a siege; as an engineer that was not his role, but would be in control of the siege operations and in the trenches. Such was his skill and acknowledged reputation, however, that commanding generals, even when Louis XIV or his son or grandson was nominally in command, would often defer to Vauban's directions.

1652   Sainte Meinhould (Lorraine), (as a Frondist)

1653   Sainte Meinhould (as a Royalist), under Marquis de Feuquières
       Saint Ghislain
       Landrecies, under Marshal de la Ferte
       Condé-sur-Escaut

1654   Stenay (Lorraine), under the Chevalier de Clerville
       Clermont en Argonne, under de la Ferte

1655   Landrecies, under de la Ferte and Marshal Turenne
       Condé-sur-Escaut
       Saint Ghislain

1656   Valenciennes, under de la Ferte and Turenne

1657   Montmédy, under de la Ferte
       Mardyk, under Turenne

1658   Gravelines, under de la Ferte and Turenne
       Ypres
       Oudenarde

1667   Tournai, under Louis XIV
       Douai
       Lille

1672   Orsoy, under Louis XIV
       Duisburg

1673   Maastricht, under Louis XIV

1674   Besançon, under Louis XIV

1675   Dole

1676   Oudenarde, under Marshal Luxembourg

1676	Condé-sur-Escaut, under Louis XIV
	Bouchain
	Aire sur Lys and Fort François, under Marshal d'Humières
1677	Cambrai, under Louis XIV
	Valenciennes
	Saint Ghislain, under d'Humières
1678	Ypres, under Louis XIV
	Ghent
1683	Courtrai, under d'Humières
1684	Luxembourg, under Marshal de Crequi
1688	Phillipsburg, under the Grand Dauphin
	Mannheim
	Frankentall
1691	Mons, under Louis XIV
1692	Namur, under Louis XIV
1693	Charleroi, under Marshal Luxembourg
1697	Ath, under Marshal Catinat
1703	Alt-Brisach, under the Duke of Burgundy

See: Rebellieau, A., *Vauban*, 1963, Appendix; also Lepage, P., *Vauban and the French Military under Louis XIV*, 2009; and Halevy, D., *Vauban, Builder of Fortresses*, 1924, for slightly different lists. *See also* the superb IGN Map Series 10, No. 923, Scale 1:100,000, 'La France de Vauban', 2009.

Appendix II

Vauban's Fortresses

The tally of fortresses that Vauban designed, adapted and improved, built and improved, or prepared plans for, is startlingly lengthy, with more than 180 that can be listed. They vary considerably in size, of course, from massive citadels to small maritime forts, and also in the scope of the engineering project that Vauban planned, instigated or actually undertook. Sources also vary quite considerably, and so prolific was his career that it is difficult to list a definitive or complete itinerary or programme of his work. A number of the smaller forts were intended to be a part of larger defensive arrangements as at St-Malo, and are sometimes grouped together and described as such. Much of the actual work was undertaken by Vauban's engineers, although to his design and plans, and a great deal of the construction was not complete, or in some cases not completed, until well after his death.

The fortresses that comprised Vauban's 'Fence of Iron' are shown in italics. Many of the fortifications remain in a good state of preservation in whole or at least part, while some have survived in merely fragmentary or limited form, and others have gone altogether. The relative value of each site, either as an example of Vauban's work, or of the theory and practice of the period, is a highly subjective judgement. No attempt has been made to indicate the present state of preservation but *see* Faucherre, N., *Les Sites de Vauban*, 2007 for most interesting comments on this point (below).

Abbéville

Aire sur la Lys

Alés

Ambleteuse

Antibes

Antwerp

Arras

Ath (Belgium)

Auxonne

Avesnes

Bapaume

Bayonne

Bazoches

Belfort

Bellegarde

Belle-Île en Mer (La Palais)

Berg op Zoom (Holland)

Bergues

Besançon

Béthune

Bitche

Blamont

Blaye (near Bordeaux)

Bordeaux

Bouchain
Bouillon (Belgium)
Boulogne
Brest
Briançon
Brisach (Alt)
Brisach (Neuf) (Germany)
Brouage (near Rochefort)
Calais
Camaret sur Mer
Cambrai
Cancale
Cannes (Île de Letins)
Carantec (Fort)
Casale (Italy)
Castelana
Cette
Charente
Charleroi (Belgium)
Charlesville
Château
Château Belin
Château d'Oleron
Château Queyras
Cherbourg
Clermont-en-Argonne
Col de Nice
Collioure
Colmar les Alpes
Concarneau
Condé-sur-Escaut
Courtrai (Belgium)
Dieppe
Dinant
Dole
Douai
Doullens
Dunkirk
Eisensheim
Embrun
Entrevaux

Exilles (Italy)
Fenestrelles
Fort Barraux (near Grenoble)
Fort Cezon
Fort Chapus
Fort Chandane
Fort de Bouc
Fort de Joux
Fort de Fouras
Fort de la Pres
Fort l'Écluse (near Geneva)
Fort la Latte
Fort le Socoa
Fort les Bains
Fort Louis
Fort Lupin (Saint Nazaire)
Fort Medoc
Fort Pate
Fouras
Freiburg (Germany)
Fuernes/Vuernes
Gap
Givet (Fort de Charlemont)
Granville
Gravelines
Grenoble
Guise
Hoedic
Huningue
Île d'Aix
Île de Ré (Sablenceaux)
Île d'Oleron
Île Houat
Kehl (Germany)
Knokke
La Fère
La Latte (Cape Frehel)
Landau
Landrecies
Landskron (near Basle)
Langres

La Prée
La Rade (Île d'Aix)
La Rochelle
Le Havre
Le Quesnoy
Lichtenbourg
Lille
Longwy
Luxembourg
Maastricht (Holland)
Mardyk
Marienbourg
Marsal (near Nancy)
Marseilles
Martray (Fort)
Mauberge
Menin (Belgium)
Metz
Mézières
Mons (Belgium)
Mont–Brezille
Mont–Dauphin
Mont–Louis
Montmédy
Montreuil sur Mer
Mont–Royal
Mouzon
Namur (Belgium)
Nancy
Navarreux
Nice
Nieuport
Nimes
Oudenarde (Belgium)
Péronne
Perpignan
Petit-Pierre (Vosges)
Phalsbourg
Philippeville
Phillipsburg (Germany)
Pignerole (Italy)

Pontarlier
Port en Bassin
Port Louis
Port Vendres
Prats de Mollo
Rochefort
Rocroi
Rosas
Roscanval
Saarlouis
Saint Paul de Vence (Cannes)
Salins les Bains
Salses
Sedan
Selestadt Sete (near Montpellier)
Seyne les Alpes
Sisteron
Socoa
St-Hippolyte (near Nimes)
St-Jean-Pied-de-Port
St-Louis (Fort)
St-Malo
St-Martin-de-Ré
Ste-Menehould
St-Omer
St-Quentin
St-Tropez
St-Vaast-la-Hogue
St-Venant
St-Vincent-les-Forts
Stenay
Strasbourg
Tareau (Carantec)
Thionville
Toul
Toulon
Tournai (Belgium)
Trarbach
Turin
Valenciennes
Verceil (Italy)

Verdun	Villefranche sur Mer (Nice)
Villefranche de Conflent	*Ypres* (Belgium)

See the very valuable *Les Sites Vauban, par Nicholas Faucherre*, listed in Montsaigeon, G., *Les Voyages de Vauban*, 2007, for interesting additional comments and notes on the list. Also, Griffiths, P., *The Vauban Fortifications of France*, 2006, Blomfield, R., *Sébastien le Prestre de Vauban, 1633–1707*, 1938, and IGN Map Series 10, No. 923, 1:100,000 scale, 'La France de Vauban', 2009.

Appendix III

Vauban's Idle Thoughts

The Great French Engineer devoted much time and thought to the social issues of his day, and set out his thoughts on a wide range of subjects in a series of well-argued papers. Vauban's own handwriting was apparently very bad, as Minister for War, Louvois, complained on a number of occasions, so the 'Idle Thoughts' were presumably dictated to Vauban's long-suffering secretary. They were intended to be notes to stimulate further thought and, perhaps, discussion. The range of subjects that caught his interest included the better use of waterways for transportation in times of peace and war, improved agriculture, growth of population and overpopulation, the planting and populating of French colonies overseas, their defence and means of remitting produce and precious metals back to France. Most controversially, (his urging that Huguenots be permitted to return to France having been ignored by Louis XIV), he suggested radical reform for the taxation system, and the publication of his text on 'A Proposal for a Royal Tythe' incurred Royal displeasure. The *Idle Thoughts of Monsieur de Vauban; a collection of Several Memoirs in His Manner on Different Subjects*[1] fell into the following broad categories:

- The Attack and Defence of Fortified Places.
- The Re-organisation of the French Army.
- Methods of Construction.
- Rural Life.
- The Colonies and the Navy.
- Political Mémoires.
- Rivers and Canals.
- Description and Numbers of the Nation.
- Various Thoughts, amongst which was an outline proposal for the establishment of an aristocracy based, not upon the fortunate accident of good birth, but upon merit – 'The Ideal of a Perfect Aristocracy' – in modern terms, in effect, a kind of meritocracy.

Appendix IV

Glossary of Siege Terms

Abattis – Sharpened branches and stakes laid in the path of an opponent to impede their progress.

Approach – Communication trench leading forward to the Parallel trenches which encircle a besieged fortress.

Banquette – Raised platform of earth or timber inside a parapet, used as a firing platform by defenders.

Bastion – Four-sided defensive work protruding from the salient angle of polygonal defensive works, able to provide flanking defensive fire.

Bastioned tower – Masonry two-tiered structure with casemates for artillery, and a flat roof on which guns could also be sited.

Battery – Emplacement of cannon and mortars.

Bonnet – Triangular work in front of the salient angle of a ravelin.

Breach – 'Practical breach' in formal defences which was capable of being mounted by a foot-soldier with both hands on his musket. The development of a breach indicated that the commander of a garrison should seek terms for a capitulation, rather than face a storm of the defences and the dire consequences that would follow.

Caltrop – Sharp iron spikes, scattered on the ground to impede the progress of both cavalry and infantry.

Camouflet – Defensive mine, designed to demolish an opponent's subterranean mining works.

Carcasse – Incendiary shell or bomb.

Casemates – Covered defensive chambers loopholed for muskets and with embrasures for artillery.

Cavalier – Earthwork, used in both defence and attack, raised to give a commanding field of observation and fire over opposing trenches.

Chamade – Drumbeat signal to indicate a desire to parley with an opponent.

Chemin de ronde – Path along the top of ramparts.

Chevaux de frise – Sharpened stakes and branches, driven into the ground to create an obstacle.

Circumvallation – Line of breastworks constructed by a besieging army, facing outwards from a fortress to guard against the approach of a relieving force.

Citadel – Heavily fortified heart of a fortress able to defend itself without outside assistance, and with a reduced garrison.

Coehorn – Small mortar used in siege works, named after the famed Dutch engineer, Meinheer van Coehorn.

Contravallation – Line of breastworks constructed by a besieging army, facing towards a fortress to guard against sorties by the garrison.

Counter-approach – Trench dug outwards from a fortress to combat the activities of besiegers.

Counter-guard – Protective work in advance of a bastion.

Counter-scarp – Slope on the outer edge of the ditch.

Covered Way – Infantry-held position running along on the rim of the counter-scarp.

Crochet – A secondary parallel in approach trenches.

Crown-work – Enlarged hornwork, with two bastioned fronts.

Curtain (Courtine) – Straight wall linking the flank of adjoining bastions.

Cuvette – Secondary trench sunk into the bed of a defensive ditch.

Defilade – Fire at the flank of an enemy, i.e. to take them in defilade (*see* **Enfilade**, below).

Demi-lune – 'Half-moon' position, a triangular detached work in the main defensive ditch.

Discretion (at) – Surrender without obtaining agreed terms in advance.

Ditch – Excavated obstacle around a fortress, formed when building up the earthworks; 'the first and the strongest defence', often filled with water.

Embrasure – Gap cut in defensive works to permit a soldier to fire through in relative safety.

Enfilade – To be fired at from a flank, i.e. to be enfiladed (*see* **Defilade**, above).

Entrenched camp – Secure base, able to provide security for a field army when attempting to halt or hinder the progress of a formal siege of a fortress.

Fascine – Tied-up bundle of sticks, used to fill an obstacle.

Fausse-Braye – Obsolete term, a low earth defensive bank, usually in a ditch at the foot of a main defensive wall.

Fougasse – Anti-personnel mine used in defences, often loaded with stones.

Gabion – Wicker basket filled with earth and stones, used to make quick temporary defences, or to protect an entrenchment from fire while still under construction.

Gallery – Widest kind of mining tunnel.

Glacis – Level ground sloping outwards away from the edge of the Covered Way.

Hornwork – Detached forward defensive work comprising two half-bastions (*see* **Crown-work**).

Lunette – Small ravelin placed in advance of the glacis.

Mantlet – Wheeled wooden screen used to protect the sappers as they worked.

Mine – Subterranean work to allow soldiers to get close to an opponent's defences (to undermine). Also, an explosive device laid underground.

Mortar – Artillery piece fired at a steep trajectory, able to search into dead ground with its fire: 'devilish, murderous, mischief-making engines' (John Evelyn). Also Coehorn, a small mortar.

Pallisades – Sharpened stakes planted hedge-like at the edge of the Covered Way to add to the defensive strength of the position. Expensive and time-consuming to make and liable to rotting, they would only be placed when a siege was imminent.

Parados – Rear-facing parapet.

Parallel – Trench dug around part of a fortress, usually one of three – 1st, 2nd and 3rd – at a generally uniform distance, to disguise from the garrison the exact point where the main blow would fall.

Parapet – Top of the defensive wall.

Perrier – Small mortar, intended to be used firing stones as an anti-personnel weapon.

Ravelin – Triangular defensive work, placed in advance of the curtain wall.

Redan – V-shaped defensive work, open at the rear.

Redoubt – Enclosed defensive work, usually square or rectangular.

Sap – Trench dug towards an opponent's defences, as in an Approach. The term 'sappers', often used for engineers, was originally applied to the men who dug the saps.

Scarp – Outer slope of a rampart.

Tenaillion – Minor defensive work to one side of a ravelin.

Trace – Plan view of a fortress (as in Trace Italienne).

Traverse – Earthwork set at right angles to the line of a trench or parapet, to limit the effect of enemy enfilade fire down the length of a trench.

Notes

Introduction

1. Chandler, D., *The Art of Warfare in the Age of Marlborough*, 1992, p. 272.
2. Halevy, D., *Vauban, Builder of Fortresses*, 1924, p. 9.
3. UNESCO World Heritage Sites Website, 2008.
4. Blaise François, Comte de Pagan (1604–1665). A soldier from the age of 12, and particularly gifted at the theory of siegecraft. Blinded in one eye by a musket ball at the Siege of Montauban in 1621, he lost the sight in the other while serving in Portugal twenty-three years later. His renowned work on siege warfare 'Les Fortifications du Comte de Pagan', was published in 1640, and was the alphabet and grammar for military engineers for many years. Pagan was primarily a theorist, unlike Vauban who was a working engineer and liked to be out on the ground seeing things for himself. The Chevalier de Ville (1596–1656) was also an influential writer; his work 'Fortifications' was published in 1629, and was reprinted many times. De Ville advocated simplicity in design, not only because this produced the most effective designs but it also saved labour and expense. He also favoured the increased introduction of ravelin outworks, forward defences placed in the defensive ditch in advance of bastions, together with the newly-introduced Dutch innovation the Hornwork (which in time expanded to become the massive fortification feature, the Crown-work, such a notable feature of fortification design in Vauban's time).
5. Vauban, S. (ed. Rothrock, G.), *A Manual of Siegecraft and Fortification*, 1969, p. 21.
6. Lloyd, E., *Vauban, Montalembert, Carnot: Engineer Studies*, 1887, p. 88.
7. Ostwald, J., *Vauban under Siege, Engineering Efficiency and martial vigour in the War of the Spanish Succession*, 2000, p. 3.
8. Halevy, p. 117.
9. Duffy, C., *Fire and Stone*, 1975, p. 96.
10. Blomfield, R., *Sébastien le Prestre de Vauban, 1633–1707*, 1938, p. 184.
11. Duffy, ibid.
12. Duffy, p. 147.
13. Halevy, p. 75.
14. Ibid., for interesting comments on the aging King's odd behaviour towards his Engineer-in-Chief.
15. Klopp, G. (ed.), *Vauban, la Pierre et la Plume*, 2009, p. 127.
16. Rebellieau, A., *Vauban*, 1962, p. 25.

Chapter 1: Fence of Iron

1. Lloyd, E., *Vauban, Montalembert, Carnot: Engineer Studies*, 1887, p. 60.
2. Holmes, R., *Fatal Avenue*, 1992, Introduction.
3. Hughes, J., *To the Maginot Line*, 1971, p. 69.
4. The term 'Pre-Carré', meaning perhaps a square or enclosed field, or quite possibly a duelling field, was first coined by Cardinal Richelieu when describing the heartland of France and the defensible borders that ought to be established for its security. It was a new concept of France as a whole entity set within its own naturally secure borders, and immune to external threats. Only later, when Vauban was hard at work to improve and strengthen the

fortresses on the borders newly-established by Louis XIV's conquests, was the term used to describe the double line of fortresses that were to hold France's northern borders in relative security. 'Fence of Iron' seems to be more apt.

5. The logic behind the defensive barrier designed and constructed by Vauban at the instruction of Louis XIV had curious parallels with that of 1920s France, faced with a war-ravaged male population of arms-bearing age, and reduced birthrate, and the prospect of a resurgent Germany. Louis XIV suffered from neither weakness, but was alert to the ever-present threat, as he saw it, of encirclement by a reinvigorated Habsburg Empire with Spain and Austria acting in unison. This was a threat that, with the added power of England and Holland, although with a divided and weakened Spain, took actual form in 1702. *See* Hughes, p. 201.

6. Ostwald, J., *Vauban Under Siege – Engineering Efficiency and Martial Vigour in the War of the Spanish Succession*, 2000, p. 5.

7. Langins, J., *Conserving the Enlightenment, French Military Engineering from Vauban to the Revolution*, 2004, p. 55.

8. Halevy, D., *Vauban, Builder of Fortresses*, 1924, p. 56.

9. Vauban, S. (ed. and tr., Rothrock, G.), *Manual of Siegecraft and Fortification*, 1969, p. 65.

Chapter 2: Siege Warfare

1. Lloyd, E., *Vauban Montalembert, Carnot, Engineer Studies*, 1887, p. 13.

2. Halevy, D., *Vauban, Builder of Fortresses*, 1924, p. 244.

3. Lloyd, p. 15.

4. The great range and destructive power of rifled artillery would cast a shadow over the value of formal geometric fortress design based on the Trace Italienne. They would remove forever the chance that the defender could outweigh the well-equipped attacker, but would not negate the concept of geometric fortress design entirely. The ever-present problems of adequate observation of fall of shot and the inherent robustness of fortress design in the most adverse circumstances would have enduring value, and be seen as late as May 1940 in the prolonged fighting for the Vauban-designed citadel of Lille. In addition, the necessity to remove all elements of dead ground, ground not covered by defensive fire and thus inviting and of value to an attacker, became an absolute requirement that was admirably served by such designs. The ability to cover dead ground with observation and fire was, and remains, a tactical imperative.

5. Chandler, D., *Marlborough as Military Commander*, 1974, p. 226.

6. Muller, J., *The Attac and Defence of Fortified Places*, 1757, p. vii.

7. The material expended by the French at the siege of Luxembourg in 1684 included, according to Vauban, 815,000 pounds of gunpowder, 75,000 pounds of slow-match, 52,500 round-shot, 5,500 explosive mortar bombs and 25,000 hand grenades. *See* Rennoldson, N., *Renaissance Military Texts, Volume I, Warfare in the Age of Louis XIV*, 2005, p. 5. Vauban's own estimate of the manpower required for the reduction of a major fortress was 32,000 infantry supported by 18,000 cavalry, with at least 10,000 pioneers and conscripted peasants to work on the siege trenches. *See* Chandler, D., *Blenheim Preparation*, 2004, p. 155.

8. Vauban, S. (ed. Rothrock, G.), *A Manual of Siegecraft and Fortification*, 1969, p. vii.

9. Duffy, C., *Siege Warfare in the Early Modern World, 1495–1660*, 1973, p. 93.

10. Duffy, C., *Fire & Stone*, 1975, p. 127.

11. Vauban, p. 30.

12. Duffy, p. 149.

13. Duffy, p. 153.

14. Falkner, J., *Marlborough's Sieges*, 2007, p. 23.
15. Duffy, *Siege Warfare in the Early Modern World, 1495–1660*, 1973, p. 93.
16. Vauban, p. 44.
17. Lloyd, p. 49.
18. Muller, p. 44.
19. Muller, p. 27. The surrender of Bouchain in 1711 led to an acrimonious exchange between the Duke of Marlborough and the French army commander, Marshal Villars, over whether or not the garrison had surrendered unconditionally, 'at the discretion' of the victors, or had submitted on agreed terms and should, as a result, be accorded the honours of war. Marlborough insisted that the former was the case, and that the garrison had surrendered without promise of special treatment. Despite the intervention of Louis XIV, who tried to browbeat the Duke with an insistence that the 'rules' in such cases be observed, Marlborough held firm, having assured himself just what the terms of submission had been, and so the garrison remained prisoners of war. These matters were taken very seriously, as reputations hung on the terms agreed: 'Everything agreed on should be looked upon as Sacred and Inviolable, and every word should be understood in its genuine sense without any forced construction.' *See* J. Muller, *The Attac and Defence of Fortified Places*, 1757, p. 203.
20. Duffy, *Fire & Stone*, p. 126.
21. Crichton, A. (ed.), *The Life and Diary of Lieutenant-Colonel J. Blackader*, 1824, p. 383.
22. Vauban, p. 54.
23. Lloyd, p. 187.
24. Falkner, p. 43.
25. Muller, p. 60.
26. Gunners in charge of the breaching batteries would not simply blaze away at the nearest fortification and hope to achieve their task by good fortune. Round-shot and gunpowder were expensive commodities and were generally used with restraint. Once the hard outer shell was broken open, the gunners would switch to explosive shell. The technique was to fire deliberately and with great care and employing reduced powder charges, so that the projectile would settle before exploding at the selected spot, with the intention to weaken the wall at that point so that it would collapse from below. This, it was hoped, would provide a convenient rubble-strewn slope, the ever sought-after 'practicable breach' up which the attackers could then scramble to gain access to the inner parts of the fortress. To go on firing with full charges was not only expensive in gunpowder, but compacted the damaged rubble without necessarily providing the slope of a practicable breach.
27. Lloyd, p. 185.
28. Reeve, J., *The Siege of Béthune, 1710*, JSHAR, 1985, p. 210.
29. Reeve, p. 206.
30. Reeve, ibid.

Chapter 3: A Typical Country Squire

1. Dates given do vary, but this is often due to the eleven days difference between the 'old' Julian and 'new' Gregorian calendars, both of which were in use at the time. So, the baptism of Vauban is generally acknowledged as 4 May 1630, but Hebbert and Rothrock in *Soldier of France*, for example, give the date as 15 May (p. 6). This neatly demonstrates the eleven days difference between the two systems.
2. Vauban's paternal great-grandfather, Emery le Prestre, was just a plain country notary or lawyer. However, he was able to purchase Burgundian noble rank, the fief of Champignoles,

with the title de Vauban in the parish of Bazoches in 1555, twenty-four years before such local arrangements were forbidden by central authority. There was a certain social stigma attached to such provincial acquired rank, perfectly valid though that rank might be, and the Duc de St Simon, an elegant and waspish adornment in Versailles society, later recalled that Vauban was 'A typical country squire of Burgundy' adding, rather meanly, that 'nothing could be shorter, newer, duller'. *See* Halevy, D., *Vauban, Builder of Fortresses*, 1924, pp. 12–14. The place of Vauban's birth was renamed in his honour on 7 December 1867, at the decree of the Emperor Napoleon III, to Saint Léger Vauban.

3. Ibid., pp. 12–13.
4. Kekewich, M. (ed.), *Prince and Peoples, France and the British Isles, 1620–1714*, 1994, p. 48.
5. Hebbert, F. and Rothrock, G., *Soldier of France, Sébastien le Prestre de Vauban*, 1990, p. 18.
6. Petrie, C., *Louis XIV*, 1938, p. 56.
7. Ibid., p. 70.
8. Duffy, C., *Siege Warfare in the Early Modern World, 1495–1660*, 1973, p. 139.
9. Duffy, C., *Fire and Stone*, 1975, p. 147.
10. Lloyd, E., *Vauban, Montalembert, Carnot: Engineer Studies*, 1887, p. 73.
11. Hebbert and Rothrock, p. 26.
12. Cronin, V., *Louis XIV*, 1964, p. 106.
13. Buckley, J., *Madame de Maintenon*, 2007, p. 230.
14. Blomfield, R., *Sébastien le Prestre de Vauban, 1633–1707*, 1938, p. 11.
15. Halevy, pp. 68–9.
16. Cronin, p. 253.
17. The roots of the accusation against Vauban, and the allegation of corruption, lay in his having signed off accounts concerned with the refortification of Brisach when he was called away at short notice to join the campaign in Flanders. Vauban apparently did not examine the documents, prepared by the Intendant of Alsace, Colbert de St Marc, in detail before adding his name – an undoubted error committed in haste. He was, however, found not to be a party to the embezzlement which was taking place amongst the contractors, and was cleared of blame. Minister Colbert (who was in something of a quandary, as a relative of Colbert de St Marc), appeared to doubt Vauban's account over the matter, but Minister for War Louvois did not, and his support lifted the Engineer out of suspicion. This was never forgotten by Vauban, and for all Louvois' domineering, sarcastic and hectoring manner the two men remained close colleagues. Louis XIV also took a keen interest in the affair, and in the explanations provided. In August 1671, he wrote at Louvois' suggestion to Vauban, that he was absolved of all the charges, and the papers on the matter were then returned to him for burning. *See also* Blomfield, p. 45, and Hebbert and Rothrock, p. 29.
18. Vauban's ambitions for the refortification of Dunkirk incorporated fortified jetties, built on the extensive and unstable sandbanks below the high-tide line. There was also an extensive protective opening leading from Dunkirk to the open sea where the entrance was doubly defended by large redoubts. 'An extraordinary work, built more than 500 Fathoms [about 3,000 feet] out to sea on a bank of shifting sand, which it was so to speak necessary to stabilize.' *See* Halevy, p. 60. Sluice gates would direct fresh water from the wet fields of Flanders to clear the harbour of silt. In many ways this was the project in which Vauban took most interest, because of the complexity of the task and the natural difficulties of the site. 'It is the greatest and finest scheme of fortification in the world [. . .] there is nothing that I have not measured at least twice.' *See* Halevy p. 27. His keen attention to anything that required notice can be seen in the employment of a mole-catcher, so that these little creatures should not damage the new embankments. The substantial fortifications of Dunkirk were to be

demolished under the terms of the Treaty of Utrecht, although the French took a remarkably long time to comply.

19. Lynn, J., *The French Wars, 1667–1714*, 2002, p. 16.

Chapter 4: The War of Devolution

1. Hebbert, F. and Rothrock, G., *Soldier of France, Sébastien le Prestre de Vauban*, 1990, p. 30.
2. Petrie, C., *Louis XIV*, 1938, p. 141.
3. Lynn, J., *The French Wars, 1662–1714*, 2002, p. 40.
4. Vauban, S. (ed. Rothrock, G.,), *Manual of Siegecraft and Fortification*, 1969, p. 47.
5. Ibid., pp. 166 and 172.
6. Hebbert and Rothrock, p. 31.
7. Halevy, D., *Vauban, Builder of Fortresses*, 1924, p. 25. *See also* Hebbert and Rothrock, p. 34.
8. Ibid.
9. Halevy, p. 32.
10. Ibid., p. 33. France and Imperial Austria eventually concluded a Partition Treaty, under which Spanish territories would be divided on an equitable basis once the invalid King Carlos II died, if he had no children, a circumstance which, given his reputed impotence and general lack of good health, seemed to be highly likely. In return, the Emperor was persuaded to remain neutral, for the time being, in the course of Louis XIV's series of wars with his near neighbours. This was a pragmatic solution to a thorny problem, but it was based on the easy assumption of lasting trust and goodwill on both sides, and almost inevitably it all came to grief in the end.
11. Halevy, p. 30.
12. Falkner, J., *Fire Over the Rock, the Great Siege of Gibraltar, 1779–1783*, 2008, p. 60.
13. Blomfield, R., *Sébastien le Prestre de Vauban, 1633–1707*, 1938, p. 67. The master-mason Simon Vollant, rather than Vauban, was the designer of the massively impressive gates at the new fortress and citadel of Lille, of which some fine examples luckily remain today. Blomfield's argument for this conclusion is quite convincing. *See also* Money, D. (ed.), *1708, Oudenarde and Lille*, 2008, p. 86.
14. Halevy, pp. 35–7. *See also* Lloyd, E., *Vauban, Montalembert, Carnot: Engineer Studies*, 1887, p. 71.
15. Weygand, M., *Turenne*, 1930, p. 162. The Franche-Comté region had been given by Emperor Charles V to his son, King Philip II of Spain, in 1556. This, in part, awakened French concern at menacing Habsburg encirclement to the south, east and the north.

Chapter 5: War with the Dutch

1. Petrie, C., *Louis XIV*, 1938, pp. 172–3.
2. Ibid., p. 175.
3. Cronin, V., *Louis XIV*, 1964, p. 194.
4. Petrie, p. 174.
5. Hebbert, F. and Rothrock, G., *Soldier of France, Sébastien le Prestre de Vauban*, 1990, p. 40.
6. Petrie, p. 176.
7. Turnbull, S., *The Art of Renaissance Warfare*, 2008, p. 196.
8. Van Der Zee, H. and B., *William and Mary*, 1973, p. 69.
9. Trevelyan, M., *William III and the Defence of Holland*, 1930, p. 207.
10. Van Der Zee, pp. 79–80.
11. Trevelyan, p. 326.
12. Ibid., p. 321.

13. Halevy, D., *Vauban, Builder of Fortresses*, 1924, p. 40.
14. Ibid., p. 41.
15. Vauban, S. (ed. Rothrock, G.), *Manual of Siegecraft and Fortification*, 1969, p. 65.
16. Hebbert and Rothrock, p. 44.
17. Langins, J., *Conserving the Enlightenment, French Military Engineering from Vauban to the Revolution*, 2004, p. 111.
18. Halevy, ibid.
19. Duffy, C., *Siege Warfare in the Early Modern World, 1496–1660*, 1973, p. 138. *See also* Carmichael-Smythe, J., *A Chronological Epitome of the Wars in the Low Countries, from the Peace of the Pyrenees in 1659 to that of Paris in 1815*, 1825, pp. 34–5.
20. Lloyd, E., *Vauban, Montalembert, Carnot: Engineer Studies*, 1887, p. 186.
21. Hebbert and Rothrock, p. 43. *See also* the Marshal Vauban Website, 2008.
22. Lloyd, p. 77.
23. Halevy, p. 44.
24. Duffy, C., *Fire and Stone*, 1975, p. 129.
25. Hebbert and Rothrock, p. 41.
26. Halevy, p. 43.
27. Carleton, G. (ed. Lawrence, A.), *Military Memoirs*, 1929, p. 46.
28. Halevy, p. 44.
29. Hebbert and Rothrock, p. 52.
30. Halevy, p. 46.
31. Hebbert and Rothrock, p. 54.
32. Carleton, p. 49.
33. Ibid., p. 51.
34. Lloyd, p. 70.
35. Ibid., p. 80.
36. Halevy, pp. 51–2.
37. The tower at Epiry still stands, an impressive structure in the Burgundian landscape.
38. Michel, G., *Le Histoire de Vauban*, 1990, p. 98.
39. Vauban, *Manual of Siegecraft and Fortification*, pp. 96–7.
40. By the Treaty of Nijmegen, the Dutch received a 'satisfaction' in the lifting of punitive French trade tariffs on their goods, but Madrid had to pay a 'satisfaction' in turn to Louis XIV for its declared aggression, in the form of relinquishing control of the Franche-Comté and several other towns in the southern part of the Spanish Netherlands. The long-term effect of this was that French borders were henceforth pushed to the north and east to a significant degree, although some of these gains, such as the fortress of Menin, would have to be relinquished by Louis XIV at the close of the War of the Spanish Succession in 1713. However, French possession of the France-Comté region firmly broke the passage of the 'Spanish Road', the valuable overland route by which Madrid had been able to pass their armies northwards from Italy to the Low Countries. This foresaw the irrevocable loss to Spain of their valuable possessions in the Low Countries, in 1706.
41. Bloch, M.-H., *The Citadel of Besançon, Fortifications of Vauban*, 2008, p. 6.
42. Rebellieau, A., *Vauban*, 1962, p. 115.
43. Kekewich, M. (ed.), *Princes and Peoples, France and the British Isles, 1620–1714*, 1994, pp. 238–9. *See also* Hebbert and Rothrock, p. 57.
44. Kekewich, ibid.
45. Ibid.

Chapter 6: An End to Glory

1. Halevy, D., *Vauban, Builder of Fortresses*, 1924, p. 58.
2. The fortress of Mont-Louis was valiantly defended by French revolutionary troops, commanded by General Dogobert, against a Spanish attack in 1797. *See* Hebbert and Rothrock, *Soldier of France, Sébastien le Prestre de Vauban*, 1990, p. 66.
3. Halevy, pp. 80–1.
4. Halevy, p. 70. *See also* Lloyd, p. 65.
5. Rennoldson, N. (ed.), *Renaissance Military Texts, Vol. I, Warfare in the Age of Louis XIV*, 2005, p. 4.
6. Hebbert and Rothrock, p. 72.
7. Rennoldson, p. 31.
8. Ibid., p. 33.
9. Halevy, p. 73.
10. Ibid.
11. Hebbert and Rothrock, p. 72.
12. Rennoldson, p. 25.
13. Ibid., p. 6.
14. Ibid., p. 133.
15. Muller, J., *The Attac and Defence of Fortified Places*, 1757, p. 181.
16. Michel, G., *Le Histoire de Vauban*, 1990, p. 196.
17. Halevy, p. 75.
18. Ibid., p. 83.
19. Halevy, p. 104.
20. Evelyn, J. (ed.), *Diary of John Evelyn*, 1818, p. 492.
21. Halevy, p. 146. The Revocation of the Edict of Nantes in 1685 remains something of a mystery, as the French Protestants, by and large, had remained loyal to the Crown throughout the turbulent times of the Fronde civil wars. In addition, Louis XIV, although meticulous in his own observances as a good Catholic, was quite undogmatic in religious matters. Vauban's principal concern over the issue was the weakening of the pool of talent from which to draw good public servants for the King, a subject he would repeatedly allude to when concerned with the adequate provision of young men for the armies, families to populate France's growing colonies overseas, and labourers available to work on his many projects to fortify the frontiers. *See also* Scafe, R., *The Measure of Greatness: War, Wealth and Population in the Political Thought of Marshal Vauban*, 2004.
22. Lloyd, pp. 93–4.
23. Halevy, pp. 196–7.
24. Ibid., pp. 88–9.
25. 'What the château of Bazoches lacks in great renown, it makes up for in imposing effect [...] The powerful bulwark that it is.' *See* Miltoun, F., *Castles and Châteaux of Old Burgundy*, 1909, pp. 48–9.
26. Halevy, p. 129.
27. 'The Heart of the Kingdom,' Vauban wrote concerning Paris, 'with well provisioned arsenals and magazines enabling a garrison to hold out for over a year.' Plans to strongly fortify the city were always regarded with some reserve by Louis XIV, remembering as he did very well the activities of the Parisians during the Fronde civil wars. This neglect is all the more surprising when it is considered that at the time, France was one of the most centralized nations in western Europe, and if Paris fell, then so did Versailles, and so did France. There was no cohesive system for defending Paris in Napoleonic times, other than

the valiant efforts of the French field armies, but in 1841–1845, at the insistence of Adolphe Thiers, the President of the Council and the Foreign Minister, Paris was belatedly provided with an outer ring of fortifications. A series of fifteen detached forts were constructed to keep an attacker's artillery at a safe distance. On the day of trial, they proved able to resist the long reach of rifled artillery and penetrating explosive shells employed during the Franco-Prussian War of 1870–1871, and Paris and its people, although bombarded, proved both courageous and resilient, unlike France's leaders at the time. The bombardment, it was recalled by an American observer, 'Had not so far the effect of hastening a surrender. On the other hand, it apparently had made the people more firm and resolute.' Horne, A., *The Fall of Paris, the Siege and the Commune, 1870–71*, 1965, p. 217.

28. Muller, pp. 57–9.
29. Halevy, p. 120.
30. Lloyd, pp. 91–2.

Chapter 7: Nine Years War

1. Hebbert, F. and Rothrock, G., *Soldier of France, Sébastien le Prestre de Vauban*, 1990, p. 113.
2. Langallerie, M., *Mémoires of the Marquis de Langallerie*, 1710, p. 15.
3. Blomfield, R., *Sébastien le Prestre de Vauban, 1633–1707*, 1938, p. 109.
4. Petrie, C., *Louis XIV*, 1938, p. 248.
5. Halevy, D., *Vauban, Builder of Fortresses*, 1924, pp. 99–100.
6. Michel, G., *Le Histoire de Vauban*, 1990, p. 348.
7. Vauban, S. (ed. G. Rothrock), *A Manual of Siegecraft and Fortifications*, 1969, p. 348.
8. Duffy, C., *Fire and Stone*, 1975, p. 141.
9. Muller, J., *The Attac and Defence of Fortified Places*, 1757, pp. 74–5.
10. Halevy, pp. 107–8.
11. Ibid., p. 113. François-Michel le Tellier, Marquis de Louvois (1666–1691). His father was the Chancellor le Tellier. From 1666 to 1691 the son was Louis XIV's formidable Minister for War, and reorganized the rather haphazard arrangements by which the French army operated. The officers were no longer able to pick and choose their own terms of service, or indeed which orders they were inclined or disinclined to accept. Soldiering in France thus became a profession, with the establishment of squadrons and regiments of a regulation size and strength. Dress, armament, colours and equipment were also made standard. The range of duties of French officers was codified, and commissariat and medical services put on a proper footing. Noble lineage kept its place but merit was also recognized, as with Vauban. The ability of Louis XIV to put large numbers of troops into the field at fairly short notice expanded considerably, from 80,000 Frenchmen under arms, with an additional 40,000 foreign hired troops during the Dutch War in the 1670s, to no fewer than 220,000 troops, most of whom were French, in service for the Nine Years War two decades later. During the years of the War of the Spanish Succession in the early eighteenth century, this number, including militia, grew to an impressive but arguably unsustainable 350,000 men (and as anecdotes often relate, occasionally women such as the redoubtable French girl Marie Mouron who was enterprising enough to enlist in two different regiments at the same time). Louvois was, perhaps, Louis XIV's greatest servant. *See also* Hatton, R., *Louis XIV and His World*, 1972, p. 66; Chandler, D., *The Art of Warfare in the Age of Marlborough*, 1972; and Falkner, J., *Marlborough's Wars*, 2007.
12. Blomfield, p. 124.
13. Halevy, pp. 110–11.

14. Hebbert and Rothrock, pp. 121–2. The young engineer, Cladech, was killed at the Siege of Valenciennes in 1693, much to Vauban's regret.
15. Halevy, p. 113.
16. Ibid., p. 57.
17. St John, B. (ed. and tr.), *Memoirs of the Duc de St Simon*, 1879, Vol. III, p. 199.
18. Crichton, A. (ed.), *The Life and Diary of Lieutenant Colonel J. Blackader*, 1824, p. 118.
19. Hebbert and Rothrock, p. 126.
20. Lazard, P., *Vauban, 1633–1707*, 1934, pp. 229–30.
21. Halevy, p. 114.
22. Ibid., pp. 114–15.
23. Childs, J., *The Nine Years War and the British Army, 1688–1697*, 1991, p. 192.
24. Petrie, C., *Louis XIV*, 1964, p. 251.
25. Halevy, pp. 138–9. *See also* Petrie, pp. 251–2.
26. Briançon Fortifications Website, 2009.
27. Halevy, p. 140.
28. The enlargement of the defences at Briançon continued long after Vauban's death. The major part of the renewed work was begun in 1721, on the order of Louis XV (during the Regency), and was supervised by Claude François de Bidel, the Marquis d'Asfeld, an assiduous follower of Vauban's methods. A great deal of effort was made, as when Vauban commenced the work, to make the most of the natural features and inaccessible nature of the defences. The huge project took thirteen years to complete, and an outer barrier of forts and redoubts was constructed – the Salettes (begun by Vauban), Troi-Tetes, Randouillet, Dauphin, Anjou, Point de Jour and Asfeld bridge. It is odd that, as Vauban knew the fortress so well, he was not called upon to take part in the operations when the place was attacked in the opening months of the War of the Spanish Succession.
29. Hebbert and Rothrock, p. 135.
30. Blomfield, p. 6.
31. Langallerie, pp. 33–4.
32. Blomfield, p. 133.
33. Horsley, W. (ed. and tr.), *Chronicles of an Old Campaigner*, 1904, p. 30.
34. Hebbert and Rothrock, p. 139.
35. Horsley, p. 33.
36. Ibid., p. 36.
37. Petrie, pp. 251–2.
38. Halevy, p. 143.
39. It was widely rumoured and widely given credence, at the time and since, that John Churchill, the Earl of Marlborough, had disclosed the plans for Tollemarch's expedition in a letter that was sent to the exiled English King James II, who lived in France. Given that the Earl was out of favour with William III at the time, and would not have had ready access to such confidential information, this all really seems very unlikely, although Marlborough did engage in some remarkably indiscreet correspondence, at times, with the exiled King. *See* Churchill, W., *Marlborough, His Life and Times*, 1947, Vol. I, p. 368.
40. Hebbert and Rothrock, p. 100.
41. Halevy, p. 146.
42. A resident of Brussels during the French bombardment wrote that 'Everyone was in a panic. Nobody knew where to hide his papers or treasure, and most of the people who were able to move took themselves to the upper part of the town, which was the remotest area from the enemy [...] Whole blocks of houses had been destroyed, and our feet were burned as we

scrambled over the still smoking ruins. Vauban disapproved of such barbaric bombardment of civilian areas, as he did with the periodic devastation of wide areas to prevent enemy armies from operating. 'I have observed,' he wrote, 'that the bombardment of Oudenarde, Luxembourg, or even Liège, have not resulted in the gain of even an inch of territory for the King, and that, on the contrary, they have consumed much valuable ammunition, besides fatiguing and wearying the troops.' *See* Halevy, p. 112 and Duffy, C., *Siege Warfare in the Early Modern World*, 1973, pp. 251–2.

43. Carleton, G., *Military Memoirs*, 1929, pp. 72–3.
44. Chandler, D. (ed.), *The Journal of John Wilson*, 2005, pp. 20–1.
45. Carleton, ibid.
46. Muller, J., *The Attac and Defence of Fortified Places*, 1758, p. 173.
47. Chandler, D., *The Art of Warfare in the Age of Marlborough*, 1988, pp. 270–1.
48. Ibid. 'Elkinberg, a Dane, who by his personal Courage and Merit had raised himself from a Private Centinell to be a Major General [...] and was particularly recommended by the King.' *See also* Kane, R., *Campaigns of King William and Queen Anne*, 1745, p. 21.
49. Chandler, pp. 270–1.
50. Ibid.
51. Langallerie, p. 45.
52. Duffy, p. 174.
53. Hebbert and Rothrock, p. 145.
54. Halevy, p. 148.
55. Hebbert and Rothrock, p. 148.
56. Langallerie, p. 51.
57. Halevy, pp. 156–7.
58. Ibid.
59. Petrie, pp. 252–3.
60. Halevy, p. 157.
61. *American Historical Review*, pp. 258–60.
62. Halevy, pp. 158–9.
63. Lloyd, E., *Vauban, Montalembert, Carnot: Engineer Studies*, 1887, pp. 85–6.
64. Blomfield, p. 104.
65. Halevy, pp. 153–4.
66. By the Terms of the Treaty of Ryswick, Louis XIV had to give up Charleroi, Ath, Courtrai, Luxembourg and Barcelona to Spain. In addition the defences at Mont-Royal, Kirn and Ebensbourg, Bitche, Nancy and Homburg were to be demolished, while Phillipsburg, Alt-Brisach and Freiburg were returned to Imperial Austrian possession.
67. Brisach, or Briesach, had been ceded to France under the terms of the Treaty of Westphalia which brought to an end the calamitous Thirty Years War. In 1697, the place was given up to Austrian control and the brand-new Vauban-designed town took shape on the western bank of the River Rhine. So well planned and strongly built was Neuf-Brisach, of a regular and symmetrical design that was not quite replicated elsewhere, that the fortifications survive, more or less intact, to the present day, with relatively minor damage and loss inflicted in 1870 by Prussian bombardment, or during the Second World War when troops used the walls for target practice. Vauban made extensive use of what is generally known as the 'Third System' of formal defence, with tower bastions and detached bastions (eight of each), and returning angles at regular intervals, to increase the volume of flanking fire that could be brought to bear upon any attacker. The work was a progressive development of the original Trace Italienne, and then Vauban's 'Second System'. The great engineer acknowledged the

progression by referring to the fortifications he designed for Neuf-Brisach as the 'Systeme de Landau'.

68. Petrie, C., *Louis XIV*, 1938, pp. 262–3.
69. Hebbert and Rothrock, p. 197.

Chapter 8: The Long Campaign

1. Petrie, C., *Louis XIV*, 1938, p. 275.
2. Van der Zee, H. and M., *William and Mary*, 1973, p. 463.
3. Chandler, D. (ed.), *Military Memoirs, Robert Parker and the Comte de Merode-Westerloo*, 1968, pp. 12–13.
4. Hebbert, F. and Rothrock, G., *Soldier of France, Sébastien le Prestre de Vauban*, 1975, p. 200.
5. Halevy, D., *Vauban, Builder of Fortresses*, 1924, p. 185.
6. Ibid., p. 184. The other Marshals of France appointed in 1703 were: Harcourt, Tallard, Rosen, d'Estres, Château-Renault, Montravel, Chamilly, d'Huxelles and Tesse.
7. Halevy, pp. 185–7.
8. Ibid., p. 186.
9. Ibid., p. 187.
10. Ibid.
11. Lloyd, E., *Vauban, Montalembert, Carnot: Engineer Studies*, 1887, p. 68.
12. Hebbert and Rothrock, p. 203.
13. Halevy, pp. 188–9.
14. Chandler, p. 185.
15. Halevy, p. 250.
16. Hebbert and Rothrock, p. 206.
17. Halevy, p. 118.
18. Scafe, R., *The Measure of Greatness, Wealth and Population in the Political Thought of Marshal Vauban*, 2004, p. 1.
19. Vauban, S., *A Project for a Royal Tythe, or General Tax*, 1706, p. iv.
20. Ibid., pp. 132–8.
21. Halevy, p. 174, also pp. 255–6.
22. Vauban, pp. 175–6.
23. Halevy, pp. 178–9.
24. Lloyd, p. 96. *See also* Halevy, p. 229.
25. St John, B. (ed.), *Memoirs of the Duc de St Simon*, 1885, Vol. I, p. 356.
26. Lynn, J., *The French Wars, 1667–1714*, 2002, pp. 64–5.
27. Falkner, J., *Marlborough's Sieges*, 2008, p. 110.
28. Kekewich, M. (ed.), *Princes and Peoples, France and the British Isles, 1620–1714*, 1994, p. 249.
29. Hebbert and Rothrock, p. 178.
30. Halevy, p. 217.
31. Hebbert and Rothrock, pp. 213–14.
32. Halevy, p. 219.
33. Lloyd, p. 63.
34. Hebbert and Rothrock, p. 237.
35. St John, B. (ed.), *Mémoires of the Duc de St Simon*, 1887, Volume I, p. 354. *See also* Halevy, p. 235.
36. Blomfield, p. 188.
37. Halevy, p. 236.

Chapter 9: The Greatest of His Services

1. Langallerie, M., *Mémoires of the Marquis de Langallerie*, 1710, p. 253.
2. Duffy, C., *Fire and Stone*, 1975, p. 131.
3. Petrie, C., *The Marshal, Duke of Berwick, 1953*, p. 232. *See also* Money, D. (ed.), *1708, Oudenarde and Lille*, 2008, Introduction.
4. Petrie, C., *Louis XIV*, 1938, p. 298.
5. Falkner, J., *Marlborough's Sieges*, 2007, p. 174.
6. Ibid., p. 177.
7. Murray, G. (ed.), *Letters and Dispatches of the Duke of Marlborough*, 1845, Vol. IV, p. 572.
8. Chandler, D. (ed.), *Military Memoirs, Robert Parker and Comte de Merode-Westerloo*, 1968, p. 84.
9. Falkner, p. 179.
10. Ibid.
11. Chandler, p. 91.
12. Falkner, p. 240.

Chapter 10: Engraved on the Soil

1. The Duke of York's victories at Beaumont and Willems in 1794, now little celebrated, were certainly well remembered at one time. When the British Army garrison was being established at Aldershot in Hampshire in late Victorian times, the South Cavalry Barracks were named Beaumont Barracks, and the North Cavalry Barracks became Willems Barracks. Modern development has swept most traces away, although some stonework remnants remain, but Willems Park (army married quarters) and Beaumont Junior School remain as some small reminder of those two days of dashing British cavalry action against French Revolutionary armies.
2. UNESCO World Heritage Centre Website, 2010. *See also* 'Resau des Sites Vauban' Website, 2010.
3. Holmes, R., *Fatal Avenue*, 1992, p. 90.
4. Blomfield, R., *Sébastien le Prestre de Vauban, 1733–1707*, 1938, pp. 58–9.
5. Lloyd, E., *Vauban, Montalembert, Carnot: Engineer Studies*, 1889, p. 213.
6. Holmes, R., *The Little Field Marshal*, 1981, p. 220.
7. Horne, A., *The Price of Glory, Verdun 1916*, 1961, p. 106.
8. Halevy, D., *Vauban, Builder of Fortresses*, 1924, p. 211.
9. Hughes, J., *To the Maginot Line*, 1971, p. 18.
10. Ibid., p. 67.
11. Horne, A., *To Lose a Battle, France 1940*, p. 110. *See also* Thompson, J., *Dunkirk*, 2008, p. 209.
12. Inevitably, not everyone admired Vauban and his methods, which some felt had over time become outmoded and dull. Pierre-Amboise-François Choderlos de Laclos (1741–1803), the author of *Les Liaisons Dangereuses*, was a particularly acid critic of the Old Engineer, and this seeming absurd heresy at what had become accepted wisdom amongst military men cost him his commission in the French Army. He was, however, reinstated with the Revolution, and ended his life with the rank of General and appointed to be the Governor of Tarento.

Appendix III: Vauban's Idle Thoughts

1. Hebbert, F., and Rothrock, G., *Soldier of France, Sébastien le Prestre de Vauban*, 1990, p. 167.

Bibliography

Most of the numerous biographies, histories and accounts of the life and career of Marshal Vauban have been written in French. This is, of course, very understandable, as he has rightly long been regarded as a celebrated French hero. Many of these works are admirable, well-informed and well-balanced with regard to his interest in fortifications on the one hand, and the capture of those same defences on the other. His interests as a social reformer, in an early sense, are also quite well covered, although it is undoubtedly Vauban's prolific military career that attracts the most notice.

As with all heroes, some of the biographical works have a tendency to verge on the over-adulatory, and discretion has occasionally to be used to ferret out the real story of Vauban and his prodigious services under Louis XIV. With the 300th anniversary of Vauban's death, a spate of fresh works appeared, and many of these are highly informative and very attractively produced. In the main, but not exclusively, they concentrate on the large number of his fortified places that remain to be seen and visited the length and breadth of France.

Some of the works in French have been subsequently translated, with rather varying degrees of success, into English, and once more a certain amount of care has to be taken when consulting them. Works written in English on the achievements of Vauban are much less common, but the biography by the eminent architect Reginald Blomfield, printed in the late 1930s, is a rare exception and well worth the effort to find, although this is heavily focussed on the technicalities of fortress design and construction. Daniel Halevy's useful but rather uncritical biography was translated into English in the 1920s, and Hebbert and Rothrock's valuable and informative work *Soldier of France* was published in 1990. Rothrock also translated into English Vauban's detailed manual on siegecraft, and this is indispensable, as the original copies are very rare indeed. The late Paddy Griffiths recently produced an attractive, colourful (in the very best sense), and informative work on Vauban's surviving fortifications in France.

Ashley, M., *Louis XIV and the Greatness of France*, 1938.
Baxter, D., *Servants of the Sword*, 1976.
Blanchard, A., *Vauban*, 1996.
Bloch, M.-H., *The Citadel of Besançon, Fortifications of Vauban*, 2008.
Blomfield, R., *Sébastien le Prestre de Vauban, 1633–1707*, 1938.
Bornecque, R., *La France de Vauban*, 1984.
Buckley, V., *Madame de Maintenon*, 2007.
Carleton, G., (ed. Lawrence, A.), *Military Mémoires*, 1929.
Carman, W., *The Siege of Lille, 1708*, JSAHR, 1940.
Carmichael-Smyth, J., *A Chronological Epitome of the Wars in the Low Countries, from the Peace of the Pyrenees in 1659 to that of Paris in 1815*, 1825.
Carnot, M. (tr.), *A Treatise on the Defence of Fortified Places*, 1814.
Chandler, D., *The Art of Warfare in the Age of Marlborough*, 1992.
Chandler, D., *Blenheim Preparation*, 2004.
Chandler, D. (ed.), *The Journal of John Wilson*, 2005 (Army Records Society).
Chandler, D., *Marlborough as Military Commander*, 1974.
Chandler, D. (ed.), *Military Memoirs, Robert Parker, and the Comte de Merode-Westerloo*, 1968.

Childs, J., *The Nine Years War and the British Army, 1688–1697*, 1991.

Childs, J., *Warfare in the Seventeenth Century*, 2001.

Churchill, W.S., *Marlborough, His Life and Times*, 1947.

Clothard, H., *Louis XIV, Louvois, Vauban, et le fortifications du nord de la France*, 1889.

Corvisier, A., *L'Armée Française de la fin de XVII siecle*, 1969.

Crichton, A. (ed.), *The Life and Diary of Lieutenant Colonel J. Blackader*, 1824.

Cronin, V., *Louis XIV*, 1964.

De La Croix, H., *Military Considerations in City Planning: Fortifications*, 1972.

Duffy, C., *Fire and Stone*, 1975.

Duffy, C., *The Fortress in the Age of Vauban and Frederick the Great, 1660–1789*, 1985.

Duffy, C., *Siege Warfare in the Early Modern World, 1495–1660*, 1973.

Ekberg, C., *The Failure of Louis XIV's Dutch War*, 1979.

Evelyn, J. (ed. Bray, W.), *Memoirs of John Evelyn comprising his Diary from 1641 to 1705–6*, 1827.

Falkner, J., *Great and Glorious Days, Marlborough's Battles*, 2002.

Falkner, J., *Blenheim, 1704*, 2004.

Falkner, J., *Marlborough's Wars, Eye-Witness Accounts*, 2005.

Falkner, J., *Ramillies 1706, Year of Miracles*, 2006.

Falkner, J., *Marlborough's Sieges*, 2007.

Falkner, J., *Fire Over the Rock, the Great Siege of Gibraltar, 1779–1783*, 2008.

Faucherre, N. and Prest, P. (ed.), *Le Triomphe de la Méthode*, 1992.

Fitzpatrick, W., *The Great Condé and the Fronde*, 1873.

Fletcher, I., *In Hell Before Daylight*, 1994.

Gottman, J., *Vauban and Modern Geography*, 1994 (American Geographical Society).

Griffith, P., *Vauban's Fortifications in France*, 2006.

Grimblot, P. (ed.), *Letters of William III and Louis XIV, and their Ministers*, 1848.

Halevy, D., *Vauban, Builder of Fortresses*, 1924.

Hatton, R., *Louis XIV and His World*, 1972.

Hebbert, F., and Rothrock, G., *Soldier of France, Sébastien le Prestre de Vauban*, 1990.

Holmes R., *Fatal Avenue*, 1992.

Holmes R., *The Little Field Marshal*, 1982.

Horne, A., *The Fall of Paris, the Siege and the Commune, 1870–71*, 1965.

Horne, A., *The Price of Glory, Verdun, 1916*, 1961.

Horsley, W. (tr. and ed.), *Chronicles of an Old Campaigner*, 1904.

Hughes, J., *To the Maginot Line*, 1971.

IGN Map Series, *La France de Vauban*, Series 10, No: 923, 100,000 scale, 2009.

Kamen, H., *The War of the Succession in Spain, 1700–1715*, 1969.

Kane, R., *The Campaigns of King William and Queen Anne*, 1745 (2008 reprint edition).

Kekewich, M. (ed.), *Princes and Peoples, France and the British Isles, 1620–1714*, 1994.

Klopp, G. (ed.), *Vauban, la Pierre et la plume*, 2009.

Langallerie, M., *Mémoires of the Marquis de Langallerie*, 1710.

Langins, J., *Conserving the Enlightenment, French Military Engineering from Vauban to the Revolution*, 2004.

Lazard, P., *Vauban, 1633–1707*, 1934.

Lepage, J.-D., *Vauban and the French Military under Louis XIV*, 2009.

Lloyd, E., 'Vauban and Modern Sieges', *The Quarterly Review*, Vol. 154, 1882.

Lloyd, E., *Vauban, Montalembert, Carnot: Engineer Studies*, 1887.

Lynn, J., *The French Wars, 1667–1714*, 2002.

Lynn, J., *A Giant of the Grande Siecle, the French Army, 1610–1715*, 1996.

Lynn, J., 'The Trace Italienne and the growth of armies: the French case', *Journal of Military History*, 1991.

Manningham, H., *A Complete Treatise of Mines*, 1756.

Mary, L., *Vauban, le maître des fortresses*, 2006.

Michel, G., *Le Histoire de Vauban* (1990 reprint edition).

Miltoun, F., *Castles and Châteaux of Old Burgundy*, 1909.

Mitford, N., *The Sun King*, 1966.

Money, D. (ed.), *1708, Oudenarde and Lille*, 2009.

Monsaingeon, G., *Les Voyages de Vauban*, 2007.

Muller, J., *The Attac and Defence of Fortified Places*, 1757.

Murray, G. (ed.), *Letters and Dispatches of the Duke of Marlborough*, 1845.

Neave, A., *The Flames of Calais*, 1955.

Norton, L., *First Lady at Versailles*, 1992.

Norton, L., *St Simon at Versailles*, 1980.

Nosworthy, B., *The Anatomy of Victory*, 1992.

O'Callaghan, J., *History of the Irish Brigades in the Service of France*, 1883.

Ostwald, J., *Vauban under Siege – Engineering efficiency and martial vigour in the War of the Spanish Succession*, 2000.

Parker, G., *The Dutch Revolt*, 1977.

Parker, G., *The Military Revolution, Military Innovation and the Rise of the War, 1500–1800*, 1996.

Parker, G., *The Army of Flanders and the Spanish Road, 1567–1659, the Logistics of Spanish Victory and Defeat in the Low Countries War*, 1972.

Petrie, C., *Louis XIV*, 1938.

Petrie, C., *The Marshal, Duke of Berwick*, 1953.

Pujo, B., *Vauban*, 1991.

Rebellieau, A., *Vauban*, 1962.

Reeve, J., *The Siege of Béthune, 1710*, JSAHR, 1985.

Rennoldson, N. (ed.), *Renaissance Military Texts, Vol. I, Warfare in the Age of Louis XIV*, 2005.

Rowe, G., *The Great Wall of France*, 1959.

Roy, I. (ed. and tr.), *Blaise de Monluc, The French War of Religion*, 1971.

Rule, J., *Louis XIV and the Craft of Kingship*, 1974.

Sautai, M., *Le Siege de la ville et de le Citadelle de Lille, en 1708*, 1899.

Scafe, R., 'The Measure of Greatness; War, Wealth and Population in the Political Thought of Marshal Vauban' (Essay), 2004.

St John, B. (tr. & ed.), *Memoirs of the Duke of St Simon*, 1879.

Taylor, F., *The Wars of Marlborough*, 1921.

Thompson, J., *Dunkirk*, 2008.

Tournoux, P., *Defense des frontiers*, 1960.

Trevelyan, G.M., *Blenheim*, 1933.

Trevelyan, G.M., *The Peace and the Protestant Succession*, 1933.

Trevelyan, G.M., *Ramillies*, 1933.

Trevelyan, G.M., *Select Documents for Queen Anne's Reign*, 1930.

Trevelyan, M., *William III and the Defence of Holland*, 1930.

Turnbull, S., *The Art of Renaissance Warfare*, 2008.

UNESCO, World Heritage Sites Website, 4 March 2010.

Van der Zee, H. and M., *William and Mary*, 1973.

Vauban, S., *A Manual of Siegecraft and Fortification*, 1688 (ed., Rothrock, G.) 1969.

Vauban, S., *A Project for a Royal Tythe; or General Tax*, 1706 (2010 reprint edition).

Vauban, S., *Le Traité de la Defense des Places*, 1771.

Virol, M., *Vauban, de la gloire du Roi au Service de l'État*, 2003.

Walsh, R., 'Notes on Sieges', *American Quarterly Review*, 1833.

Warmoes, I., *La Musée des Plans-Reliefs*, 1997.

Wentzler, C., *Architecture de Bastion, l'art de Vauban*, 2000.

Weygand, M., *Histoire de l'Armée Français*, 1938.

Weygand, M., *Turenne, Marshal of France*, 1930.

Weygand, M., *Vauban*, 1933.

Wright, J., 'Sieges and Customs of War at the opening of the 18th Century', *American Historical Review*, 1933–34.

Index